THE POLITICS
OF PALESTINIAN
NATIONALISM

A RAND CORPORATION RESEARCH STUDY

THE POLITICS
OF PALESTINIAN
NATIONALISM

William B. Quandt, Fuad Jabber,
Ann Mosely Lesch

UNIVERSITY OF CALIFORNIA PRESS
BERKELEY, LOS ANGELES, LONDON

University of California Press
Berkeley and Los Angeles, California
University of California Press, Ltd.
London, England
Copyright © 1973, by
The Rand Corporation
ISBN: 0-520-02336-6 (cloth)
0-520-02372-2 (paper)
Library of Congress Catalog Card Number: 72-89791
Printed in the United States of America

CONTENTS

v

            by Fuad Jabber   155

    1. The Resistance Movement before the Six-Day War   157
    2. The Arab World after the Defeat   176
    3. The Arab Regimes and the Palestinian Revolution   186
    4. The Resistance in Crisis   199

       Bibliography   217
       Index   225

MAPS

FIGURES

TABLE

PREFACE

Palestinian nationalism, the subject of this book, is alleged by some observers not to exist. We believe that it does exist and that it has been neglected for too long by students of the Middle East. The idea of Arab statehood in Palestine, which has been the object of Palestinian nationalism since the 1920s, has been embodied in a bewildering variety of political parties and movements. Twice in modern history, Palestinian nationalism has been a strong and dynamic factor in the Middle East, first in the decades of the 1920s and 1930s, then again in the 1960s, especially after the Arab-Israeli war of 1967.

It is the most recent manifestation of Palestinian nationalism that receives primary attention in this study. The earlier period, however, is analyzed in an introductory section, both to provide historical perspective and background and to illustrate some of the basic patterns in Palestinian political life that have persisted into the present.

Political developments within the Palestinian community, and particularly the rise of the Resistance movement, are the subject of Part II. Problems of political organization and leadership are dealt with in detail, and the effects of dependence on other Arab states for support are analyzed. Because the Palestinian movement has been so much at the mercy of inter-Arab politics, this topic receives special attention in Part III. Inevitably, Parts II and III cover some of the same ground and repeat some information, but in the first instance the focus is on internal political developments, while in the second it is on the inter-Arab political context and its impact on the Resistance movement.

The authorship of each section has been kept separate, for although this has been in many ways a collaborative effort, each author has a distinctive point of view that we have sought to preserve rather than compromise through joint authorship. We have all commented on and contributed to each other's sections, but the responsibility ultimately lies with the individual author.

A note on transliteration from Arabic is required. Apart from a few commonly known names (e.g., Nasser, Hussein, Hashemite), we have adopted a simplified version of standard transliteration which is meant to be sufficiently accurate for scholars and relatively close to normal pronunciation to be useful for the layman. Special markings for "alif" are not used, and "ayn" is represented by an apostrophe only within a word, not at its beginning. When names appear, the "al-" prefix is only maintained if the entire name is given. Although we have sought for consistency and accuracy, we realize that our idiosyncratic system may leave some readers unsatisfied, but—we hope—not confused.

Finally, we must acknowledge with thanks the help of many friends and colleagues in the course of our research. They will recognize their valuable contributions without our having to list them by name, for to do so would be a lengthy process indeed.

The research in Part I by Ann Lesch was carried out in preparing a doctoral dissertation for Columbia University, entitled "The Frustration of a Nationalist Movement: Palestine Arab Politics, 1917–1939." Her chapter in this book was written at the request of the senior author. Much of the research in Part II was sponsored by the Office of the Assistant Secretary of Defense for International Security Affairs, whose support is gratefully acknowledged. Part III was written by Fuad Jabber for the Rand Corporation. While various parts of the book, therefore, reflect different sources of support, in all cases the authors alone are responsible for the views expressed.

Santa Monica, California
September 1972

ABBREVIATIONS

ALF	Arab Liberation Front
ANM	Arab Nationalist Movement
AOLP	Action Organization for the Liberation of Palestine
OAP	Organization of Arab Palestine
PASC	Palestine Armed Struggle Command
PDFLP	Popular Democratic Front for the Liberation of Palestine
PFLP	Popular Front for the Liberation of Palestine
PFLP-GC	Popular Front for the Liberation of Palestine, General Command
PLA	Palestine Liberation Army
PLF	Palestine Liberation Front (Jibril)
PLF	Popular Liberation Forces (Commando Wing of PLA)
PLO	Palestine Liberation Organization
POLP	Popular Organization for the Liberation of Palestine
PPS	Parti Populaire Syrien—same as SSNP
PPSF	Palestinian Popular Struggle Front
PRFLP	Popular Revolutionary Front for the Liberation of Palestine
SSNP	Syrian Social Nationalist Party

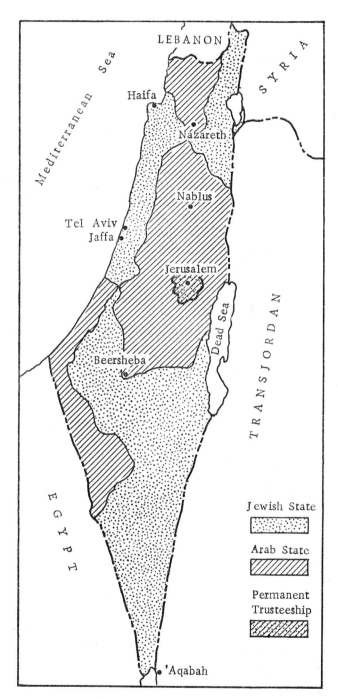

MAP 1. U.N. General Assembly's Plan of Partition with
Economic Union (1947)

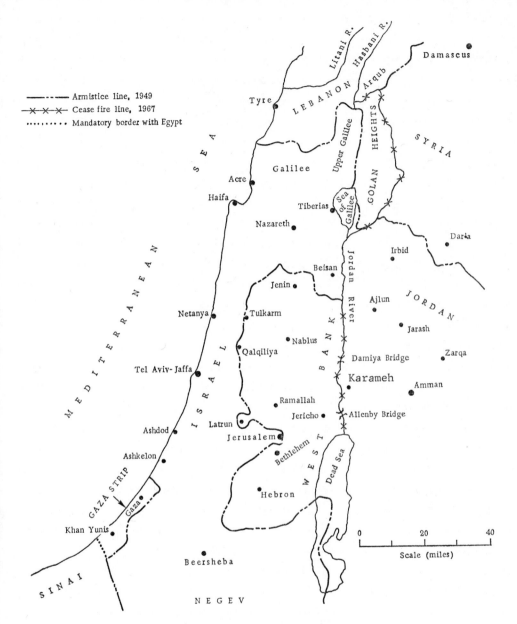

Litani R.
Hasbani R.
Damascus
Tyre
LEBANON
Arqub
Upper Galilee
GOLAN HEIGHTS
SYRIA
Galilee
Acre
Haifa
Sea of Galilee
Tiberias
Dar'a
Nazareth
Irbid
SEA
Beisan
Jordan River
Ajlun
JORDAN
Jenin
Jarash
Netanya
Tulkarm
MEDITERRANEAN
Qalqiliya
Nablus
Zarqa
Damiya Bridge
Tel Aviv-Jaffa
WEST BANK
Karameh
Amman
Ramallah
ISRAEL
Jericho
Allenby Bridge
Ashdod
Latrun
Jerusalem
Ashkelon
Bethlehem
Dead Sea
GAZA STRIP
Hebron
Gaza
Khan Yunis
0   20   40
Scale (miles)
Beersheba
SINAI
NEGEV

MAP 2. Palestine and Surrounding Area

THE POLITICS
OF PALESTINIAN
NATIONALISM

INTRODUCTION

Palestine has been an object of conflicting political claims and intense religious attachment for millennia. This small, arid land, located between the eastern shores of the Mediterranean and the Jordan River, has been ruled and coveted by Jews, Christians, and Muslims, all of whom have found historic and strategic rationales for their mutually exclusive demands.

The struggle over Palestine has attracted an unusual degree of international attention and outside interference, particularly in the twentieth century. In its most recent phase, this conflict has pitted indigenous Palestinian Arabs against immigrant Jews and their offspring. In organizational and ideological terms, the clash has been between Palestinian nationalism and Zionism, both of which have sought nationhood within Palestine. Until the 1930s, few observers would have doubted the eventual emergence of an Arab-dominated state in Palestine. By the 1970s, however, the Jewish state of Israel was firmly established in all of Palestine, with little prospect of its relinquishing control over any territory in the near future.

The apparent failure of the Palestinian nationalist movement does not imply the lack of Palestinian national feelings. True, some Palestinians have remained attached to nonnational loyalties such as the family or village, while others have found in Arab nationalism a broader and more satisfying ideology than Palestinian nationalism. Nonetheless, across a broad social spectrum Palestinians agree that Palestine is essentially Arab and that it should be

1

governed by Arabs. Consensus on this goal has been constant since at least the beginning of the British mandate in 1922, but the means for attaining this goal have been the object of intense controversy.

A specific Palestinian nationalism has flourished in two brief periods separated by nearly two decades of relative quiescence. The first period was during the mandate and especially in the 1930s, when Palestinian opposition to both Zionism and British repression culminated in three years of violence from 1936 to 1939. Part I of this study, "The Palestine Arab Nationalist Movement Under the Mandate," concentrates on these early years of Palestinian nationalism, tracing the development of political style from petition to protest and then to full-scale rebellion. Political problems of organization and leadership were serious and contributed to the inability of the Palestinians to prevent the establishment of the state of Israel. But the more important reason for this failure in the 1940s was the limited resources at the disposal of the Palestinians compared with those of their enemies, the Zionists in particular.

The second major period of Palestinian nationalism, the subject of Parts II and III, began with the defeat of the established Arab regimes of Egypt, Jordan, and Syria—the "custodians" of the Palestine cause—in the Six-Day War of June 1967. In the ensuing four years, Palestinian guerrilla organizations carried out armed raids against Israel, challenged the authority of the Jordanian and Lebanese regimes, rivaled Egypt's President Nasser in prestige, hijacked international aircraft, and finally provoked a civil war in Jordan in September 1970 that threatened to embroil the superpowers in direct confrontation. Within the Palestinian "diaspora," they mobilized large-scale material and political support, asserted their claim to political leadership of the scattered community, and gained control of existing Palestinian political institutions.

In Part II, "Political and Military Dimensions of Contemporary Palestinian Nationalism," internal developments after 1967 affecting the Palestinians are analyzed, with particular emphasis on the growth of the guerrilla movement. Several distinct Palestinian guerrilla organizations emerged in this period which were committed to the idea of armed struggle against Israel. But rather than producing a unified movement, contemporary Palestinian nationalism has spawned several groups competing for resources and loyalty. This factionalism has roots in Palestinian society and political culture as well as in concrete historical experiences of the recent past.

Contemporary Palestinian nationalism has stimulated a search by Palestinians for coherent goals and ideologies. In contrast to an earlier view that the liberation of Palestine would result from

Arab unity, Palestinians now argued that their struggle to regain Palestine must be engaged without delay and that it would be the catalyst for change and unification in the Arab world. This assertion has pushed the Palestinian movement to the fore in the Arab-Israeli struggle, and Palestinian commando leaders have sought not only recognition of their claim to represent all Palestinians, but also a veto power over any proposed settlement of the Arab conflict with Israel.

In addition to emphasizing Palestinian autonomy and self-reliance, guerrilla spokesmen have tried to give a progressive social content to their national struggle. Marxist groups have stressed the need for fundamental economic and social change as a precondition for success in transforming Palestine into a nonsectarian democratic state. The role of Jews in such a state has been widely debated, with the result that Palestinians have begun to face realistically some of the issues involved in the conflicting claims of two peoples to the same territory.

The ambitious objectives of the Palestinian nationalists have far surpassed their capabilities to attain them. Heavily dependent on non-Palestinian sources of support for the conduct of the armed struggle and facing a well-armed and efficient enemy in Israel, the guerrillas have been unable to pose a serious military threat to their ostensible opponent. Instead, by 1970 they had shifted attention from attacks on Israel to confrontation with King Hussein's regime, whose authority over its predominantly Palestinian subjects was threatened by the strong pressure of the guerrillas in Jordan. Unable to maintain discipline and unity in the face of impending conflict, the guerrillas were poorly prepared to cope with the full-scale hostilities that erupted in Jordan in September 1970. This crucial event resulted in a major setback for the guerrillas.

The Jordanian civil war highlighted the importance of inter-Arab politics for the Palestinian nationalist movement. Dependent in its early stages on Arab governments for resources and protection, the Resistance movement had nonetheless managed to attract sufficient mass support after 1967 to offset this dependence somewhat. But as the guerrilla groups developed into a strong, well-armed movement enjoying widespread popular backing, various Arab regimes inevitably sought to gain influence and control over this new political force. In Part III, "The Palestinian Resistance and Inter-Arab Politics," the complex network of relations among the Palestinians and the Arab governments in Egypt, Syria, Jordan, and Lebanon is analyzed. As the guerrilla movement sought to overcome its dependence on Arab regimes by pursuing an activist course and by diversifying its sources of support, the Palestinians became a threat to the status quo, not so much within the occupied territories of Palestine as within the countries bordering on Israel. Consequently, Arab regimes became interested in controlling or using the Palestinian movement, in some cases mainly for political advantage, in others as a prudent insurance against its revolutionary potential. The tensions between the guerrillas and the established order reached their peak in Jordan in 1970, and in the aftermath of the September 1970 civil war the guerrillas began to lose both popular backing and effective protection from other Arab governments. The political climate created by American and Egyptian initiatives for a settlement of the conflict with Israel further eroded the strength of the Palestinian movement. In this weakened state, the guerrillas could not prevent their expulsion from Jordan in July 1971. This reversal of fortunes forced the movement back into a situation of heavy dependence on Syria, somewhat on the pattern of the pre-1967 period.

Despite the immense problems encountered by Palestinian nationalists, they have succeeded in keeping the Palestinian Arab cause alive. Although weak, poorly organized, and prone to factionalism, the Palestinian movement has the support of most Palestinians and Arabs, for the simple reason that it is seen as representing the victims of a great historical injustice. Whether the Palestinians will one day attain some of their goals, and in particular the creation of a state of their own within Palestine, is problematical. It depends to a large degree on the Palestinians themselves and their political and organizational capabilities. It also depends on other Arab states, and in particular Jordan, where at least the principle of Palestinian self-determination and autonomy is now recognized. But the realization of a Palestinian state also depends on Israel, where the Palestinian case is generally viewed with deep suspicion and hostility. Finally, within the international community, the major powers, with the exception of China, have been cautious in their dealings with the Palestinians, preferring to view their claims in humanitarian rather than nationalist terms. In view of these obstacles to Palestinian nationalist aspirations, one must be skeptical of their realization in the near future. But Palestinians have not forsaken their homeland and are unlikely to acquiesce in its permanent control by Israel. Consequently, one can be sure that so long as the Palestinian national identity remains unfulfilled, Palestinians will continue their struggle with the modest means available to them. This will help to ensure that the Middle East remains an area of tension and conflict rather than peace and development.

PART I
THE PALESTINE ARAB NATIONALIST MOVEMENT UNDER THE MANDATE

BY

ANN MOSELY LESCH

The nationalist movement of the Arabs in Palestine developed in the 1920s and 1930s in reaction to British control over the country and to the rapid expansion of the Jewish community and its political aspirations. After briefly considering Britain's commitments and dilemmas in Palestine and the development of Zionism in the interwar years, this chapter traces the early course of Arab nationalism in Palestine. It analyzes the interaction between different groups in the society, and the tactics pursued by the Arab politicians, from the initial delegations and nonviolent efforts to oppose the British policies through the general strike of 1936 and the full-scale revolt of 1937–1939. The revolt marked the peak of Arab efforts, after which the community was demoralized and factionalized, unable to prevent the partition of its homeland or the flight of 1948.

BRITISH IMPERIALISM

Although Britain's main imperial interests were centered in India, the Ottoman Empire's alliance with Germany in World War I made Palestine important as the left flank of the route to India through the Suez Canal. After the failure of the Gallipoli campaign against the heart of the Ottoman Empire, Britain decided to advance through the Arab territories of Mesopotamia and Palestine. To ensure the support of the Arab inhabitants against the Ottoman forces, Britain enlisted the aid of Husayn, the sharif of Mecca, who had long chafed under Ottoman overlordship. Husayn's son, Amir Faysal, led bedouin and regular Arab troops which harassed the Ottoman forces strung out along the Hijaz Railroad leading from Constantinople to Mecca. He kept part of the Ottoman army immobilized there while General Allenby thrust north along the coast, reaching Jerusalem in December 1917 and Damascus the next fall. In return for Faysal's support, Britain promised to uphold the Arab's claim to independence, within boundaries broadly defined in the Husayn-McMahon correspondence of 1915–1916. The correspondence only explicitly excluded

British interests in Mesopotamia and Aden and French interests in the region to the west of the Syrian towns of Damascus, Homs, Hama, and Aleppo, areas that the British government did not consider to be purely Arab.[1]

By the end of the war, Britain had entered into several contradictory commitments concerning Palestine. In a secret agreement reached with the French government and czarist Russia in 1916 (the Sykes-Picot agreement), the Ottoman Empire was to be divided among Britain, France, and Russia into spheres of control and paramount interest. Palestine was to be administered internationally because of the special interests in its Christian holy places. Still another agreement had promised the Zionists a "national home" in Palestine. The Balfour Declaration of November 1917 stated, "His Majesty's Government view with favour the establishment in Palestine of a national home for the Jewish people, and will use their best endeavours to facilitate the achievement of this object, it being clearly understood that nothing shall be done which may prejudice the civil and religious rights of the existing non-Jewish communities in Palestine, or the rights and political status enjoyed by Jews in any other country." Furthermore, Britain and the Allies had made several statements stressing the modern principle of national self-determination, which tended to support the Husayn-McMahon correspondence pledge of Arab independence. President Woodrow Wilson's wartime Fourteen Points contained broad pledges to support the principle of self-determination and the rights of small nations, themes that were echoed in the Covenant of the League of

1. The exact areas included in the promise to Husayn by Sir Henry McMahon, British high commissioner in Egypt, have been the subject of intense disagreement. The Arabs understood the commitment as excluding the area of present-day Lebanon and areas to the north along the Syrian coast. Others, primarily British officials and Zionists, have insisted that the area excluded from the proposed Arab independent state was defined as the area to the west of the *willaya* (district) of Damascus. Since the *willaya* of Damascus extended far to the south of the city and included much of what later became known as Transjordan, this interpretation insists that Palestine was deliberately excluded from the Arab independent state and consequently could be promised to the Zionists under the Balfour Declaration. This latter interpretation was never accepted by the Arabs and is filled with inconsistencies. Recent contributions to this debate are Isaiah Friedman, "The McMahon–Hussein Correspondence and the Question of Palestine," *Journal of Contemporary History*, Vol. 5, No. 2 (1970), and Arnold Toynbee, "The McMahon–Hussein Correspondence: Comments and a Reply," *ibid.*, Vol. 5, No. 4 (1970), and Friedman's rejoinder in the same issue.

Nations. Concrete promises to let the Arabs decide their own political destiny were contained in the British declaration to Syrian Arab spokesmen in June 1918, the British army's recruiting campaign in Palestine that year, the Anglo-French declaration to the peoples of Syria and Mesopotamia of November 1918, and the terms of reference of the Paris Peace Conference's special commission appointed in the spring of 1919, of which only the American section (the King-Crane Commission) toured Palestine and Syria.

British Foreign Secretary Lord Balfour admitted that the pledges were irreconcilable. In the summer of 1919, he pressed for the imposition of a settlement which was primarily based on the Sykes-Picot agreement, but which granted the Arabs autonomy in portions of the promised area of independence and upheld the Balfour Declaration in Palestine. He noted that "the contradiction between the letter of the Covenant and the policy of the Allies is even more flagrant in the case of the 'independent nation' of Palestine than in that of the 'independent nation' of Syria. For in Palestine we do not propose even to go through the form of consulting the wishes of the present inhabitants of the country. . . . The Four Powers are committed to Zionism." [2] As an official in the Foreign Office minuted, this conclusion ignored the problem of reconciling the Arabs to the loss of Palestine; Balfour proposed to give Palestine to the Zionists "irrespective of the wishes of the great bulk of the population, because it is historically right and politically expedient that [Britain] should do so. The idea that the carrying out of these programmes will entail bloodshed and military repression never seems to have occurred to him." [3]

And so the French assumed direct control of both the Lebanon littoral and the Syrian interior, forcibly ejecting Faysal from Damascus in July 1920. Although the Arabs obtained nominal independence in Iraq and Transjordan, and autonomy in the Arabian peninsula, they continued to argue that Palestine was included in the area promised independence. And Britain's denial of that argument contributed signally to their loss of faith in British pledges. [4]

2. Memorandum by Lord Balfour, September 19, 1919 (FO 371/4183/2117/132187).

3. Minute by Kidston, Middle East Department of FO, September 22, 1919; *ibid.*

4. Many British officials agreed privately with the Arabs that Palestine had not been clearly excluded from the area of Arab independence. Major Hubert Young of the Middle East Department in the Colonial Office wrote in February 1923, "The root of the whole opposition [to our Palestine policy] is the fact that Palestine is predominantly an Arab country

The Balfour Declaration itself contained serious ambiguities, and Britain failed to define or set measurable limits to the Jewish national home. The Zionists read the declaration as a pledge by the British government, and later by the League of Nations, to establish a Jewish state in Palestine, and maintained that this pledge overrode any secondary obligations on the part of the British to protect the non-Jewish population.[5] Lord Curzon noted in January 1919 that Dr. Chaim Weizmann, the president of the Zionist Organization, had telegraphed to his deputy in Palestine that the "whole administration of Palestine shall be formed as to make of Palestine a *Jewish Commonwealth* under British Trusteeship" (italics added by Lord Curzon), to which Lord Curzon commented that a "commonwealth" means "a state" or "an independent community," concluding, "what then is the good of shutting our eyes to the fact that this is what the Zionists are after, and that the British Trusteeship is a mere screen behind which to work for this end?" [6]

The Arabs, however, argued that the declaration was merely a statement of sympathy for the Zionist movement, and that its realization was conditional on the nonprejudice of the rights and position of the population already living there, which was overwhelmingly Arab. Such rights and position would be violated by extensive immigration and land purchase and especially by the possibility of the Arabs becoming a minority in the country.[7]

The British government itself was never consistent in its interpretation of the Balfour Declaration. Some leading statesmen stated frankly that they had promised a Jewish state to the Zionists. Other officials, acutely conscious of the reality of Arab existence and aspirations in Palestine, attempted to win Zionist acceptance of a more limited conception of their position there. As a Colonial Official noted in 1921, "It is clearly useless for us to endeavour to

---

and that the reservation by which we intended it to be excluded when we promised King Hussein to recognise and support the Independence of the Arabs was never fully understood by him and is not, in fact, very easy to support in the actual text of the document upon which we rely." Minute on telegram from the High Commissioner, February 11, 1923 (CO 733/42).

5. Bernard Joseph, *British Rule in Palestine* (Washington, D.C.: Public Affairs Press, 1948), offers a forceful, legalistic argument to this effect. Joseph was a leading Zionist official.

6. Minute by Curzon on January 26, 1919, referring to Weizmann's telegram to Eder of December 17, 1918, which was attached to the FO file (FO 371/4153/275).

7. W. T. Mallison, Jr., "The Balfour Declaration," in Ibrahim Abu-Lughod, ed., *The Transformation of Palestine* (Evanston: Northwestern University Press, 1971).

lead Dr. Weizmann in one direction if he is told quite a different story by the head of the government. Nothing but confusion can result if HMG [His Majesty's Government] do not speak with a single voice." [8] The Colonial Office, supported by the cabinet, tried to define British policy as one of building up "in Palestine a commonwealth, based upon a democratic foundation, in which all sections of the community will enjoy equal political rights." [9] The white papers of 1922 and 1930 asserted that Britain had obligations to the two communities, which necessitated their sharing the country as a biracial commonwealth. However, such hope of compromise faded as the Arab and Zionist nationalist movements became increasingly militant and estranged in the 1930s. The recommendation of partition by a Royal Commission in July 1937 formally acknowledged the incompatibility of Britain's obligations to the two communities and the impossibility of their being reconciled within one country. Partition into small Arab and Jewish states appeared to be the only way to meet their conflicting national ambitions and to extricate Britain from its predicament. Military repression against the Arab community for the next two years, and attempts to establish a unitary government through the white paper of 1939 and diplomatic efforts at the end of World War II, only postponed and made more violent the final partition of 1947–1948.

THE ZIONIST MOVEMENT

The Zionist movement grew out of both an ancient messianic attachment to the land of Israel and a modern political reaction to anti-Semitism and economic discrimination, particularly in Eastern Europe. It viewed the establishment of an autonomous Jewish state, to which Jews could freely immigrate, as essential for the future of the Jewish people and for the normalization of their position in the contemporary world of nation-states.

Founded officially at the Basle congress in 1897, the movement developed in ignorance of conditions in Palestine. Many Zionists readily accepted the slogan "a land without a people for a people without a land," despite the obvious presence of a half million Arabs, whose families had been rooted to the soil for millennia. Even after small groups of colonists settled in Palestine and met

8. Minute by J. E. Shuckburgh, Middle East Department, CO, late November 1921 (CO 733/15).

9. Quotation from the draft formula submitted by the CO to the ZO and the Arab delegation on December 17, 1921, as a basis for further discussions (CO 537/854).

Arab opposition to their land purchases and political pretensions, the Zionists tried to ignore the local population. Ahad Ha'am, a Zionist who supported the cultural renewal of the Jewish people in Palestine, criticized in 1914 the political Zionists who "wax angry towards those who remind them that there is still another people in Eretz Israel that has been living there and does not intend at all to leave." [10]

Dr. Weizmann argued that Palestine was designed to solve "a world-wide problem" and therefore "the rights which the Jewish people has been adjudged in Palestine do not depend on the consent, and cannot be subjected to the will, of the majority of its present inhabitants." He maintained that "the Balfour Declaration and the Mandate have definitely lifted [Palestine] out of the context of the Middle East and linked it up with the world-wide Jewish community and the world-wide Jewish problem." [11] Thus the Zionists refused to let the British grant the Palestine Arabs any role in setting immigration quotas or in influencing other aspects of the development of the Jewish national home. Weizmann's contempt for the first Arab delegation to London was apparent in his one discussion with them at the Colonial Office, in which he adopted the attitude "of a conqueror handing to beaten foes the terms of peace." [12]

He outlined the projected development of the autonomous Jewish community in Palestine (the Yishuv) in a lengthy memorandum to the Colonial Office as early as August 1921, in which he described the colonization planned for the next three years. The Yishuv would be doubled or tripled by the addition of from ninety to one hundred and fifty thousand immigrants in preparation for the eventual Jewish majority. He suggested that the Zionists should "begin by creating a majority in certain districts," mentioning Jerusalem, Jaffa–Tel Aviv and the coast up to Haifa, and the Jordan valley–Tiberias-Safad region. "Garden suburbs" would surround the towns so that the community would be agriculturally self-sufficient. A hydroelectric power complex on the Jordan River would provide the basis for industrial development. And special Jewish military protection would enable the community to exist and expand as an entity wholly independent of the Arab population.[13]

10. Quoted by Erskine B. Childers at the opening of his essay, "The Wordless Wish," in Abu-Lughod, ed., *Transformation of Palestine*, p. 165.

11. Weizmann personal letter to Shuckburgh, March 5, 1930 (CO 733/187/77105).

12. Note by CO official E. Mills on the joint meeting, November 30, 1921 (CO 537/855).

13. Memorandum dated August 17, 1921 (CO 733/16).

In addition to these guidelines, which were substantially followed, land bought by the Jewish National Fund was held as the inalienable property of the Jewish people, with the result that Arabs could no longer find a means of livelihood on it. The exclusive employment of Jews in Jewish businesses and on Jewish farms, termed "the conquest of work," was enforced by militant pickets and constituted another aspect of this economic policy. The Zionist Organization developed autonomous executive institutions in Palestine which paralleled the government departments, as well as a separate elected general assembly and executive (Va'ad Haleumi) for the Jewish *millet* (religious community). It clandestinely organized and equipped a military force, the Haganah, which protected the colonies and Jewish urban quarters and would ultimately assume control of most of the country itself. Despite heated Arab objections, Zionist-supported organizations acquired major economic concessions, including the provision of hydroelectric power from the Jordan and Awja rivers, the extraction of mineral salts from the Dead Sea, the drainage and settlement of the Hulah marshes, and reclamation of the sand dunes along the Mediterranean coast below Haifa. As the Jewish population increased from 11 percent in 1922 to 16 percent in 1931, then doubled in absolute number to 28 percent in 1936, it became possible for an immigrant to live entirely within a Jewish community, dependent in no respect on the Arab majority and coming into only incidental contact with Arabs.[14] He lived within a society that stressed the Jews' absolute right to possess Palestine as their own without considering whether the Arabs might have comparable or prior rights.

The Zionist officials traded on their strong position in London. Individual spokesmen could contact the Colonial Office, cabinet members and members of Parliament at almost any time on any issue. In contrast, the rare trips by Arab delegations and prominent individuals to London permitted only sporadic presentation of the Arab viewpoint to officials and the English public. The Zionists also utilized secret negotiations to attain their ends: the negotiations between a cabinet committee and the Zionist Organization in the winter of 1930–1931, which resulted in substantial concessions to the Zionist position on immigration rights and exclusive hiring policies, are the prime example of this approach, undertaken without concern for the repercussions of such secret conclaves on Arab opinion.[15]

14. Janet Abu-Lughod, using official census data, has carefully surveyed demographic changes in Palestine in "The Demographic Transformation of Palestine," Ibrahim Abu-Lughod, ed., *Transformation of Palestine*.

15. Minute by Dr. Shiels, Parliamentary Under Secretary, February 3, 1931 (CO 733/197/85050).

Zionist officials in Palestine tried to buy the support of prominent Arabs, to subsidize Arabic newspapers, and even to form political parties that would follow their lead. At first some notables did join the National Muslim Societies, formed by the Zionist Organization in 1921, in the hope of obtaining public office, but they immediately lost their popular influence. And others who had joined in hopes of obtaining government posts or low-interest loans withdrew once it was apparent that no posts or loans would be forthcoming. The Agricultural Parties of the mid-1920s also collapsed when the Zionist Organization withdrew its subsidy and did not help the members to obtain agricultural loans or establish a much-needed agricultural bank. These efforts only left a legacy of bitterness and failed to win over any genuine support for the Zionist position in the Arab community.[16]

ARAB NATIONALISM IN PALESTINE

Until the end of World War I, Palestine was divided into several districts, and the local inhabitants considered themselves part of a broadly defined Syria. When Amir Faysal established a government in Damascus in October 1918, the Palestine Arabs' aspirations focused on him, and many young men served in his government and army. The local political clubs that sprang up in the wake of the British occupation drew together for an All-Palestine Conference in February 1919, which supported the inclusion of Palestine in an independent Syria and elected delegates to the First Arab Congress, held in Damascus later that spring. But Faysal's fall in July 1920 resulted in a swift reorientation of Palestinian political attention and aspirations. A Palestinian nationalism emerged which was concerned with problems caused by Zionist aspirations, problems that were not faced by the other Arab countries. (Figure 1 outlines the development of Arab political organizations within Palestine.) This reorientation was evident as early as the winter of 1920–1921 in the demands of the Third Arab Congress at Haifa. As presented by the first Muslim-Christian delegation to London in the summer of 1921, they may be summarized thus: (1) formation of a national government responsible to a parliament elected by the

16. See criticism of such methods by Leonard Stein, a Zionist official in London, in his letter to Col. Frederick Kisch, the Zionist Political Secretary in Palestine, June 12, 1923; Central Zionist Archives (CZA), S25/665; and apologia by Chaim Kalvarisky, an early settler who was the main organizer of these societies, in his letter to ZO, London, July 2, 1923; CZA, Z4/2421.

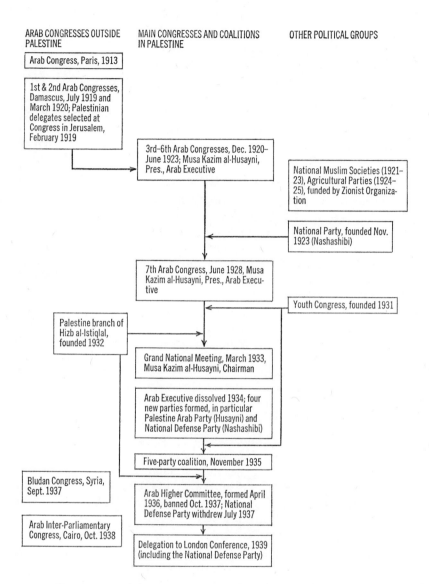

FIG. 1. Arab Political Organization in Palestine, 1919–1939

native population, Muslim, Christian, and Jewish; (2) abolition of the Jewish national home principle; (3) an end to Jewish immigration until the national government is formed, which would then decide on immigration policy; (4) Palestine to be governed according to prewar Ottoman law, not the postwar British regulations; (5) Palestine not to be separated from the neighboring Arab states.[17] These demands were developed at length in a letter from the delegation to Colonial Secretary Winston Churchill, which noted, concerning the Balfour Declaration:

> The Balfour Declaration was made without our being consulted and we cannot accept it as deciding our destinies. . . .
>
> The Declaration should be superseded by an Agreement which would safeguard the rights, interests and liberties of the people of Palestine, and at the same time make provision for reasonable Jewish religious aspirations, but precluding any exclusive political advantages to them which must necessarily interfere with Arab rights. . . .
>
> It is the claim of the Zionists that the People of Palestine, after practical experience, will recognize the advantage to the country of Zionist immigration. If that be so, the Jews may be confident that the future immigration policy of [the National Government in] Palestine would not be unfavourable to them: but if the immigration policy of the Zionist Organization proves detrimental to the Palestine people, this policy should be regulated, not in the interests of the Zionists, but of Palestinians.[18]

There remained a striking continuity in the Arabs' basic demands throughout the mandate period, but the underlying feelings grew more bitter and desperate as Jewish immigration and land purchase increased and as the possibility of independence under an Arab government receded. In 1935 the British high commissioner wrote that the Arabs' hostility was rooted in their belief that they were promised independence after the last war. Instead, the Balfour Declaration and the mandate were imposed on them, and the government reneged on its promise of independence and neglected to encourage even local autonomy. "To this sense of injustice," he noted, "must now be added a genuine feeling of fear that the Jews will succeed in establishing themselves in such large numbers that in the not distant future, they will gain economic and political control over the country." [19]

17. Muslim-Christian Delegation statement, handed to the Colonial Secretary in London, August 12, 1921 (CO 733/14).
18. Letter from the Delegation to the Colonial Secretary, October 24, 1921 (CO 733/16).
19. Sir Arthur Wauchope (High Commissioner) to the Colonial Secretary, December 7, 1935 (CO 733/278/75156).

The "national demands" of the six-month general strike in 1936 called for suspension of Jewish immigration, prohibition of land sales to Jews, and the formation of a national government responsible to a representative council. By then, the Arabs' aim was not to drive the Jewish community out of Palestine but to make the Jews realize that they formed part of a predominantly Arab area and that they would have to come to terms with the Arabs in order to continue to live there. One articulate Arab expressed his countrymen's viewpoint: "The feeling is *not* that if the British will go we will kill the Jews; the feeling *is* if the British go the Jews will be less arrogant and less grabbing and we will be able to live with them." [20]

The Palestinian Arab national movement grew out of the Arab social environment and therefore had great endurance, if not, in the end, success. The pyramidal family and clan network, which built on relationships of support and protection from the village level through local potentates to leading families at the district level, offered the means of rapid articulation of opinion and mobilization of all levels of society.[21] The main political parties were based on this structure, the parties of the particularly influential Husayni and Nashashibi families having ties throughout the country. However, this structure made it difficult to unify the national movement. Since each leading family had a political power base in client villages or town quarters, it felt itself the equal of the others and bargained vigorously before forming alliances. Even then the alliances shifted rapidly, on the basis of personal and family differences rather than policy. The most enduring and damaging split occurred between the Husaynis and Nashashibis. Hajj Amin al-Husayni served not only as mufti of Jerusalem, but as president of the Supreme Muslim Council, an organization established in early 1922 to control Islamic religious, legal, educational, and endowment programs. His elder relative, Musa Kazim al-Husayni, presided over four delegations to London and all the Arab congresses, until his death in 1934. He had been mayor of Jerusalem in 1920, when the British ousted him for his outspoken stand on national issues. Raghib an-Nashashibi replaced Musa Kazim Pasha as mayor, thereby winning Husayni enmity and the charge of collaborating with the British. After his defeat in the

20. Musa al-Alami, Personal Secretary to the High Commissioner, in a long memorandum to the CO, September 1933, on the political situation, enclosed in a dispatch of the High Commissioner to the CO, December 23, 1933 (CO 733/257/37356).

21. Jacob Shimoni, *The Arabs in Israel*, 1947 (translated from Hebrew in 1956 by the Human Relations Area Files), pp. 423–425.

municipal election of 1934, Raghib Bey formed his own political party, which took a moderate stand toward the British and allied itself with Amir Abdallah of Transjordan. The bargaining, the shifting alliances, and the Husayni-Nashashibi split tended to conceal the underlying unity of national feeling and the concern among all groups for preserving the Arab identity of Palestine.[22]

Another division, which had socioeconomic importance but far less political salience, lay between the peasantry (*fallahin*) and the landowning class. The Zionists tried to play on this division by sponsoring Agricultural Parties in the mid-1920s, and the British hoped that improved economic conditions would cause the *fallahin* to reject political leaders drawn from the landlord class. But in practice the Zionists were unable to provide the tangible rewards necessary for the parties' success, and the British found the peasantry's economic position deteriorating rather than improving. The *fallahin* felt remote from the political infighting among the Arab elite, but they responded readily to the basic national demands. Land purchases by Zionist companies from absentee landlords and indebted *fallahin* made them anxious to restrict further land sales. Two large farmers' congresses in 1930 and 1931 articulated a wide range of rural grievances, but in general the more politically sophisticated elite presented their concerns before the high commissioner and the Colonial Office. The villagers' fear and antagonism were acted out directly in the 1921 attacks on Zionist colonies in the Jaffa district, and in the 1929 violence that swept through several towns. *Fallahin* formed the backbone of the 1936–1939 revolt, during which they served as guerrilla fighters, supplied the

22. Even in the early years of the mandate an important individual rapidly lost his influence within the Arab community if he was known to cooperate with Zionist leaders. Haydar Tuqan of Nablus, for example, apparently thought that the Zionists could help him to gain either an appointment as mayor of Nablus or a seat on the advisory council in Jerusalem, and that the Zionist Organization could provide loans to benefit his political clients. (Miller, Nablus dispatch to Eder, Zionist Commission, Jerusalem, July 16, 1922; CZA, S25/4380.) But the Zionists failed to provide either positions or loans for him, and so Haydar Bey lost both the tangible benefits of association with the Zionists and his personal standing in the Arab community. As Chaim Kalvarisky, the Zionists' principal liaison agent with the Arabs, wrote: "In past days, Chidur Bek [Haydar Bey] was a man of importance in his town, a member of Parliament in Constantinople, and Mayor of the Municipality. Since the occupation, and since it became known that he is a friend of the Jews, he has lost all hope of obtaining any post whatever, even an honourary one." (Kalvarisky dispatch to Political Department, ZO, London, June 4, 1923; CZA, Z4/2421).

townspeople with essential foodstuffs, and provided sanctuary for the rebel bands.

A third social division lay between the Muslims and Christians, the latter one-eighth the size of the Muslim community and further divided into several sects. Over three-quarters of the Christians lived in the twenty-three main towns in the 1920s, whereas only a quarter of the Muslims were urban dwellers. Similarly, 71.5 percent of the Christian men over the age of seven were literate in 1931, as against 25.1 percent of the Muslim men.[23] Thus, the Christians formed an important element in the commercial, agricultural, educational, and government life of Palestine, and the Muslim majority sometimes resented their influential role. However, the Christians were accorded at least proportional representation in the Arab congresses, on the Arab Executive, and on the delegations, in order to stress the secular basis of Arab nationalism. They also sent separate delegations to Rome and the Balkans to plead the Arab case. When political parties were established in the mid-1930s, the Catholics tended to gravitate to the Husayni party, and the Greek Orthodox politicians to the Nashashibis, a tendency based on traditional protective arrangements.

They remained anxious about potential anti-Christian actions on the part of the Muslims and therefore caucused separately before Arab congresses and presented a united front on such issues as the legislative council. They were particularly anxious at the tone of the December 1931 international Muslim conference convened by Hajj Amin al-Husayni in Jerusalem, which stressed the city's role as a center of Muslim culture and religious revival. British officials noted this anxiety and used it as an excuse for maintaining the communal basis of the electoral franchise in municipal politics and in plans for a legislative council. The two communities did display, however, a common front on the one issue that overrode all others—the fear of Zionism and a determination to maintain the Arab character of Palestine.

Finally, the generational differences within the Arab political leadership played an important political role. The older politicians tended to be more conciliatory, more willing to work within legal channels than the young men. In the early 1920s this difference was expressed in the contrast between the moderate Muslim-Christian Society and the young men of an-Nadi al-Arabi and Muntada al-Adabi. The former led the opposition to British attempts to estab-

23. Lister G. Hopkins, "Population," in Said B. Himadeh, ed., *Economic Organization of Palestine* (Beirut: American Press, 1938), pp. 12 and 36; figures from Palestine Census 1931, Vol. I, p. 206.

lish a legislative council but shied away from engaging in the extralegal tactics of nonpayment of taxes and violent demonstrations, which were advocated by some of the members of the two clubs. By the 1930s the young men of these clubs had themselves joined the established older generation, and a younger generation, which had matured entirely within the mandate period, which was frustrated at its lack of career opportunities in Palestine, and which placed direct blame on the British government, mobilized itself through a variety of movements such as the Boy Scouts, Arab Young Men's Congress, and Hizb al-Istiqlal al-Arabi (a branch of the Pan-Arab movement), and formed the spearhead of the rebels in the late 1930s. These men still worked within the general framework of the Palestinian movement, accepting the authority of the Arab Executive as the Arabs' spokesman vis-à-vis the British until the death of its octogenarian president, Musa Kazim al-Husayni, in 1934. The impact of the generational division was reduced by the Arabs' deferential culture. Respect for one's father and for an elder statesman who consulted the other leaders and expressed the general consensus remained powerful forces, drawing together the differing drives of the young and old in a politically effective manner.

There were also external institutional obstacles to the political unification of the Arabs resulting from British policies which hindered the development of permanent, structured organs to articulate the Arab viewpoint. In the first place, the Arabs could not form a communal (*millet*) body because, unlike the Jewish community, the Arabs were divided into two religions, and separate *millet* organs had to be established for the Muslims and the several Christian sects. Since this divided the common front which the Arab nationalists wished to preserve, the communal institutions were never allowed to assume the central political role that they could play in the Jewish community in Palestine. Even the powerful Supreme Muslim Council, which controlled the Muslim religious courts and endowments, never became synonymous with the nationalist movement.

Second, the British would not recognize the Arab political organizations, in particular the Arab Executive (1920–1934) and Arab Higher Committee (formed in 1936), as the official spokesmen of the Arab community, despite the evidence that the general public fundamentally supported their position. The refusal was ostensibly made on the grounds that the leaders were not elected by the population at large, but government officials acknowledged in private that "nonrecognition" was not due to any question of their representative character among the people but to the fact that "it [the Arab

Executive] opposes the principles embodied in the Mandate." [24]
An Arab assembly would only be considered "representative" by
the British if it did not issue resolutions contrary to the mandate,
which included the Balfour Declaration.[25] This requirement placed
the Arab leaders in an impossible dilemma, inasmuch as accepting
the stipulation and supporting the mandate would have resulted in
losing their popular backing and their stature as leaders of the
Arab community. In crises, the British did negotiate with the Arab
leaders as the de facto spokesmen of their community, but in quiet
periods the British could ignore the Arab political bodies or encourage moderates to develop opposition groups.

Finally, there was no legislative council in Palestine to provide
a constitutional forum to air grievances or to allow legitimate communication with the British rulers. The Arabs had rejected an
offer of a council in 1922–1923 because they hoped that the entire
mandatory machine could be overturned. When the Arab leaders
decided in the late 1920s to support the establishment of a council
so long as that did not imply acceptance of the mandate itself, it
was the turn of the Zionist Organization to oppose the council,
partly on the grounds that the Arabs could agitate more effectively
if they had such a forum. One contemporary commentary noted:
"Under a semi-parliamentary regime [the British government would]
be forced to heed [the Arabs'] protests, inasmuch as they would
have that guise of representative opinion that they can now be said
to lack." [26]

Thus the Arab community lacked institutions recognized by the
British rulers, unifying communal organs, and a role in a wider
representative forum. Despite these obstacles, which added to the
tensions inherent in Palestinian society, the common motivation
to oppose the British and Zionists generally overcame the divisions.
Cohesion and mobilization tended to vary directly with the degree
of threat perceived by the Arabs from the Zionist movement: when
the threat seemed minimal in the mid-1920s, the Arab movement
was most susceptible to internecine strife, and its leaders felt they
could indulge in conflicts over elections for municipal councils and
the Supreme Muslim Council. But these squabbles were papered
over in 1928 as the Arabs perceived that the threat from the Zionist movement had again increased. The rapid immigration of Jews

24. Memorandum prepared by Government House, Jerusalem, on an
Arab Executive Report, March 28, 1921 (CO 733/13).
25. Political Report, January 1921 (FO 371/6374).
26. Commentary in *Near East and India*, London, December 15, 1932,
entered into CO records (CO 733/223/97258).

in the early 1930s was paralleled by unprecedented mobilization among the various elements of the Arab community (including even the secluded Muslim women). Although the leaders of the half-dozen political parties had barely formed a common front by the time the 1936 strike broke out, the spontaneous public uprising maintained the lengthy strike and later a full-scale rebellion, even after the party leaders had been deported and the Arab Higher Committee proscribed.

THE PAN-ARAB DIMENSION OF PALESTINIAN NATIONALISM

Palestinian leaders felt that they must involve the rest of the Muslim and Arab worlds in their struggle in order to win any diplomatic results. Therefore, the Arab Executive sent delegations to the Hijaz, Egypt, Iraq, Iran, and India. The Hijazi delegations were particularly important opportunities to address the general populace assembled in Mecca for the annual pilgrimage, not just the official classes. In the early years, the Palestinians had hoped that Amir Faysal would found an Arab federation whose size would reduce the Palestinians' fear of being swamped by Jewish immigrants. Faysal's ejection from Damascus in 1920 and his father's loss of the Hijaz to Ibn Saud in 1924 destroyed these hopes. The Palestinians had, however, succeeded diplomatically to the extent that the sharif Husayn rejected Britain's demand that he recognize the Zionist policy in Palestine and insisted that the British "establish in Palestine as soon as possible a Native Representative Government." [27] But the terms of Husayn's treaty with Britain were not agreed on before he lost control of the Hijaz.

27. Direct quotation from the draft Anglo–Arab treaty, in High Commissioner's dispatch to CO, November 16, 1923 (CO 733/51). At the Cairo conference in March 1921 the British government decided that a principal condition for maintaining Amir Husayn's financial subsidy should be his ratification of the treaties of Versailles and Sèvres, which would mean accepting the mandatory principle and the Balfour Declaration. Although Husayn tentatively recognized these principles in his negotiations that summer with T. E. Lawrence, substantial pressure from Palestinian leaders induced him to harden his position in correspondence with London from the spring of 1923 through the summer of 1924. He proposed that a national government representing all the inhabitants in Palestine be established, which would permit regulated Jewish immigration on humanitarian grounds and also retain Arab political rights. The negotiations remained deadlocked over this issue and were abruptly ended by Husayn's forced abdication as Ibn Saud's forces approached Mecca in early October 1924. George Antonius, *The Arab Awakening* (New York: Capricorn Books, 1965), pp. 332–334; Aaron S. Klieman, *Foundations of British Policy in the Arab World: The Cairo Conference of 1921* (Baltimore: Johns Hopkins Press, 1970), pp. 121–122, 223.

On another diplomatic front, the Palestinians hoped that the Turkish leader Mustafa Kemal would support them in his peace negotiations with the European powers at Lausanne in late 1922. The first article of the Turkish National Pact had called for plebiscites in the Arab parts of the former Ottoman Empire, but the Palestine delegation to Lausanne found that the negotiations avoided the issue of their fate.

The Arabs could not afford to send delegations to League of Nations sessions in Geneva, although the Arab Executive did submit memoranda to the Permanent Mandates Commission (PMC). The Executive had to rely on a group of Syrian exiles who had formed a Syro-Palestinian Committee there. But the committee's influence was limited, and it was compromised in Palestinian eyes for its contacts with the Zionists in the 1920s and with Italian Fascists in the 1930s. When Iraq and Egypt joined the League in the 1930s, the Palestine Arabs finally had spokesmen who could at least present their viewpoint, if not lobby effectively for it.

Two Palestinian leaders were particularly active in promoting Pan-Arab and Pan-Islamic support for Palestine. Awni Abd al-Hadi, who had worked closely with Faysal in 1919–1920, formed the Palestine branch of Hizb al-Istiqlal al-Arabi (the Party of Arab Independence) in 1932. His plan to rally Pan-Arab sentiment at a congress in Baghdad fell through after Faysal died in 1933. But he maintained useful contacts with political leaders in Iraq and Saudi Arabia. Hajj Amin al-Husayni gained international stature through his efforts to make al-Haram ash-Sharif in Jerusalem a principal center of Muslim culture, a campaign which culminated in the international Muslim congress of December 1931. The congress included not only official delegates and *ulama*, but representatives of middle-class lay societies such as the Young Men's Muslim Associations, and Shi'a leaders from Iran and Iraq. Hajj Amin also headed a mission to Mecca in 1934, which contributed to the resolution of a border war between Saudi Arabia and the Yemen and earned him goodwill in those countries.

Hajj Amin and Awni Bey were able to utilize these contacts in 1936 when they persuaded the kings of Iraq, Saudi Arabia, Yemen, and Transjordan to appeal for an end to the general strike in the hope that their diplomatic influence with Britain would result in a political settlement favorable to the Palestine Arabs. This direct involvement in the Palestine conflict expanded during the next summer, when the Palestine Arabs called on the kings to protest the Royal Commission's recommendation of partition, and in the fall, when a congress of over four hundred politicians was held in Bludan, Syria. The delegates, largely drawn from Palestine, Syria, and Lebanon, stressed their opposition to any partition of Palestine and their support of political and economic measures to block Zionism. For the first time non-Palestinian Arabs were included in responsible positions, as part of a new executive committee and as organizers of a network of local Defense of Palestine committees.

In October 1938, at the height of the revolt, another congress was convened, this time in Cairo, which drew together politicians from a dozen Arab and Muslim countries and marked the first active involvement of the Egyptian government and politicians in the Palestine issue.[28] Although its resolutions fell short of the Arab-unity program Awni Bey had desired, it did send a delegation to London, which helped to persuade Britain to convene a conference in London in February 1939 that would include delegates from the Arab states as well as from the Palestine Arabs and the Jewish Agency.

Britain expected that the Arab ministers attending the London conference would exert a moderating influence on the Palestine Arab delegation. The ministers did try to find common ground between the British and Palestine positions on immigration, minority rights, and the period of transition to independence. But they were also confronted by extreme Zionist claims, and discovered that Britain was unwilling to grant majority influence to the Palestine Arabs in any future independent state. They therefore supported the Palestine delegation's position at the close of the conference, rejecting the British offer as not precise enough to assuage the Palestinians' fears.

In the late 1940s, this official involvement was translated into diplomatic activities through the Arab League (formed in 1945) and Arab delegations to the United Nations, and then into military support in 1948–1949. In general, the Arab rulers were more willing to compromise with the Zionists than were the Palestinians, since the vital interests of their countries were not at stake in the conflict. The military and diplomatic hold that Britain and previously France retained over them further limited their foreign policy initiatives. Finally, the political divisions among the rulers and the poor condition of their armies restricted severely the effectiveness of the military operations which they undertook to prevent the partition of Palestine.

28. Elizabeth Monroe, *Britain's Moment in the Middle East* (Baltimore: Johns Hopkins Press, 1963), pp. 122–123, on the Cairo congress. Dispatches from Gilbert MacKereth (British Consul, Damascus) to FO, September 11, 14, 1937, and Chief Secretary dispatch to CO, September 25, 1937, on the Bludan congress (CO 733/353/75718/35).

PHASES OF THE PALESTINIAN NATIONALIST MOVEMENT

The basic difficulty confronting the Palestine Arabs may be summarized in this question: How could a small, traditionally organized and impoverished people gain its independence against the combined weight of the British Empire and the determined Zionist movement?

Peaceful Resistance

Until the mid-1920s the Arab leaders thought that they could persuade the British to relinquish the Zionist aspects of their rule and grant the Arabs a measure of self-government. They used various methods of persuasion and obstruction to make their position clear. The modes of persuasion included sending petitions to the colonial secretary and the Permanent Mandates Commission (PMC) of the League of Nations, as well as to local officials, and sending special delegations to London, Geneva, and Lausanne. Modes of obstruction included demonstrations, one-day general strikes, and the refusal of offers of a legislative council, an advisory council, and an Arab agency because they all implied acceptance of the Balfour Declaration as the basis of Palestinian political life.

Every year the Arab Executive (formed in late 1920) sent lengthy memoranda to the PMC. However, these communications had to be submitted to the Palestine government first, which then passed them on to the Colonial Office and the PMC with its own comments attached. Therefore the Arabs had no way of approaching the PMC directly, and the British could always rebut their criticisms. After the Arab leaders met briefly with Colonial Secretary Winston Churchill when he passed through Palestine in late March 1921, they realized the importance of taking their case directly to London. An eight-man delegation spent nearly a year there attempting to persuade the Colonial Office to grant Palestine independence. The high commissioner for Palestine did persuade the Colonial Office to discuss its constitutional plans with the delegation and to present to them a clarification of British policy, which attempted to meet their criticisms. But the Churchill white paper of July 1922 retained the essence of the Balfour Declaration and remained too far removed from their aspirations to be acceptable. Further smaller delegations were sent to Lausanne and London at the time of the renegotiation of the European peace treaty with Turkey, 1922–1923, and to London in the summer of 1923 while a special cabinet committee deliberated on policy toward Palestine, but neither delegation achieved any tangible results.

The earliest demonstrations were held in February and March 1920, the former to protest the first official public reading of the Balfour Declaration in Palestine, and the latter to support the proclamation of Syrian (and Palestinian) independence by the Second Arab Congress in Damascus. The religious celebration of Nabi Musa (the Prophet Moses) a month later degenerated into violent attacks on the Jewish quarter of the Old City of Jerusalem. And violence briefly flared up in Jerusalem on November 2, the anniversary of the Balfour Declaration. Throughout the mandate period, that anniversary was marked as a day of mourning, with shops closed, newspapers appearing with black borders, and black crepe paper festooned on buildings. By the 1930s, December 9, the anniversary of Britain's "liberation" of Jerusalem in 1917, was also declared a day of mourning. Another one-day strike was held in July 1922 to protest the League of Nations' support of a Palestine mandate based on the Balfour Declaration. And all Arab public figures except the mayors boycotted the ceremony in September 1922 when the high commissioner took the constitutional oath.[29] A complete boycott was also maintained against Lord Balfour when he came to Palestine in the spring of 1925 to dedicate the Hebrew University, on the invitation of the Zionist Organization.

Although some prominent Arabs participated in the advisory council established by the high commissioner in the fall of 1920, they did so in their individual capacities, not as spokesmen of the general population, and on the understanding that it was a temporary institution, soon to be superseded by constitutional representative organs. The high commissioner also invited forty-six Arab leaders to meet with him in August 1921 as a Muslim-Christian consultative committee. The first meeting was well attended, but only six came to the second meeting, because the delegation, just arrived in London, had urgently telegrammed that the committee's cooperation with the government was undermining the delegation's efforts to obtain fundamental constitutional changes. Furthermore, the Arabs had been willing to participate in the committee only on the condition that political issues be excluded from its purview, and they were irritated that the high commissioner immediately raised the question of constitutional reform as an issue suitable for them to discuss.[30]

The constitution which the British offered the Palestinians in the

29. Political Report, July 1922 (CO 733/24). Political Report, September 1922 (CO 733/26).

30. Political Reports, August and September 1921, and High Commissioner's telegram to CO, September 29, 1921 (CO 733/6).

fall of 1922 contained the hated Balfour Declaration and provided that the British official members of the projected legislative council plus the Jewish representatives would always carry a majority. In addition, the high commissioner could veto legislation, and the council could not discuss immigration, which would be considered by a special advisory commission composed of the three religious communities. The commission could only propose immigration policy to the high commissioner, who did not have to follow its advice. The organization and powers of the legislative council did not reassure the Arab politicians; aside from providing them with a political forum, it gave them no means to counter or limit the Zionist policy. On the contrary, its acceptance would mean capitulating to the Zionists on fundamental political points. As the Arab Executive proclaimed, "By accepting [the council] there will be clear proof of [the nation's] acceptance of the Mandate and of the present Zionist policy." [31] All groups except the Zionist-funded National Muslim Societies boycotted the February–March 1923 elections for secondary electors; and rather than form a clearly unrepresentative council, the high commissioner canceled the next stage of elections and substituted an appointed advisory council to provide the administration with nonofficial advice.

The Arab politicians agreed to participate in the new advisory council so long as participation did not imply acceptance of Britain's Zionist policy or involve discussion of political issues, as they had stipulated in regard to the previous advisory council and the abortive consultative committee. However, the wording of Britain's Amending Order-in-Council made it appear that the advisory council was a constitutional substitute for the legislative council; and so, under heavy pressure from the Arab Executive, the ten moderates (including Raghib an-Nashashibi) withdrew their tentative acceptance.

The British government tried one more ploy, offering an Arab agency in the fall of 1923, which was publicized as a parallel to the Jewish agency established by the mandate, but which really lacked comparable powers and rationale.[32] The members of the Arab agency were to be appointed by the high commissioner, not chosen by the Arab community itself; it would not be mentioned in the mandate instrument, unlike the Jewish agency; it would

31. Arab Executive proclamation, February 3, 1923, enclosed in Political Report, February 1923 (CO 733/43).

32. The idea of an Arab agency was formulated by the Cabinet Committee on Palestine, July 1923 (CO 733/58). On the Arabs' reaction, see High Commissioner's telegram to CO, October 11, 1923 (CO 733/50).

not have the international support and funding or the colonizing drive which were behind the Jewish agency; and its acceptance would have meant that the Arabs saw the Arab and Jewish communities as being of equal standing in Palestine, whereas their fundamental premise was that Palestine was and should remain an Arab country. With the refusal of these palliatives, the Palestine Arabs hoped that Britain would see that "the only remedy to the present state" was "the establishment of a national representative government in Palestine." [33] Although the Arabs considered that their election boycott showed "the world that we are a nation worthy of the life of liberty and complete independence," [34] the government in London viewed the Arabs as stubborn, negative, and intractable, and decided not to make any more political offers to them, hoping to break the authority of the Arab Executive over the Arab community.[35]

The Arabs' attempts to influence British policy through delegations, political strikes, and election boycott appeared a failure by the mid-1920s. Although the Palestine government took seriously this evidence of discontent, the actions failed to have an impact on the government in London, from which fundamental policy changes would have to come. As a result, the Arab movement began to split between those who felt that the best strategy would be to grasp any available levers of power in Palestine in order to influence policy, and those who held that total opposition and anomic violence would force the British into rethinking their policy. In the mid-1920s the moderate viewpoint prevailed, partly because this was the one period in which Arab fears of being swamped by immigrants appeared illusory. The economic depression of 1926–1927 resulted in Jewish emigration actually exceeding immigration in 1927, and the Zionist Organization could barely provide dole for all the unemployed people thronging the streets of Tel Aviv. Even the prominent Zionist official Leonard Stein wrote as early as June 1923 that the Zionists' dream of a vast immigration had vanished and they must face reality and readjust to the idea of remaining "a Jewish island in an Arab sea," hardly able to keep pace through

33. Arab Delegation memorandum to His Majesty's Government, circulated in Palestine, August 1923, enclosed in Political Report, August 1923 (CO 733/49).

34. Arab Executive Declaration, April 15, 1923, enclosed in Political Report, April 1923 (CO 733/45).

35. Minutes by CO officials mid-October 1923; and Colonial Secretary telegrams to High Commissioner, October 17 and November 16, 1923 (CO 733/50 and 51).

immigration with the natural increase in the Arab population.[36]

As a result of their increased confidence, the Arab politicians sharply contested the elections for the Supreme Muslim Council in 1926 and those for the municipal councils in 1927. The Supreme Muslim Council elections were annulled by the courts on a technicality which provided the high commissioner with the opportunity to balance the factions by appointing two Husayni supporters and two Nashashibi supporters to the interim council. However, Hajj Amin continued to maintain final authority as the permanent president of the council. The municipal elections were largely won by the moderate Nashashibi faction in towns in which the Jewish bloc vote could be brought to bear on its side (notably in Jerusalem, Haifa, Safad, and Tiberias). The Arabs felt that they could afford the luxury of political infighting at this time, without sacrificing their broader position vis-à-vis the Zionists. The different factions even joined in private discussions with a government official in the summer of 1926 to formulate a new constitutional proposal, but the talks foundered because the government could not agree to the amount of autonomy desired by the Arabs and because it did not consider the negotiators to be the official spokesmen of the Arab community.[37]

Radicalization

Arab fears revived in 1928 when Jewish immigration and economic life took an upward turn, the British confirmed the Zionist concession for extracting salts from the Dead Sea, the Jewish National Fund expanded its land purchases, and the Zionist Organization was enlarged to include the financially prosperous non-Zionists in the United States in an umbrella organization, the Jewish Agency. These fears led the Arab community to compose their political differences and to convene a long-postponed congress in July 1928 which elected a forty-eight-man Executive incorporating all the factions. They also attempted to accelerate the constitutional discussions with the Palestine government. Some of the Arab Executive leaders even indicated in the spring of 1929 that they might accept a nominated advisory council along the lines of the one they had rejected back in 1923.[38] But the August 1929 violence aborted constitutional discussions.

36. Leonard Stein confidential letter to Colonel Frederick Kisch, June 12, 1923 (CZA, S25/665).

37. *Palestine Bulletin,* Jerusalem, September 16, 1926. Zionist Organization, London letter to Kisch, July 23, 1926 (CZA, S25/665).

38. High Commissioner, Sir John Chancellor, dispatch (secret) to Shuckburgh, June 14, 1929 (CO 733/167/67105).

The outbreak had its roots in the long-festering difficulties between the Muslim and Jewish communities over the Wailing Wall, which was legally Muslim property and sacred to Muslims as part of al-Haram ash-Sharif. The prophet Muhammad was said to have tethered his horse inside the wall while he ascended to heaven to appear before Allah. Al-Quds (the Holy), as Jerusalem is known in Arabic, became the holiest city after Mecca and Medina. Al-Aqsa Mosque and the Dome of the Rock, both within al-Haram ash-Sharif, were especially venerated. Jews also venerated al-Haram as the site of the Temple destroyed by the Romans. The Wailing Wall was the only remaining part of the Temple, and Jews came to it to pray and lament. Their customary right of access under the Ottoman regime did not, however, include the right to bring the full accoutrements for a religious service there. With the revived spirit and militancy of the Jewish community in 1928, their interest in expanding their rights and perhaps even acquiring the wall area increased correspondingly.[39] An incident at the wall on the Day of Atonement, in September 1928, in which a police officer removed a screen during the service, was blown up into a political campaign to secure additional rights at the wall. The situation escalated rapidly out of control, with the Muslims asserting counter-rights at the wall and the British unable to impose a mutually acceptable compromise. The final catalyst was added to the heated atmosphere in mid-August 1929 when youths from Tel Aviv staged a political demonstration at the wall, singing "Hatikvah" (the Jewish national anthem) and raising the Zionist flag. Muslim counterdemonstrators the next day destroyed Jewish prayer-petitions inserted in crevices in the wall. And unrelated violent incidents escalated into rapidly spreading attacks on Jewish communities in Jerusalem, Hebron, and Safad during the next weeks.

The bloody outbreak was evidence of the extreme anger of the Arab public, but its immediate impact was politically counterproductive. The British government and the Zionists cited it as evidence of the Arabs' backwardness, their unpreparedness for independence, and the consequent need to maintain a firm hold on Palestine. On the other hand, British officials realized thereafter

---

39. For an able summary of the conflict, including British, Muslim, and Jewish letters and protests since 1918, see memorandum by Sir Ronald Storrs, 1925, enclosed in High Commissioner dispatch to CO, October 31, 1925 (CO 733/98). Note, in particular, Weizmann's letter to Ormsby-Gore, May 1, 1918, proposing that the Jewish community purchase the Wailing Wall and the area in front of it.

that the Arabs must have a constitutional means to express their grievances if another outbreak were not to occur.

The outbreak also resulted in a rapid increase in political mobilization among the Arab community. A Women's Congress, an all-Palestine congress, farmers' congresses, and youth congresses followed each other in rapid succession that winter, each group articulating its own particular grievances as well as stressing the basic national demands and fears. The Arab Executive sent a blue-ribbon delegation to London in the spring of 1930, composed of Musa Kazim al-Husayni (then age eighty-two), Hajj Amin al-Husayni, his distant cousin Jamal al-Husayni, Raghib an-Nashashibi, Awni Abd al-Hadi, and a leading Christian, Alfred Rock. They demanded that the government stop immigration, make land inalienable, and establish a "democratic Government in which all inhabitants will participate in proportion to numbers." [40] When the government predictably rejected these demands, offering only to study the land and immigration issues further and to introduce certain constitutional changes, the delegation abruptly left London "with impression that Arab case will not justly be solved by British Government influenced by Zionists," as they telegraphed home. "Whereas we are convinced that continuation in usurping our rights in favour of Zionist policy means our extirpation as nation and consequent disappearance from our country and question for us is one of life or death we believe our people will fight this policy with all nonviolent means." [41]

The Arabs' faith in British policy was briefly restored in the summer of 1930 by the serious consideration given to the Wailing Wall issue by the international commission appointed by Britain and the League of Nations, and by a report on the land shortage in Palestine which was supported by a government white paper in October. The Arab Executive submitted detailed reports on the white paper and land policy to the government in late December, and canceled the day of mourning on Balfour Day that year. However, secret negotiations between the Jewish Agency and a special cabinet committee resulted in Britain's repudiating a substantial part of the white paper. The letter from Prime Minister J. Ramsay MacDonald to Weizmann in February 1931, which sealed the negotiations, acknowledged the right of Jewish institutions to hire

40. Arab Delegation telegram to the Arab Executive, received May 12, 1930, quoted in High Commissioner telegram to CO, May 14, 1930 (CO 733/187/77105).
41. *Ibid.*

only Jews and lease land only to Jews, and it emphasized that the economic absorptive capacity of only the Jewish sector of the economy was the criterion for immigration quotas. The shock of Britain's capitulation to Zionist pressure caused lasting reverberations throughout the Arab community.

The "black letter," as the Arabs dubbed it, marked a turning point in the Arabs' attitude. They lost faith in Britain, and the younger generation lost faith in the Arab Executive's moderate pressure tactics. A conference of three hundred young politicians in August 1931 pressured the Arab Executive into taking a strong stand against a projected development scheme, the arming of Jewish colonies by the British for self-defense, and the idea of having to apply to the government for permission to hold demonstrations.[42] The Palestine branch of Hizb al-Istiqlal al-Arabi, the Young Men's Congress, and the scout groups called for active steps on the part of the Arabs against both British and Zionists. Scouts patrolled the Mediterranean coast for a short period to prevent illegal Jewish immigrants from landing and to underline their accusation that the British government was not trying to prevent this immigration. Awni Abd al-Hadi pressured other Arab leaders into resigning from government advisory committees in the fall of 1932, thereby wrecking the high commissioner's hope of fostering nonofficial ties with the administration.[43]

The Arab Executive convened a Grand National Meeting in Jaffa in March 1933 which, despite acrimony between the Husayni and Nashashibi factions, called for the gradual introduction of noncooperation with all aspects of the government. As a result, the Arabs boycotted both the colonial secretary and General Allenby during their visits that spring, although they were anxious to discuss legislative council proposals with the colonial secretary and had jubilantly welcomed Allenby as their liberator in 1917. The Young Men's Congress and Istiqlal then stepped up pressure on the Arab Executive. They induced it to sponsor demonstrations in Jerusalem and Jaffa in October 1933, which violated the government ban on demonstrations and led to serious clashes with the police. Finally, when the Histadrut (Jewish Labor Federation) picketed Jewish orange groves, building sites, and businesses that

42. High Commissioner telegrams to CO, August 17 and 19, 1931 (CO 733/209/87353).

43. High Commissioner dispatch to CO, October 4, 1932, and Colonial Secretary memorandum to the Cabinet, November 3, 1932 (Co 733/219/97105/2).

hired Arabs, Arab political groups organized counter-pickets [44] and stepped up their propaganda in favor of boycotting Jewish produce.

Rebellion

By the early 1930s, a few Arabs had begun to consider covert paramilitary operations as a way to counter the Zionists, distract the British, and call attention to the seriousness of Arab grievances. An early example was a small band of outlaws from Safad called the Green Hand Gang, which hid in the remote mountainous country in northern Palestine in late 1929. It attempted to harass the Jewish quarter of Safad and indulged in banditry on the roads. The group was broken up by massive police and military action in early 1930,[45] but it foreshadowed the guerrilla groups of the late 1930s.

Even before the 1929 riots, Shaykh Izz ad-Din al-Qassam had formed secret revolutionary cells in Haifa. He was in contact with both the discontented educated youths, through his presidency of the Haifa Muslim Society, and the dispossessed *fallahin* crowding into the shanty-towns on the coast north of Haifa, for whom he acted as religious leader. Shaykh al-Qassam criticized the anomic violence of 1929 as self-defeating and maintained that maximum political effect could only be attained by building up dedicated cadres and hitting carefully selected targets. The Ikhwan al-Qassam first came to public attention with its hand-grenade attack on a house in the Nahalal colony in December 1932. In early November 1935 the shaykh took to the hills with a few followers to call the peasantry to revolt, but he was killed only a week later in a gun battle with British police. After his death, he became a "martyr" to the Arab cause, eulogized throughout the country, and his idea of militant action began to gain wider currency. Qassamite actions served as the catalyst to both the general strike of 1936, which occurred after a band robbed and killed Jewish travelers, and the massive arrest of nationalist leaders in the fall of 1937, following the assassination of a district commissioner, which was widely attributed to Qassamites.

Despite this rapid political and military radicalization, which

44. High Commissioner dispatch to CO, December 25, 1933 (CO 733/250/37211). Also his dispatches to CO in September 1934 (CO 733/257/37356).

45. High Commissioner dispatch to CO, February 22, 1930, reports on the gang's actions at length (CO 733/190/77171). On Shaykh al-Qassam, see Subhi Yasin, *The Great Arab Revolt in Palestine 1936-1939* (in Arabic) (Cairo: Dar al-Kitab al-Arabi, 1959), pp. 30-42.

increased in direct proportion to the rapidly mounting Jewish immigration, which peaked at over 60,000 in 1935, the more established leaders on the Arab Executive continued to press for the formation of a legislative council and for legislation to restrict land purchases. The Arab Executive itself dissolved after the death of Musa Kazim Pasha in 1934, as he had held it together solely by his personal influence and prestige in the previous two or three years. The politicians reorganized into a half dozen political parties, of which the most important were the National Defense Party sponsored by Raghib an-Nashashibi, who lost his position as mayor of Jerusalem in 1934, and the Palestine Arab Party under Hajj Amin's relative, Jamal al-Husayni. Despite bickering, personal animosity, and tendencies to overbid each other, all but the Istiqlal joined together to present the "national demands" to the high commissioner in November 1935 and to discuss the details of another legislative council proposal which he outlined that winter. These discussions continued right up to and past the opening weeks of the April general strike. Even after Zionist pressure in London resulted in the House of Commons' resolution that criticized the establishment of a legislative council in Palestine as "premature," the party leaders hoped that a further delegation to London could persuade the government to implement the council proposal.

The General Strike and Uprising, 1936–1939

Armed robbery and the shooting of three Jews by a Qassamite group on the Tulkarm road, the night of April 15, 1936, followed by a highly political, inflammatory funeral demonstration in Tel Aviv and the killing of two Arabs in a hut near Petah Tikvah, precipitated the general strike. Groups in Jaffa and Nablus initiated the call to strike, and all the towns rapidly formed "national committees" to coordinate the effort. The leaders of the five parties only gave up plans to send a delegation to London on April 21, forming the Arab Higher Committee on April 25, with Hajj Amin al-Husayni as its president. This was the first time that he assumed responsibility as the leader of the Arab movement.

Local national committees, traffic strike committees, Arab "national guard" units, labor societies, Muslim and Christian sports clubs, boy scouts, the Jaffa boatmen's association, women's committees, and various other local groups directed different aspects of the strike under the loose coordination of the Arab Higher Committee. The national committees held a congress on May 7 which called for civil disobedience, the nonpayment of taxes, and stoppage of municipal government.[46] The government banned further congresses scheduled for August and September. And so, with communications seriously hampered, the Arab Higher Committee could obtain the local groups' support for ending the strike in October only by sending its members to the different towns to consult with them directly.

Virtually all Arab business and transportation ceased during the strike. Basic agricultural work continued, of course, as the urban population had to be fed. Distribution centers for grains, fruits, and vegetables were established in towns for that purpose. Government officials contributed 10 percent of their salaries to the strike fund,[47] rather than join the strike, since the Arabs feared that their positions would be taken by Jews. These Arab officials provided a substantial portion of the strike funds. Frustration built up among the officials to such an extent that the high commissioner permitted Musa al-Alami (then a government advocate in the legal department) to circulate a memorial among the senior officials which expressed their support for the national demands and the precondition of suspending immigration, in order to head off their resigning. Many of the municipalities closed down on June 1, and the Supreme Muslim Council continued only its religious functions.

Sporadic violence began in May, after the British announced a new immigration quota, and built up during the summer despite heavy British punitive measures, which included demolishing a large section of Jaffa, imposing collective punishments on villages, and detaining suspects without trial. Individual acts of sabotage, such as wire-cutting and crop-burning, expanded into engagements of small guerrilla bands with the military. By June the high commissioner wrote home that the situation was "a state of incipient revolution," with "little security or control of lawless elements . . . outside principal towns, main roads and railways." [48] The Syrian guerrilla leader Fawzi al-Qawuqji came to Palestine in August at the head of a band of Syrians, Iraqis, and Palestinians, which con-

46. High Commissioner telegrams to CO, May 23 and 28 1936 (CO 733/310/75528). In the May 23 telegram Wauchope described the Arab Higher Committee's influence as "limited," and noted that "its function is to deal with broad questions of policy and is not directly concerned with organization of strikes."

47. High Commissioner telegram to CO, May 4, 1936 (CO 733/307/75438/1).

48. High Commissioner telegram to CO, June 2, 1936 (CO 733/297/75156).

ducted operations in northern Palestine against the British military and helped train Palestinian youths in guerrilla warfare. The Palestinians never had any illusions about their military capacity in relation to the British. It was always clear that the British could crush the one or two thousand *mujahidin* if they tried, but the Arabs felt that the British public would not tolerate such repression, as it ultimately had not tolerated it in Ireland.

The strike lasted nearly six months, longer than any other general strike in the Middle East or Europe. Syrian nationalists had just wrung significant concessions from the French after a fifty-day strike, and so the Palestinians were optimistic about the effectiveness of this pressure tactic. The precondition of suspending immigration during negotiations to form a national government was not unprecedented, as the high commissioners had suspended immigration in the wake of the 1921 and 1929 riots. However, the British government not only refused to suspend immigration this time, but in May it announced the next six-month labor immigration quota. The British offer of a Royal Commission which would investigate the political situation as soon as the strike ended and order was restored seemed an insufficient basis for ending the strike. The Arabs had already experienced several commissions of inquiry and expert investigations upon whose conclusions the government had failed to act. Thus, the deadlock persisted throughout the summer, despite mediation attempts by Amir Abdallah of Transjordan and Nuri Pasha as-Said, the foreign minister of Iraq.

The Arabs realized that the Jewish community benefited economically from the Arab strike by increasing its independence from the Arab economy. A notable example was the jetty built at Tel Aviv, because the Jaffa port was closed down by the strike. That realization, in addition to the British government's increased threats of military repression in early September, made the Arab political leaders fear that the strike had become counterproductive. Therefore the Arab Higher Committee suggested that the Arab kings issue an appeal to end the strike, which the committee formally accepted in mid-October 1936. The strike ended without the precondition being met, and the leaders only hoped that the Royal Commission would take the Arab position seriously and present a favorable report which the government would actually implement.

The Arab kings had to intercede a second time to end the Arab Higher Committee's boycott of the Royal Commission, a boycott called because the colonial secretary insulted the Arabs by announcing the new labor immigration quota on the same day as the departure of the commission for Palestine in November 1936.

The Arab community was shocked by the commission's recommendation of partition, published in July 1937, and angered at the revelations at the Zionist congress in August that Weizmann had discussed with the colonial secretary the ways to alter the partition boundaries so as to favor the Jewish community.[49] Both the Arab Higher Committee and the Nashashibi faction, which had just broken ranks, publicly rejected the idea of partition, although in private Raghib Bey indicated that he would accept partition on more favorable terms, in the hope of becoming prime minister under Amir Abdallah in a united Transjordanian-Palestinian Arab state. District commissioners filed reports on the increasing alienation of the populace from the British, especially in the Galilee, which was to fall under Jewish rule even though only a minute proportion of the population was then Jewish.[50] But the public and the political organizations took no further political initiative, seemingly stunned to inaction. The British tried to nip any organized opposition in the bud by attempting to arrest Hajj Amin on July 17 while he attended a meeting of the Arab Higher Committee; but he had already left by the back door.[51]

As anomic violence and political murders began in September, the British used the assassination of the Galilee district commissioner as the pretext for a wholesale roundup of nationalist leaders. The Arab Higher Committee and local national committees were proscribed, Hajj Amin was removed from the presidency of the Supreme Muslim Council, and the members of the Arab Higher Committee were deported to the Seychelles or forbidden to return to Palestine. Rather than serving as the final blow to the nationalist movement, the arrests catalyzed the local people. After two weeks of shock, violence broke out throughout Palestine—wire-cutting, shooting, burning—the work of uncontrolled and uncontrollable villagers. As the new district commissioner for the Galilee observed, the arrests had eliminated all the responsible local leaders on whom

49. Colonial Secretary's notes on his discussion with Weizmann, July 19, 1937, and communications to CO from Weizmann, July 20 and August 18, 1937 (CO 733/352/75718/21).

50. District Commissioner Andrews' report for July 1937 noted the "shock and incredulity" of the Arabs in Galilee at the partition plan, especially as only .001 percent of the rural population of Acre subdistrict and 4 percent of Safad subdistrict was Jewish. He concluded, "that the Arab population should ever be reconciled to the scheme is clearly too much to hope." Report enclosed in High Commissioner dispatch to CO, August 5, 1937 (CO 733/351/75718/6).

51. High Commissioner telegram to CO, July 19, 1937 (CO 733/352/75718/9).

British officials had relied to control mobs, cool passions, and articulate grievances.[52] Local military bands sprang up, which coalesced into regional groups. There was little coordination and considerable rivalry between the regional commanders. The commanders also vied for support from Damascus, where the rump Arab Higher Committee had established itself and attempted to supply military equipment and funds for the *mujahidin*. Hajj Amin had escaped to Beirut, where he lived under surveillance of the French, but was able to continue as the political and moral leader of the movement, if not to guide its day-to-day operations.

The rebellion peaked in the summer and early fall of 1938, encompassing the whole countryside from the far north down to Beersheba. Rebels infiltrated the towns to such an extent that the General Officer Commanding reported that "the situation [in September] was such that civil administration and control of the country was, to all practical purposes, nonexistent." [53] The government offices, post offices, banks, and police stations in such central towns as Ramallah, Bethlehem, and Nablus closed down during the summer.[54] Beersheba was evacuated by the military in early September and was reoccupied only in late November. The Old City of Jerusalem had to be placed under a five-day siege in mid-October before the rebels could be rooted out.

To counter the popular insurrection, the British government continually increased the number of troops in the country, built a wire fence along the border with Syria to reduce the infiltration of men and supplies from the north, and introduced a pass system in November 1938, which required all drivers to register before they were allowed on roads outside the towns. These restrictive measures, in addition to constant searches of villages, demolitions of houses where rebels or weapons may have been hidden, internment of hundreds of suspects in concentration camps without trial, and daily small engagements with groups of *mujahidin,* wore down the rebel forces. However, it was largely the publication of the

52. Sir Alec S. Kirkbride, *A Crackle of Thorns* (London: John Murray, 1956), pp. 100–101.

53. General Haining, GOC, Report to War Office, November 30, 1938, paragraph 14; St. Antony's College, Oxford, private papers collection.

54. A fascinating eye-witness account of the rebellion was provided by Miss H. W. Wilson, a young British woman who taught at the Bir Zayt school near Ramallah from the fall of 1938 until the summer 1939. She described her experiences with the rebels, and the difficulties faced by the villagers, caught between the rebel demands and British retaliation, in her diary, which is on file at St. Antony's College, Oxford, in the private papers collection.

Woodhead Partition Commission report in November 1938, which found the various partition plans technically infeasible, and the British government's accompanying announcement that it would reassess the whole political situation at a Round Table Conference in London, that made the revolt begin to lose its momentum. Once again politicians and villagers felt that there might be an alternative to armed revolt. As a result, the *mujahidin* began to have to coerce villagers in order to obtain material support, and political assassination against suspected collaborators increased dramatically. When Raghib an-Nashashibi's cousin Fakhri Bey announced in November 1938 that he opposed Hajj Amin's leadership of the Palestine movement and demanded at least half the seats on the Palestine delegation to the London conference, terrorists increased their attacks on supporters of the Nashashibi faction, which was viewed by then as a traitorous element in the country.[55]

The Round Table Conference was attended by the Zionists, Palestinian Arabs, and official Arab delegations from Egypt, Iraq, Transjordan, Saudi Arabia, and the Yemen. The Jews and Arabs met separately with the British negotiators, and both sides rejected the white paper issued by the British at its close.[56] Many Palestinians felt privately that they should accept the white paper, as it came close to realizing their objectives. Under its terms, Palestine would become independent in ten years if conditions permitted, the Arabs would have to approve Jewish immigration after

55. The political assassination of Arabs by Arabs began during the 1936 strike and increased in the 1937–1939 revolt. Those assassinated fell roughly into three categories: (1) active opponents of the revolt or lukewarm supporters, such as police detectives, informers, those who continued to trade with Jews, and those merchants and landlords who resisted making monetary payments to the terrorists; (2) those involved in the court case, as investigators or witnesses for the prosecution, against a Qassamite group accused of murders at the Nahalal colony in 1932; (3) political opponents of Hajj Amin al-Husayni: some officials in al-Haram ash-Sharif, some politicians who were on good terms with Amir Abdallah, and especially supporters of the Nashashibis. As a result, Raghib an-Nashashibi and other prominent members of the Defense Party went into self-imposed exile from August 1938 until the spring of 1939, Fakhri Bey being one of the few to remain in Palestine. His public statements against Hajj Amin accelerated these assassination attempts in late November and December 1938, since he placed the Defense Party openly on the side of the government against the revolt. *Palestine Post*, Jerusalem, 1936–1939, *passim;* Lloyd-Phillip report to the Chief Secretary, October 5, 1938, on conditions in the Southern District, St. Antony's College, private papers collection.

56. The minutes of the London conference are contained in FO 371/23223–23232.

a five-year quota was filled, and extensive restrictions would be introduced concerning Jewish land-purchases from Arabs. However, Hajj Amin held out against the paper because it did not contain a guaranteed time-limit and especially because it explicitly forbade his returning to Palestine; anyone who publicly accepted the paper would have, in effect, publicly rejected his leadership.

Aftermath

In the end, the white paper proved to be a Pyrrhic victory for the Arabs. By 1939 the Jewish community was too strong and too mobilized to be contained. It responded to the white paper with strikes, bombs in Arab markets, terrorist attacks on a few Arab villages, increased clandestine military training, and massive propaganda efforts in Geneva, Britain, and especially the United States. The 1937–1939 deportations, arrests, fines, deaths by bullet or hanging, and serious economic destruction had broken the Arab community, politically and economically. Exhausted, and without effective leadership within the country, the Arabs could neither act politically during World War II nor counter the Jewish revolt at its close.

Serious divisions among the Husaynis, the Nashashibi-Abdallah alliance, and the Istiqlalists prevented the formation of a common front.[57] The Husayni supporters were in disarray because Hajj Amin had fled to Germany, where he collaborated with the Axis powers, Jamal al-Husayni was detained in Southern Rhodesia, and other politicians were closely supervised by the British in Palestine. The Nashashibis initially supported active cooperation with the British war effort, but fell silent after Raghib's cousin Fakhri Bey was assassinated in late 1941. Political activity was forbidden during most of the war, and so the Istiqlal leaders attempted to organize indirectly through the Arab National Bank, left-wing labor societies, and Arab chambers of commerce, the only remaining institutions.

The Arab states had to intervene to impose a semblance of unity on the Palestine Arab movement. In 1944 the Syrian leader Jamil Mardam induced the Istiqlal and Husayni leaders to accept the appointment of Musa al-Alami as the Palestine delegate to the Alexandria conference, which was to draw up plans for a League of Arab States. Alami then took charge of Arab League efforts to establish information offices abroad and promote land-buying in

57. J. C. Hurewitz, *The Struggle for Palestine* (New York: Norton, 1950), *passim*, on the period from 1939 to 1948.

Palestine, earning the enmity of both the Husaynis and Istiqlalists for his refusal to place his activities under their control. Again, in the fall of 1945, Mardam imposed a twelve-seat Arab Higher Committee on the Palestine politicians. But it was reorganized by Jamal al-Husayni after he returned to Palestine the next spring. He expanded the committee to twenty-eight members, one-third from the Husayni camp, one-third from other parties, and one-third representing various economic groups. The Istiqlal refused to participate and formed a rival Arab Higher Front in June. The Arab League then intervened for the third time, seizing upon the opportunity of Hajj Amin's sudden return to Cairo from detention in France in late May to form an Arab Higher Executive under Hajj Amin and Jamal Bey; it soon reverted to the title Arab Higher Committee. The British officially recognized this body as the Arab spokesman that winter when it was included in the second stage of a conference with Arab states, the first stage of which had been held in September 1946. The Arab League provided funds to maintain its activities and placed Musa al-Alami's projects under its supervision. But Hajj Amin was not allowed to return to Palestine.

No concrete plans were laid in Palestine to oppose either the recommendations of the Anglo-American Committee of Inquiry in May 1946 for a unitary state with no restriction on Jewish land-buying and the immediate admission of 100,000 Jewish refugees from Europe, or the United Nations Special Committee's recommendation of partition in September 1947. And the Arab states only sketched general plans for diplomatic and military support. Local national committees, which had led the 1936 strike, were not revived until December 1947, weeks after the U.N. General Assembly supported the partition plan. And it was not until April 1948 that the Higher Committee proposed that Arab civil servants assume control of their departments once Britain evacuated Palestine in May. Efforts were made to renew guerrilla warfare in the countryside under Abd al-Qadir al-Husayni, the son of Musa Kazim Pasha, who had led *mujahidin* in 1936–1939, and Fawzi al-Qawuqji, the commander of 1936, who headed the Arab League-sponsored Arab Liberation Army. But the Haganah offensive in April broke their hold over communications routes, killed Abd al-Qadir, and overran such major Arab centers as Acre, Haifa, Tiberias, Safad, and Jaffa, all before the British officially withdrew on May 14 and the state of Israel was proclaimed.

In the ensuing fighting between Israel and the Arab armies, only the seacoast around Gaza and the central hill region were held by the Arabs. The Arab Higher Committee formed a "government of all Palestine" in Gaza in late September 1948, with Hajj Amin as president of the Assembly, which was recognized by most of the Arab states. But Amir Abdallah countered by annexing the hill areas, held by his troops, and confirmed his alliance with Raghib an-Nashashibi by appointing him military governor of this area, thereafter known as the West Bank.

The Palestinians had been caught in an impossible situation throughout the mandate period. Unable to persuade the British rulers to grant them independence by petitions, reasoned memoranda, or delegations,[58] they found themselves also unable to exercise effective pressure through obstructive tactics or violence. The other Arab countries that had been placed under mandatory rule had obtained at least internal autonomy without resorting to such extreme, prolonged violence, even though they had far less cohesive nationalist movements and far less mobilized populations. But the aspirations and pressure of the Zionist movement blocked the realization of Arab aims in Palestine. Over time, as the Royal Commission of 1937 reported, the two communities grew more estranged rather than less, and so the possibility of rapprochement receded. By the 1930s the British lost control of the situation, and followed a nonpolicy of drift and reflex military repression. The Zionists never dared to accept the idea of remaining a minority in a predominantly Arab area, and the Arabs in turn never dared to accept the legitimacy of the Jewish community, because that would have meant accepting Zionism and its implication of ultimate Jewish rule.

58. A final effort to persuade the United Nations to uphold the Arab case was made in 1947 under the direction of Musa al-Alami, the Palestinian representative at the Arab League in the mid-1940s. This document, largely drafted by Albert Hourani, has recently been republished as *The Future of Palestine* (Beirut: Hermon Books, 1970).

PART II

POLITICAL AND MILITARY DIMENSIONS OF CONTEMPORARY PALESTINIAN NATIONALISM

BY

WILLIAM B. QUANDT

I

THE ECLIPSE OF
PALESTINIAN NATIONALISM,
1947-1967

By refusing the terms of the British white paper of 1939, Palestinian Arab leaders lost the possibility of obtaining international support for a unitary Arab-dominated state in Palestine. Eight years later, in 1947, when Palestine's future was again addressed by the British, much had changed. World War II had shattered Britain's ability to maintain a far-reaching empire; the United States and the Soviet Union had emerged as the major powers of the postwar era; and Nazi Germany's extermination of the European Jews had shocked the conscience of the Western world.

In Palestine, the beneficiary of these developments was the Zionist community. More determined than ever to create an independent state, the Zionists could count on widespread sympathy at least for a liberal policy of permitting immigration to Palestine of the Jewish survivors of the holocaust, if not for immediate Jewish statehood. The United States government, which had previously played little part in the Palestinian drama, strongly supported increased immigration to Palestine and tried to convince the British to open the doors of the mandate to at least a hundred thousand Jews.[1]

1. An excellent treatment of the 1947–1949 period in Palestine is contained in J. Bowyer Bell, *The Long War: Israel and the Arabs Since 1946* (Englewood Cliffs, N.J.: Prentice-Hall, 1969), chaps. 2–11.

PARTITION

By early 1947, the British government realized that neither a negotiated settlement nor an equitable compromise could be found for the conflicting Arab and Zionist claims to Palestine. Unable to resolve the problem, and lacking the resources or determination to maintain the mandate indefinitely by force, the British announced in February 1947 that they would turn over the Palestine problem to the newly formed United Nations. In the ensuing months, an ad hoc committee examined several possible solutions and finally recommended the partition of Palestine into two states, one Jewish and one Arab, within a context of economic union. The proposed Jewish state was to include not only the areas of predominant Jewish settlement, but also a number of Arab-inhabited areas, such that nearly half of the population of the envisaged Jewish state would have been Arab.[2] Needless to say, the Arabs did not find this an appealing compromise and were adamantly opposed to the plan. But partition gained the support of both the United States and the Soviet Union, as well as the Zionists, and after intense bargaining, lobbying, and pressure at the United Nations, the partition plan was approved by the required two-thirds vote on November 29, 1947.

J. Bowyer Bell has summed up the dilemma of the Palestinians during this period:

> In retrospect it is all too easy to point out the Arab blunders, their missed opportunities, their intransigence. It is only just, however, to note that it is easy to urge compromise of another's principle, to urge someone else to give up half a loaf of his own bread. Surely the Arab argument had much justice. Shorn of biblical quotations, emotional references to the "final solution," and loaded statistics, the Zionist case looked no stronger, and probably somewhat weaker, than the Arab case to disinterested observers. To the Arabs the demand for an Arab Palestine seemed neither novel nor extreme; it seemed just and in accordance with international practice. That there were two competing "rights" all agreed; but that what had been the feebler, the minority, position could be chosen seemed incredible. Whittled down to basics, the Zionist position was that, given the Palestine dilemma, they would settle for half whereas the Arabs unfairly continued to demand all. It was ingenious, it was evil, and it threw the entire Arab argument into the wrong frame of reference. More devas-tating still, it proved effective.[3]

2. See map 1 for the proposed partition lines.
3. Bell, *Long War*, p. 67.

The First Arab-Israeli War

The vote at the United Nations favoring partition was the opening move in a new phase of the struggle for Palestine. No plan for implementing partition existed. The British remained in control of the territory, but had made clear their intention to evacuate their troops in the near future. It soon became obvious that partition would not be accomplished peacefully, but would rather depend on the outcome of fighting between the Zionists and the Arabs. While benefiting from the legitimacy conferred on a Jewish state in Palestine by the U.N. vote, the Zionists recognized that they would have to rely primarily on themselves to create the state.

From late 1947 to the time of British withdrawal on May 14, 1948, the Zionists sought to augment their defenses, to procure arms, and to defend all Jewish settlements. The proposed partition lines made little sense to either Jews or Arabs, and neither side felt constrained to respect them. In Zionist eyes, the Arab rejection of the idea of partition relieved the Jews of any obligation to confine their state to arbitrarily determined lines drawn by the United Nations. If the Arabs had their way, no Jewish state at all would exist in Palestine. To ensure the viability of the state in such hostile conditions, the Zionists required as much territory in Palestine as they could control with their small forces, and as few Arabs in those territories as possible. To Jews, this was an issue of survival, not of expansion and the uprooting and expulsion of the Arab population.

During the early months of 1948, Jewish regular and irregular forces succeeded in defending most Jewish settlements. Despite British constraints on the intercommunal fighting, clashes were frequent, and by spring Zionists had scored some notable military successes and had perpetrated at least one major atrocity by massacring over two hundred Arab villagers at Dayr Yassin on April 19. Fear spread among Palestinians, and some began to flee to safer refuge in Transjordan. With the fall of Haifa to Jewish forces later in April, and the local Arab leadership's reluctant decision to evacuate the remaining Arab population of the city rather than submit to Jewish domination, the stream of refugees took on major proportions. The advantages to the embryonic Jewish state of reducing the number of Arabs within its borders did not go unnoticed, and soon after British withdrawal in mid-May the Zionists sought systematically to expel the remaining Arabs in areas under their control.

After British withdrawal, a new dimension in the fighting was the intervention of a small number of regular army troops from surrounding Arab states, most notably Egypt and Transjordan. In no sense was this a massive, coordinated onslaught. In fact, inter-Arab rivalries seriously affected the conduct of the war in the months after the military involvement of the Arab states. The Egyptians, as well as some Palestinians, were nearly as intent on preventing the Transjordanian Arab Legion from controlling the Arab parts of Palestine as they were on containing and, if possible, eliminating the newly formed Jewish state of Israel.

Israel, officially created on May 15, 1948, and rapidly recognized by the United States and the Soviet Union, was a state without fixed frontiers. At war with its Arab neighbors as well as with the Palestinian Arab population from the day of its birth, Israel successfully survived the first four weeks of fighting. The balance of forces had been about equal, and few territorial changes were registered prior to the first cease-fire in mid-June. During the ensuing truce, Israel rapidly augmented her military power by acquiring arms abroad, and when fighting again erupted, the advantage lay with the Israelis. Cease-fires and fighting succeeded one another, until by the end of 1948 the Arab forces were exhausted and prepared to negotiate an armistice. By then, however, the state of Israel encompassed much more territory than the original partition plan had envisaged, including the Upper Galilee, the Negev, and half of Jerusalem. Within these lines, the Arab population now stood at about 150,000, where formerly it had contained at least 800,000. Some of the refugees from Israeli-controlled territory were relocated within Palestine in the Egyptian-administered Gaza Strip or on the West Bank, while others fled to Transjordan, Syria, and Lebanon. The miserable conditions in which the refugees lived in subsequent years contributed significantly to the mood of despair and frustration that marked the Palestinian community. In time, these conditions provided breeding grounds for a militant form of nationalism and recruits for political movements willing to resort to violence to regain Palestinian rights.[4]

With the formal armistice agreements ending the fighting between the Arab states and Israel, the Palestinian dimension of the Arab-Israeli conflict receded into the background. No Palestinian Arab state had been formed as envisaged in the U.N. partition resolution. Instead, Egypt became the guardian of the Palestinians

4. On the Palestine refugees, see Don Peretz, "The Palestine Arab Refugee Problem," in Paul Y. Hammond and Sidney S. Alexander, eds., *Political Dynamics in the Middle East* (New York: American Elsevier, 1972).

in the Gaza Strip, while Transjordan's King Abdallah formally annexed the West Bank and east Jerusalem in 1950, thereby creating the Hashemite Kingdom of Jordan. In the absence of any movement toward a final peace agreement between Arabs and Israelis in the following years, activist Palestinians turned to the surrounding Arab states to promote their cause.

PALESTINE AS AN ARAB CAUSE, 1949–1967 [5]

Palestine had become an Arab problem during the late 1940s and remained at the center of inter-Arab politics for the next two decades. During this period, however, Palestinian organizations, parties, and leadership were secondary to the plethora of Arab political movements. In the 1950s, a new generation of Palestinian activists, those who had been too young to participate as leaders in the struggles of the 1930s, came of age. These young intellectuals, many of whom were Christians, were susceptible to the proposition that Arab unity was the road to the liberation of Palestine. But this new generation was geographically dispersed, and consequently few Palestinians worked together in the 1950s and early 1960s in their search for an Arab solution to the Palestine problem. Instead, some found themselves associated with the Muslim Brotherhood, others with the Syrian Social Nationalist party (SSNP),[6] still others with the Arab Ba'th Socialist party or the Arab Nationalist movement (ANM). Many were attracted to the leadership of Egypt's President Gamal Abdul Nasser, especially after 1956, while others accepted positions within the Jordanian establishment and became influential politicians within the Hashemite regime.

Politically minded Palestinians in the 1950s and early 1960s differed not only in their opinions of the Jordanian regime as the representative of the Palestinians, but also with respect to ideological and organizational questions. The more militant Palestinians, those who rejected Jordanian authority, were members of groups identified with all shades of the ideological spectrum. What they had most in common was a conspiratorial, clandestine style of operation and a vision that generally went beyond Palestinian nationalism to at least Syrian nationalism (SSNP), if not integral Arab unity under Egyptian leadership (ANM). Each of these militant factions was also strongly opposed to the others. Once again,

5. In Part III, "The Palestinian Resistance and Inter-Arab Politics," added attention is given to the pre-1967 Arab context in which Palestinian nationalist leaders functioned.

6. Also known as the Parti Populaire Syrien (PPS).

these conditions did little to foster a sense of purpose and unity among the emerging Palestinian elite.

PALESTINIAN ARMED STRUGGLE:
REACTIONS TO THE JUNE 1967 DEFEAT

The Arab defeat in the war with Israel in June 1967 accelerated the development of a Palestinian national movement free from the control of Arab governments. The immediate lesson of the defeat was that the state of Israel could not be destroyed by conventional war led by existing Arab regimes. Consequently, the Palestinians, insofar as they hoped to achieve some of their nationalist goals, determined to take the lead in managing their own affairs. A few Palestinians, as early as the mid-1950s, had created small clandestine groups that sought to keep the Palestinian cause alive. The secession of Syria from the United Arab Republic (UAR) in 1961 had been a blow to the idea of integral Arab unity, and some Palestinians had been quick to draw the conclusion that reliance on Arab unity to recover the losses in Palestine might mean an indefinite postponement of their struggle. Several Palestinian groups in the mid-1960s carried out commando raids against Israel in the hope of setting off a conflict between Israel and the Arab states.

It was precisely to curtail this type of irresponsible activity that the Arab League, and especially Egypt, had created the Palestine Liberation Organization (PLO) in 1964. Led primarily by old-guard Palestinian nationalists, the PLO was recognized by the Arab League as the official representative of the Palestinian people. Popular armed struggle was clearly not part of its program. Instead, a conventionally trained and equipped army was assembled and stationed in Egypt, Iraq, and Syria.

The June 1967 defeat discredited not only the Arab regimes but also the PLO, whose verbal extremism had not been matched by military successes during the brief war. For those Palestinians who wished to continue the struggle, the essential questions were whether to concentrate first on building up an effective political organization and then resort to armed struggle within Palestine, or to use violence and armed attacks against Israel as the means of organizing the Palestinian masses. The former strategy was favored by self-styled radicals, but the obstacles to mobilizing the Palestinians in the absence of visible signs of activism were formidable. Most important was the fact that Israel had seized more territory in the 1967 war, this time including all of Palestine. Nearly half of the

Palestinians now lived under Israeli control, despite the exodus of over two hundred thousand refugees from the occupied West Bank to the East Bank of Jordan.[7]

Neither social conditions nor political realities favored the launching of a Palestinian armed movement in late 1967. The social base was as weak and divided as it had ever been, and the elite, after two decades of political life that partook of all the conflicts and contradictions of the Arab world, was ideologically and organizationally fragmented. The legacy of the first two periods of Palestinian national deveolpment weighed heavily on the post-1967 leaders. Armed struggle and self-reliance emerged as key concepts behind actions in this period, but both concepts represented rejection of past experiences more than an adaptation to reality: armed struggle could only be effective if it were coupled to feasible political objectives; self-reliance risked encouraging the Arab states to abandon the Palestinian cause in the name of narrow national interest or implied that Palestinians would demand aid and support from Arab states, but would refuse all political guidance and control in return.[8]

Palestinian nationalism in its current phase continues to articulate the goal of self-determination and independence. The obstacles to attaining some variant of this goal are both external and internal. Israel's overwhelming power, compared with the limited capabilities of the Palestinians, is the major impediment to full success. Dependence on outside sources, primarily the Arab governments, for arms, funds, and territory in which to organize is a further constraint on effective military or political action. Finally, Palestinian society remains physically dispersed and culturally fragmented, providing a narrow base of recruitment for Palestinian organizations. Since 1967, Palestinian leaders have sought to resolve many of these problems, with occasional successes and notable failures.

7. The circumstances of departure for the new refugees of 1967 are studied by Peter Dodd and Halim Barakat, *River without Bridges: A Study of the Exodus of the 1967 Palestinian Refugees* (Beirut: Institute for Palestine Studies, 1968).

8. A perceptive Algerian observer, Lakhdar Brahimi, notes in *Révolution Africaine* (Algiers), No. 356 (December 18–24, 1970), pp. 16–17, that most Arab states were suspicious of Fatah (Palestine National Liberation Movement) before 1967 because "for the first time, a Palestinian organization presented itself as exclusively Palestinian, with exclusively Palestinian objectives. A revolutionary attitude because it was totally unorthodox." See Part III for more information on Arab views of the Palestinian guerrillas.

2
ORGANIZATIONAL DEVELOPMENTS, JUNE 1967 TO SEPTEMBER 1970

The June 1967 war was a disaster for the Arab states involved in it, as well as for many Palestinians, who either fled their homes and were unable to return or were obliged to live under Israeli military occupation. Nonetheless, Palestinian nationalism as an idea, and the political organizations based on this sentiment, were presented with new opportunities in the aftermath of the war. Arab leadership was disoriented or nonexistent, and it seemed unlikely that the international community would do much to help the Palestinians. Consequently, Palestinian leaders, many of whom in earlier years had subordinated their political activities to the cause of Arab unity, began to call for the creation of Palestinian organizations that would be independent of control by Arab states. The old slogan that Arab unity was the road to the liberation of Palestine was reversed to read that the liberation of Palestine would be the path to Arab unity. This renewed sense of Palestinian self-respect and determined activism contrasted with the low state of morale in other Arab countries after the June defeat and provided a focus for political activity, especially among Palestinians in Jordan and Lebanon.

The overwhelming need after 1967 was to create an organizational structure that could represent and direct the growing sentiment of "Palestinianism." All other activities and goals became subordinate to this organizational imperative. Armed struggle, ideology, elaboration of long-range goals, and the development of a

viable diplomatic posture were distinctly secondary to the requirements of building an organization that could claim to speak on behalf of Palestinian interests. The struggle for legitimacy and representativeness was paramount, but entailed the more mundane
organizational tasks of raising funds, acquiring arms, developing a
territorial base, and gaining international recognition.

In asserting their right to speak for the Palestinians, the organized
commando groups had to compete with similar claims on the part
of traditional West Bank leaders, independent groups of intellectuals, and Palestinians within the Jordanian establishment. The
position of the West Bank leaders was weakened by their ambiguous
status under Israeli occupation, as well as by their traditional
rivalries. Few could speak for more than a local constituency. Other
contenders for the right to represent Palestinian interests were even
more severely hampered by the lack of a political base. Consequently, the organized commando movements were able to make a
plausible claim to represent the largest segment of the politically
aware portion of the Palestinian population. But who spoke for
the commandos?

While the Resistance movement as a whole enjoyed considerable
popularity in the early years,[1] serious difficulties arose as a result of
fragmentation and factionalism within the movement itself. Immense efforts were required to deal with divisive tendencies. Alliances were formed and broken; conflicts over authority were
resolved, only to erupt again. Steps toward unity were offset by
the proliferation of autonomous groups that formed around individual leaders or represented the interests of various Arab states.
Finally, the movement faced the agonizing dilemma that as it grew
in strength and authority, it also became more of a threat to the
existing state interests of the Arab regimes than to Israel.[2] A weak
and disorganized movement might be tolerable and even aided by
Arab regimes, but a unified and growing organization could present
a severe challenge, particularly to the seemingly vulnerable political
systems of Jordan and Lebanon.

Faced with formidable constraints on their efforts to build effec-

1. The Palestinian commando movement is generally referred to by
Arabs as the Resistance (al-muqawamah), probably in recognition of the
primary function of armed struggle in the Palestinian context.

2. Lakhdar Brahimi has stated: "In fact, a serious problem exists for
the Palestinian Resistance, and it does not help to deny it. In the short
and medium term, at least, the interests of the Palestinian people and
their aspirations do not coincide with the goals and the preoccupations of
the existing regimes in certain Arab countries." Révolution Africaine
(Algiers), No. 356 (December 18–24, 1970), pp. 16–17.

tive organizations based on Palestinian national feeling, the commando organizations in 1967–1968 initially accepted the proliferation of small groups. Two widely shared sentiments indicated tolerance toward these potential competitors. First, it was generally felt that armed struggle should precede the mobilizing and organizing of the masses. Thus, when recruits and funds began to pour in, no single, cohesive organization was already in existence. Instead, unification remained to be achieved by means of armed action.[3] Second, the largest of the commando groups decided not to eliminate smaller competitors by force, but rather to try to persuade them to accept the leadership of the main groups. If persuasion were to fail, then perhaps the splinter groups could become covert allies in struggles against other rivals. A decision to crush rival groups, as the Algerians had done in their war for independence, would have risked jeopardizing the commando movement's claim to representativeness and might have led to clashes with the Arab regimes that maintained an interest in the small groups.[4] Thus, the organizational requirement of maintaining popular support and the dependency of the fedayeen (literally, "self-sacrificers") on Arab regimes for aid and protection led to a tolerance of division and diversity within the Palestinian movement that, ironically, threatened to undermine its effectiveness and eventually even its claim to legitimacy. To overcome these dangers, it became necessary to build coalitions and alliances among the many autonomous groups that made up the Resistance movement.

The political style that emerged in the process of trying to create a unified nationalist movement reflected the social divisions and fragmented authority in Palestinian society. In the absence of a recognized central authority, and in the presence of many competing groups, alliances proved to be unstable and individuals moved from one group to another, often with little regard for ideology. Political alignments were unpredictable, which predisposed each group toward defensive maneuvers to protect against a sudden shift in the balance of power. Friends could always become enemies, and enemies might eventually become useful allies.[5]

3. *A Dialogue with Fateh,* Palestine National Liberation Movement, 1969, p. 31.

4. A detailed theoretical and empirical analysis of the role of coercion in unifying nationalist movements is found in William B. Quandt, "Palestinian and Algerian Revolutionary Elites: A Comparative Study of Structures and Strategies," paper presented to the Annual Meeting of the American Political Science Association, September 1972.

5. John Waterbury, in *The Commander of the Faithful* (New York: Columbia University Press, 1970), p. 162, describes a similar process in

In such an environment, leaders feel obliged to keep options open while building their organizational strength. To illustrate the primacy of organizational requirements in the development of the Palestinian Resistance movement since 1967, it is necessary to trace the growth of the major groups and to describe the many efforts to achieve unity.

THE PALESTINE NATIONAL LIBERATION MOVEMENT—FATAH

The largest and most important of the fedayeen organizations is the Palestine National Liberation Movement—Fatah.[6] Several reasons account for Fatah's organizational success compared with other Palestinian groups. First, Fatah has been led by a small but relatively cohesive group of nationalists, several of whom have worked together for over a decade. Second, Fatah has developed a broad, nationalist appeal that can encompass supporters and recruits from nearly all ideological perspectives. Third, Fatah has declared its intention of avoiding inter-Arab quarrels, thus allowing it to receive aid and arms from Arab regimes as diverse as Saudi Arabia, Kuwait, Algeria, Syria, and Egypt. Finally, the simplicity of Fatah's nationalist political goals makes them understandable to the large mass of poorly educated Palestinians. By contrast, other groups have often engaged in highly sophisticated ideological debates that have little meaning to most potential recruits.

Fatah can trace its origins to a small number of Palestinians who lived in the Gaza Strip during the mid-1950s. Some of these young men had actively participated in the war of 1948–1949, but not as prominent leaders. As early as 1955, a few of Fatah's future leaders may have joined in fedayeen raids on Israel from Gaza. The 1956 Suez war found some of these Palestinians fighting with Egyptian troops against British, French, and Israeli attackers. Education in

Morocco as follows: "Political disputes should not be pushed to the breaking point, for that erases an option and closes a door. The rival may someday be in a position to influence the well-being of the group and it is imperative to have contacts with all rivals. Alliances are fluid, and personnel move easily from one to another or enjoy multiple membership. It is difficult to attribute political or programmatic coloration to most groups, and, because there is so little commitment to a political program involved, movements among them are not judged as morally reprehensible. Dogmatic stances are avoided, and the dogmatist is either acting or a fool."

6. The name Fatah, meaning "conquest," is an acronym formed by reversing the order of the first letters of the Arabic name of the Palestine Liberation Movement—Harakat at-Tahrir al-Filastini.

Egyptian or Lebanese universities, followed by residence in Kuwait, completed the formative years of Fatah's core leadership.[7]

By the fall of 1959, Fatah was beginning to publish its views, although not openly under its own name. The essential point in Fatah's argument was that the liberation of Palestine was primarily a Palestinian affair and could not be entrusted to the Arab states. At best, the Arab regimes could provide aid and protection, and if the occasion arose they might also contribute their conventional armies. But Palestinians were to take the lead in the battle with Israel. The Algerian war of liberation was cited as an example of what might be done in Palestine.

By the early 1960s, the idea of armed struggle was gaining popularity with the small number of Fatah recruits, many of whom were well educated and articulate. Contacts with the Syrian government intensified the development of the idea of popular armed struggle, both as a means for mobilizing the Palestinians and as a way of forcing the Arab regimes to follow the lead of the Palestinians in regaining the usurped homeland. In January 1965, Fatah began military operations against Israel, and numerous communiqués were issued by al-Asifah, the name given the military forces of Fatah.

The June 1967 war, but not its outcome, was consistent with Fatah's objective of drawing the Arab regimes into the confrontation with Israel. The overwhelming nature of the Arab defeat in 1967 provided the opportunity for Fatah to emerge as one of the few active, dynamic forces in the Arab world. By late August 1967, Fatah had taken the step of deciding to begin a campaign of armed attacks against Israel. This decision was explicitly made over the objections of those who thought more time should be devoted to political organization and the creation of bases on the occupied West Bank and in Gaza. An important element in Fatah's policy at this time must have been the desire not to be outflanked by other activist Palestinian groups and not to be sold out by the Arab regimes as part of a peace settlement with Israel. Both of these fears led to the conclusion that armed action must begin, even in the absence of a solid organizational base. If precedents were needed, one could again turn to the Algerian case, where the revolution

7. On Fatah's origins, see *A Dialogue with Fateh,* pp. 28–30; *Jeune Afrique,* No. 383 (May 6–12, 1968), pp. 47–51; Gilbert Denoyan, *El Fath Parle: Les Palestiniens contre Israel* (Paris: Editions Albin Michel, 1970); Ehud Yaari, "Al-Fath's Political Thinking," *New Outlook,* Vol. II, No. 9 (November–December 1968); Ehud Yaari, *Strike Terror: The Story of Fatah* (New York: Sabra Books, 1970). More detail on Fatah's leadership is found in chapter 3.

had also begun without an organized infrastructure. The hope, of course, was that action would bring support, and that with time a unified movement would emerge from the struggle. The dangers of passivity, and the very real difficulties of establishing bases under Israeli occupation, further dictated this choice of strategy.

What is remarkable is that Fatah grew as rapidly as it did.[8] Confronted with a relatively traditional and badly fragmented society from which to recruit followers, and lacking firm support from any Arab regime, Fatah nonetheless managed to create an activist, dynamic image of itself that began to attract Palestinians, especially those not living under Israeli occupation. Early in 1968, while still a small and vulnerable movement, Fatah was able to capitalize on its alleged "victory" at the East Bank Jordanian town of Karameh in March to win support and recruits. Reality was of less importance than the symbolism of resistance to Israeli attacks, and, whatever the circumstances, it was true that Israel had suffered comparatively heavy casualties at Karameh.

The UAR and President Nasser began to pay more attention to Fatah after Karameh.[9] During the spring, Fatah broke with its tradition of anonymity and collective leadership and named Yasir Arafat (Abu Ammar) as its spokesman.[10] Publicity and propaganda were now recognized as important components of Fatah's political strategy. In the summer of 1968, Fatah's political stature was great enough for President Nasser to have decided to include Arafat as part of a UAR delegation that visited the Soviet Union.[11]

The growth of Fatah's popularity and strength entailed risks as well as benefits. Fatah was obliged to create functionally distinct organizations, which left it open to accusations from the more extreme Palestinian groups of having abandoned the armed struggle. Fatah was also beginning to challenge Jordanian authority by its mere existence, thereby inviting reprisals. The Jordanians had made it clear that they would tolerate fedayeen activity only along the Jordan River, and preferably within the occupied territories.

8. By the fall of 1970, Fatah's strength was generally estimated at approximately ten thousand armed men. In addition, an unknown number of popular militia forces were attached to Fatah.

9. Michael Hudson, "The Palestinian Arab Resistance Movement: Its Significance in the Middle East Crisis," *Middle East Journal*, Vol. 23, No. 3, (Summer 1969), p. 301. See also Part III, pp. 178–179.

10. Despite Arafat's growing prominence after being named Fatah's spokesman, it was apparent that other Fatah leaders continued to consider themselves Arafat's equal. See *Fatah*, Vol. 1, No. 1 (October 15, 1969), p. 2; see also Denoyan, *El Fath Parle*, p. 42.

11. *An-Nahar Arab Report*, Vol. 1, No. 27 (September 7, 1970), p. 2.

Jordanian troops were even willing to support fedayeen actions along the cease-fire lines, as the battle of Karameh had shown. Unauthorized actions that brought Israeli reprisals against Jordan, and fedayeen contempt for law and order in Jordanian towns, went beyond the limits of Jordanian tolerance. The first armed clash between the commandos and the Jordanian forces occurred in November 1968, but was rapidly settled.

A second problem for Fatah as it grew in strength was how to deal with the other fedayeen groups that had proliferated after the 1967 war. By the end of 1968, Fatah sought to translate its numerical superiority into authority over the Palestinian movement. At the fifth session of the Palestine National Congress, held in Cairo in February 1969, Fatah managed to win control of the Palestine Liberation Organization (PLO) and elected Yasir Arafat chairman of the executive committee. Several fedayeen groups, as well as the military forces of the PLO, the Palestine Liberation Army (PLA), were reluctant to accept Fatah's leadership, and minor crises of authority erupted. Fatah's position was already well founded, however, and smaller fedayeen groups felt obliged to turn to Fatah to arbitrate their own internal disputes.

During 1969, Fatah sought to consolidate its authority through the PLO, while expanding into new areas of activity, especially in southern Lebanon. Once again, battles with the established authorities occurred, and Fatah leaders proved to be flexible enough to accept compromises worked out with UAR support.[12]

Efforts at unifying the commando movements under Fatah's leadership were begun in earnest late in 1969. By early 1970, modest accomplishments had been achieved, in part because of another clash with the Jordanian army in February, which had exposed the danger of disunity. Fighting with Jordanian forces again occurred in June 1970, this time on a much larger scale. Fatah had tried to avoid these conflicts, but had been drawn in by the actions of more radical groups. Nonetheless, Fatah leaders maintained close contact with King Hussein and his military commanders, and together Fatah and the Jordanians brought the fighting to an end on terms acceptable to them, if not to the more militant fedayeen.[13]

12. The crises provoked by the commandos in Lebanon are analyzed by Michael Hudson, "Fedayeen Are Forcing Lebanon's Hand," *Mid East,* Vol. 10, No. 1 (February 1970), pp. 7ff.

13. *An-Nahar Arab Report,* Vol. 1, No. 16 (June 22, 1970), pp. 1-2, reported that Fatah and the Vanguards of the Popular Liberation War (Sa'iqa) were aligned against the Popular Front for the Liberation of Palestine (PFLP) and the Arab Liberation Front (ALF) in trying to end the fighting.

THE POPULAR FRONT FOR THE LIBERATION OF PALESTINE:
ITS PRECURSORS AND OFFSHOOTS

During the 1950s, when the future leaders of Fatah were concluding that Palestinians must reassert control over their national struggle, an opposite point of view was being put forward by the Arab Nationalist movement (ANM). The ANM, which included a number of Palestinian intellectuals, stressed the primacy of Arab unity and cooperation as a necessary precondition for the liberation of Palestine. Students at the American University of Beirut in the late 1940s and early 1950s had debated these issues and in time had formed a political organization around a Palestinian of Greek Orthodox background, Dr. George Habash. The Arab Nationalist movement remained weak and decentralized, with small regional groups organized in several parts of the Arab world. Other Pan-Arab movements, such as the Ba'th party, were distinctly hostile to the ANM. Perhaps as a means of balancing Ba'thist influence in Syria, the non-Ba'thist head of Syrian intelligence, Colonel Abd al-Hamid Sarraj, seems to have offered the ANM some means of support in return for carrying out political activity against the Hashemite regime in Jordan.

In 1957, Habash was obliged to flee from Jordan to Syria after the eviction of the nationalist Nabulsi government. By 1959, the ANM had become strongly Nasserist in orientation, in return for which it received some support from the UAR. For several years the ANM remained nationalist and relatively nonideological, devoted to the idea of Arab unity and the liberation of Palestine, as its motto "Unity, Liberation, Revenge" implied. By 1963, however, a younger generation within the ANM was seeking to develop a more rigorous ideological posture along Marxist-Leninist lines, and evidence of a possible split in the movement was beginning to appear. Later, in 1965, Egypt sought to incorporate the ANM into the framework of the branches of the Arab Socialist Union that were to be established throughout the Arab world. Not wanting to lose their identity through such a merger, the leaders of the ANM resisted, and by early 1967 President Nasser had written off the ANM as a reliable political instrument of his Arab policy.

Several minor Palestinian groups with uncertain connections to the ANM had surfaced by 1965–1966. One, representing the younger and more militant faction of the ANM, had given itself the name "the Vengeance Youth," under the leadership of an East Bank Jordanian student from the American University of Beirut, Nayif

Hawatmah.[14] Its first military operation was carried out in May 1967.

In addition to the political organizations associated with the ANM, two Palestinian groups led by military men came into existence during this period. The first, led by a Palestinian named Ahmad Jibril, who had been an officer in the Syrian army, called itself the Palestine Liberation Front (PLF).[15] To this organization belonged the "Abd al-Qadir al-Husayni," "Abd al-Latif Shruru," and "Izz ad-Din al-Qassam" branches, which conducted several military actions against Israel from late 1966 until the June war.[16]

As early as 1965, contacts between Jibril's group and Fatah were made, and some exchange of funds and military training took place. This early cooperation seems to have been superseded in September 1966 when the Ba'thist regime in Syria began to sponsor Jibril in an effort to oppose Fatah's growing prominence. About the same time a second group, called Heroes of the Return, appeared under the leadership of an officer in the Palestine Liberation Army, Wajih al-Madani. Some links may have existed between Jibril and the Heroes of the Return.

After the June 1967 war, several efforts were made to coordinate the activities of these groups and to explore the possibilities of working with Fatah and the Syrian Ba'th. By August 1967, however, Fatah and the Ba'th had decided to pursue their own courses, and this led the fragments of the Palestinian branch of the ANM and the military groups to consider uniting. During December 1967 and January 1968, negotiations led to the merger of the Palestinian part of the ANM, the Vengeance Youth, the Heroes of the Return, and Jibril's PLF. The new coalition, initially under the leadership of George Habash, was named the Popular Front for the Liberation of Palestine (PFLP).[17] (See figure 2.)

In contrast to Fatah's doctrine of unity through armed struggle, the PFLP and its major antecedents had emphasized the need for organization and planning prior to the stage of using violence. After

14. Hawatmah traces his differences with Habash back as far as 1963. See *Jeune Afrique*, No. 429 (March 24–30, 1969), pp. 52–53.

15. See *An-Nahar Arab Report* (Backgrounder), Vol. 1, No. 13 (June 1, 1970), and *An-Nahar Arab Report*, Vol. 1, No. 1 (March 9, 1970), p. 2.

16. *Jeune Afrique*, No. 450 (August 19–25, 1969), p. 30.

17. The first statements by the PFLP were carried by *At-Taliah* (Kuwait), December 13 and December 20, 1967. The PFLP was said to consist of the Heroes of the Return, the PLF, and the ANM. The only Arab supporters of Palestinian Resistance in the occupied territories were said to be President Nasser of Egypt and President Arif of Iraq. No mention was made of Syrian support.

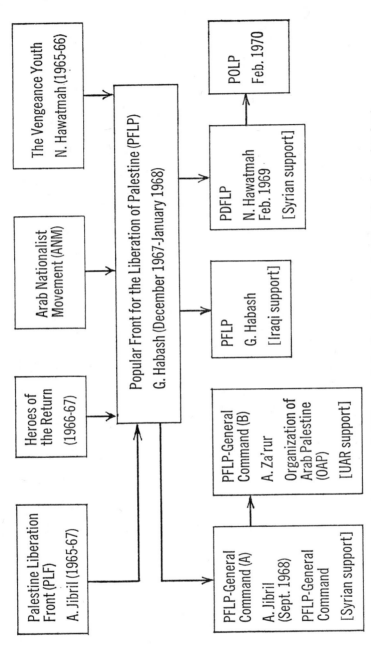

Fig. 2. Precursors and Offshoots of the Popular Front for the Liberation of Palestine.

the 1967 war, the politically intact parts of the ANM tried to set up cells in the Gaza strip and on the West Bank and succeeded in smuggling in small quantities of arms. Soon, however, the PFLP was obliged to follow Fatah's lead of engaging in direct armed action in order to gain visibility and popular support. In addition, Israeli control in the occupied areas made the task of building a political infrastructure an unusually costly undertaking.

A second difference between the PFLP and Fatah involved their respective orientations toward Arab regimes. Growing out of the Arab Nationalist movement, the PFLP tended to emphasize the integral links binding the Palestinian cause to the broader objective of revolution in the Arab world. Such an orientation made it particularly difficult for the PFLP to gain necessary aid from Arab governments while still maintaining its autonomy. Fatah's success in obtaining assistance from conservatives and radicals alike could not be matched by the PFLP, which consequently remained relatively small and underfinanced.

The PFLP also suffered from the familiar fragmentation of Arab radical political movements. During 1968, the major components of the PFLP began to drift apart. This tendency was accelerated by the arrest of the PFLP's leader, George Habash, while he was on a visit to Syria in the spring of 1968 seeking permission for PFLP raids on Israel from Syrian territory and the release of arms intended for the PFLP that Syria had intercepted.[18] During the seven and one-half months of Habash's imprisonment in Syria, the "left-wing" of the PFLP, composed largely of young men around Nayif Hawatmah, sought to take over the PFLP. While able to outvote the Habash faction in PFLP congresses, the self-styled Marxist-Leninist left was unable to enforce discipline over the movement. The esoteric ideological quarrels between the "left" and the "right" concerning, among other things, the role of the "petite bourgeoisie" in the revolutionary struggle led to the defection of two important military leaders of the PFLP, Ahmad Jibril and Ahmad Za'rur, in the fall of 1968.[19] Jibril's group, which had been responsible for the hijacking of an Israeli plane to Algiers in the summer of 1968, prob-

18. Fayiz Qaddura and Ali Bushnaq were arrested along with Habash. A month later, Ahmad al-Yamani was also jailed by the Syrians.

19. Jibril's group, the PFLP-General Command, is well described in *Jeune Afrique*, No. 450 (August 19–25, 1969). Jibril enjoyed a reputation for being a good military strategist. It has been alleged that his group was responsible for blowing up a Swissair flight en route to Israel in the spring of 1970.

ably received support from Syria after its split with the PFLP.[20] Jibril's followers used several names to identify their group, including the PFLP-General Command (A), the al-Aqsa Fedayeen Front, and, finally, the PFLP-General Command. Another military faction alienated by the ideological debates within the PFLP, but unwilling to follow Jibril's lead, was formed around Za'rur and initially took the name of PFLP-General Command (B). Za'rur's group, with support from the UAR, eventually called itself the Organization of Arab Palestine (OAP).[21]

The most important split within the PFLP occurred after Habash's escape from Syrian prison in November 1968. His efforts to reassert his authority over the PFLP led to bitter disputes with the left wing organized around Nayif Hawatmah. Clashes were frequent in January and February 1969, with the better-armed Habash faction using force to intimidate the younger, more ideologically sophisticated dissidents. Finally, the warring factions turned to Fatah for help in mediating their dispute, and late in February 1969 the Popular Democratic Front for the Liberation of Palestine (PDFLP) was recognized by the PLO as a separate commando group under Hawatmah's leadership.[22] The PDFLP won control of the party newspaper, *al-Hurriyah*, obliging the PFLP to publish its own journal, *al-Hadaf*. Further accentuating the split between the two groups was the PDFLP's acceptance of aid from Syria, while

20. It was reported in *An-Nahar Arab Report,* Vol. 2, No. 3 (January 18, 1971), p. 1, that the Syrian regime of Nur ad-Din al-Atasi had given 8 million Syrian pounds to Jibril's group to carry out armed actions against Lebanon. By mid-1970, Jibril may have substituted Iraqi support for Syrian.

21. Some confusion at this time grew out of the fact that different factions of the PFLP continued to issue statements in the name of the PFLP. For example, one of Jibril's supporters denied any links between the PFLP and the ANM, which he accused of interfering in the affairs of Arab states. The following day, the main body of the PFLP denounced his unauthorized statement in their name. See MENA Damascus to MENA Cairo, October 2, 1968, and October 3, 1968; see also Beirut RNS, October 10, 1968. The texts of some of these communiqués have been published in *Palestine Arab Documents,* 1968 (in Arabic) (Beirut: Institute for Palestine Studies, 1970), especially pp. 233, 266, and 762.

22. The PFLP and PDFLP have been carefully studied by Gérard Chaliand in *La Résistance Palestinienne* (Paris: Editions du Seuil, 1970), and in "Le Double Combat du F.P.L.P.," *Le Monde Diplomatique,* July 1970, p. 6ff. See also the article entitled "The Resistance: Commandos on the Left," *Action,* June 8, 1970, p. 5. The PDFLP describes its origins in "Democratic Popular Front for the Liberation of Palestine," Committee for Solidarity with the Palestinian Revolution, November 1969.

the PFLP received support from Syria's bitter rival, Iraq.[23] A final, insignificant split took place within the PDFLP the following year with the formation of the little-known Popular Organization for the Liberation of Palestine (POLP).[24]

SYRIAN, IRAQI, AND OTHER COMMANDO GROUPS

During 1968 and 1969, the number of commando groups grew rapidly. In addition to Fatah and the four major offshoots of the Arab Nationalist movement, at least five other distinct groups existed by 1970. As the Palestinian commando movement gained in prestige and popularity, both individual Palestinian nationalists and established Arab regimes sought to increase their influence within the movement by creating new groups of fedayeen.[25] Some proved to be little more than names on paper, but several enjoyed sufficient support to gain recognition, either because of the strength of their sponsors or because they might be used as allies by Fatah or or the PFLP.

The most important of the commando groups created after June 1967 was the Syrian-sponsored Vanguards of the Popular Liberation War, commonly known as Sa'iqa (meaning "lightning bolt").[26] The Ba'th party of Syria had decided as early as fall 1967 to withhold primary support from either Fatah or the ANM. During 1968, the Syrians created Sa'iqa as their own commando force. By the end of the year, Sa'iqa, drawing on Syrian funds and arms, had created a relatively large and well-equipped force, surpassing the PFLP in size.

Sa'iqa's organization was considerably more hierarchical and rigid than other commando groups, reflecting the training given by regular Syrian army officers. Politically, Sa'iqa initially tended to side with Fatah, supporting the doctrine that the liberation of Palestine must precede the settling of ideological quarrels. Sa'iqa

23. Iraqi support for the PFLP may have been temporarily suspended in June 1970. At that time Iraq became unusually critical of the commandos. See *Le Monde,* June 25, 1970.

24. MENA Damascus to MENA Cairo, February 23, 1970.

25. Muhammad Anis, an Egyptian observer, has deplored the fact that "some organizations are under the direct control of one government or another from which they receive their instructions. This is an extension of an odious phenomenon in the history of the Palestine problem—the guardianship of the Arab governments over the Palestinian revolution." *Al-Katib,* April 1970, pp. 2–8.

26. See Abdallah Schleifer's interview with Dafi Jamani of Sa'iqa in *Jeune Afrique,* No. 438 (May 26–June 1, 1969), pp. 30–31.

was generally hostile to the PFLP, reflecting Syrian attitudes toward a former rival, the ANM, but was usually cooperative with Hawatmah's PDFLP and particularly with Jibril's PFLP-General Command. A major difference between Sa'iqa and these fedayeen groups, however, was the presence of a large proportion of non-Palestinians in their ranks.

Sa'iqa grew rapidly during 1969, probably at the instigation of the Syrian regime and out of a desire to profit from the expansion of fedayeen activity in southern Lebanon. By the end of 1969, PLO officials in Beirut acknowledged that Sa'iqa was the most rapidly growing fedayeen organization, especially in Lebanon.[27]

The rate of Sa'iqa's growth in late 1969 seems to have been related in part to internal Syrian political quarrels. Salah Jadid, deputy head of the Ba'th party and leader of its civilian wing, had seen his authority whittled away by Defense Minister Hafiz al-Asad during 1969. In response, Jadid seems to have tried to turn Sa'iqa into an armed instrument for his own political ambitions against the military wing of the Ba'th party.[28] Asad in turn developed close links to the leaders of the Palestine Liberation Army stationed in Syria and in particular to Colonel Uthman Haddad.

When Jadid was finally ousted by Asad in November 1970, changes also took place in Sa'iqa's leadership, reflecting the dependent nature of its existence. Because of this dependence, Sa'iqa, despite its size and military potential, was not able to play an important independent political role within the Palestinian movement. Nonetheless, both Fatah and the PFLP tried at various times to win Sa'iqa to their point of view. Sa'iqa responded in understandable fashion, sometimes siding with Fatah, sometimes with the more radical groups.

Syrian efforts to gain influence within the Palestinian commando movement triggered similar activity on the part of the rival Ba'th regime in Iraq. Having come to power in July 1968, the Iraqi Ba'th was late in entering the Palestinian arena. Quarrels with Fatah, as well as a desire to compete with Syria, led the Iraqis to form the

27. Interview with author, March 1970. See also *Africasia*, No. 23 (September 28, 1970), pp. 20–21. Sa'iqa's rapid expansion was doubtless related to the comparatively generous rewards that Sa'iqa could provide its recruits. *An-Nahar Arab Report*, Vol. 1, No. 10 (May 11, 1970), p. 1, claimed that Sa'iqa paid each commando double the rate of an ordinary Syrian soldier.

28. Jadid's desire to use Sa'iqa as his personal instrument to attain power was reflected in his repeated claim that only Sa'iqa could put an end to "the corruption of the regime and the opportunism of party members." *An-Nahar Arab Report*, Vol. 1, No. 3 (March 23, 1970).

TABLE

MAJOR PALESTINIAN COMMANDO GROUPS: SUMMER 1970

Commando Groups	Major Source of Aid
I. LARGE GROUPS (5,000–10,000 armed men)	
1. Palestine National Liberation Movement—Fatah (Military forces—al-Asifah)	Diverse (Libya, Syria, Kuwait, Saudi Arabia, Algeria, private Palestinian)
2. Palestine Liberation Army (PLA) Popular Liberation Forces (PLF)	Arab League through Palestine Liberation Organization (PLO)
3. Vanguards of the Popular Liberation War (Sa'iqa)	Syrian Ba'th Party
II. MIDDLE GROUPS (1,000–3,000 armed men, including militia)	
4. Popular Front for the Liberation of Palestine (PFLP)	Iraq
5. Popular Democratic Front for the Liberation of Palestine (PDFLP)	Syria
III. SMALL GROUPS (100–500 armed men)	
6. Popular Front for the Liberation of Palestine—General Command (PFLP–GC)	Syria; later Libya and Iraq
7. Arab Liberation Front (ALF)	Iraq
8. Organization of Arab Palestine (OAP)	UAR
9. Action Organization for the Liberation of Palestine (AOLP)	UAR, Kuwait
10. Palestinian Popular Struggle Front (PPSF)	Miscellaneous
11. Popular Organization for the Liberation of Palestine (POLP)	UAR, miscellaneous
12. Al-Ansar	Arab Communist Parties

Arab Liberation Front (ALF) early in 1969. Fatah offices in Iraq were closed, and the ALF quickly became involved in the rivalry between Fatah and the PFLP. Unlike Sa'iqa, the ALF was not sufficiently well equipped or well manned to command the respect of other fedayeen groups. Its numbers in Jordan never seem to have surpassed several hundred armed commandos.

Two other commando organizations attracted small followings beginning in 1968 and 1969. The Palestinian Popular Struggle Front (PPSF) was formed in early 1968 around an old-guard Palestinian nationalist, Bahjat Abu Garbiyya, member of the PLO executive council of 1964. Small amounts of support came from Iraq and perhaps the UAR. The PPSF existed less because it represented an important segment of Palestinian opinion than because it might prove to be a useful ally or a disguised spokesman for the positions of the larger groups. The second group, with this same characteristic, was the Action Organization for the Liberation of Palestine (AOLP), led by Dr. Isam as-Sartawi, an American-trained heart surgeon. Sartawi had tried to work with Fatah, had then contacted the Iraqis and the ALF, and had finally decided to form his own group in February 1969. Assistance came primarily from the UAR, and perhaps from Kuwait as well. The more radical fedayeen groups suspected that Fatah was using the AOLP to attack the PFLP, but Sartawi was not merely Fatah's spokesman, as was demonstrated by his brief approval of the UAR acceptance of a United States–sponsored cease-fire with Israel in July 1970.

The last group of commandos to be formed reflected the desire of the Moscow-oriented communist parties of the Arab states to be represented in the political bodies of the Palestinian movement. In March 1970, the creation of al-Ansar (the Partisans) was announced, and a small armed force was established. The major fedayeen groups, however, with the exception of the PFLP and the PDFLP, initially refused to recognize al-Ansar as a legitimate Palestinian movement.[29] (See table for a listing of the major commando groups and estimates of their armed strength and their primary sponsors.)

THE PALESTINE LIBERATION ORGANIZATION

In January 1964, the Arab states agreed on the desirability of creating and supporting a Palestinian organization. At the time, it was widely believed that this decision reflected President Nasser's wish

29. Habash disclosed his positive attitude toward al-Ansar in *an-Nahar* (supplement), June 21, 1970. He predicted that it would become "an integral part of the Resistance movement."

to keep the Palestinian problem under his own supervision. The congress of Palestinian representatives that met in May 1964 did little to create the image of an independent and militant movement about to start the Palestinian revolution.[30] Instead, over four hundred Palestinians from a wide variety of backgrounds met and charged Ahmad ash-Shuqayri with selecting an executive committee for the Palestine Liberation Organization. In addition, the congress adopted the text of a National Charter.

The executive committee selected by Shuqayri was composed of fifteen middle-aged, generally well-educated professional men.[31] The PLO was charged with establishing a conventional army, the Palestine Liberation Army (PLA), recruited from among the Palestinian population and stationed in Egypt, Syria, and Iraq. Funds for the PLO were to be supplied by members of the Arab League.[32] With time, a bureaucratic and not very dynamic organization had been created, and Shuqayri had earned some notoriety as an irresponsible propagandist.

It was evident in the latter part of 1966 that an internal leadership crisis was brewing in the PLO. Shuqayri's autocratic style and his complete dependence on Cairo—which was held accountable among the Palestinians for his opposition to commando activities against Israel—elicited demands for a more even distribution of authority within the organization from PLO officials in Beirut and Damascus. Prominent in the opposition to Shuqayri were the director of the PLO bureau in Beirut, Shafiq al-Hut, and the PLA commander in chief, General Wajih al-Madani, both of whom were closely linked to the Heroes of the Return.

The struggle for power eventually led to the dissolution of the PLO's executive committee by Shuqayri and its replacement by a "revolutionary council" that would "prepare the people for the battle of liberation." This attempt to dislodge the dissidents and preempt the call to revolutionary warfare backfired, and opposition

30. PLO leaders admitted that they counted on the Unified Arab Command to direct the struggle for Palestine. Commando action was seen as dangerous and irresponsible because it would expose Arab countries to Israeli reprisals before they were militarily prepared for war. See *Jeune Afrique*, March 11–17, 1968, p. 31.

31. Sadat Hassan, "Introducing the Palestine Liberation Organization" (New York: PLO publication, n.d.).

32. A PLO official in Lebanon, Shafiq al-Hut, complained that the PLO received only about 10 percent of what the Arab League had promised in the way of aid. (*Jeune Afrique*, March 11–17, 1968, p. 31.) Budget figures are given in *An-Nahar Arab Report*, Vol. 1, No. 16 (June 22, 1970), pp. 2–3. Libya has been one of the few countries to honor its commitment to the PLO.

to Shuqayri intensified. By mid-February 1967 there were reports of a widespread movement in Palestinian circles designed to reassert the principle of collective leadership within the PLO and come out in full support of fedayeen action.[33] Shuqayri retreated and on February 26 announced the formation of a new executive committee, which included among its members the commander in chief of the PLA. Internal friction did not subside, however. In May, Shuqayri tried to remove Shafiq al-Hut from his key position in Beirut by transferring him to the PLO bureau in New Delhi, an action that Hut strongly resisted and to which he reacted by publicly accusing the PLO chairman of trying to purge all elements in favor of collective leadership. Shafiq al-Hut's position was widely supported.[34] These internal problems of the PLO remained essentially unresolved until December 1967, when they were instrumental in bringing about Shuqayri's demise from the organization.

When Shuqayri was relieved of his position at the head of the PLO at the end of 1967, efforts were already under way to work out a viable relationship between what remained of the PLO establishment and the new Palestinian forces embodied in the Resistance movement. In January 1968, Fatah invited several small fedayeen groups to Cairo to talk about plans for unity.[35] Simultaneously, the PLO executive committee, under the leadership of its acting chairman, Yahya Hammuda, was attempting to organize a meeting of the Palestine National Congress to deal with the issues of restructuring the PLO and unifying fedayeen action.

Representatives of the PLO traveled extensively during the first half of 1968. In February, it had been decided to form a new National Congress of one hundred members to replace the large, and by now unrepresentative, congress selected before 1967. Meetings with Fatah and the PFLP during March secured their tentative agreement to participate in the new congress, but troublesome issues concerning representation remained. The convening of the congress was announced several times, always to be postponed.

Since early 1968, the PLO executive committee had faced difficulties in disciplining the PLA.[36] This issue, amounting to a direct

33. *Al-Hurriyah* (Beirut), February 20, 1967.

34. *Al-Anwar* (Beirut), May 13, 1967.

35. The twelve groups invited by Fatah are named in a Middle East News Agency dispatch, Cairo, January 5, 1968. Included were the PLO, PLF, PFLP, PPSF, and Sa'iqa. The other groups listed did not remain in existence as independent entities.

36. In January 1968, the post of commander in chief of the PLA was abolished. In July, a new chief of staff was appointed, but the PLA rejected the decision and arrested the new commander. The dispute is

challenge of the PLO's authority by its armed forces, preoccupied the executive committee as it planned for the National Congress meeting. Finally, by late May 1968, the executive committee announced agreement on the allocation of seats in the congress among the PLO, the PLA and its recently created commando wing, the Popular Liberation Forces (PLF), Fatah, and the PFLP, as well as several independent Palestinians.[37]

Fatah seemed unenthusiastic about the coming meeting, arguing that the PLO should consist primarily of armed fighters, not "armchair revolutionaries."[38] The PFLP, already suffering from internal quarrels in the absence of some of its leaders, who had been arrested by the Syrians, was also reserved in its attitude toward the PLO. Syria appeared particularly hostile to the PLO, and at the time of the congress, Syria's own commando organization, Sa'iqa, was conspicuously absent.

When the Palestine National Congress finally met in Cairo from July 10 to July 17, little was achieved beyond the drafting of a new National Charter by the PLO establishment. The executive committee resigned, but no agreement could be reached on a new ruling body for the PLO, so the old executive committee was reappointed for another six months, pending a full-scale reorganization of the PLO. Fatah immediately made clear its dissatisfaction with the results of the congress.[39]

During the following six months a great deal of maneuvering occurred within the commando movement. The PLO was caught up in a prolonged crisis involving the PLA's refusal to accept the appointment of Abd ar-Razzaq Yahya as commander in chief. The PFLP underwent a series of splits, which became apparent as several groups began to use the name PFLP to denounce others of the same name. A similar phenomenon existed with respect to groups calling themselves Sa'iqa. The Syrian-sponsored Sa'iqa frequently found its name adopted by splinter movements. Meanwhile, Fatah periodically announced that it had absorbed some unknown faction or group with an unlikely sounding title. In short, the major Palestinian groups were all seeking to improve their bargaining positions before the next meeting of the Palestine National Congress early in 1969.

---

mentioned in the following sources: MENA Damascus to MENA Cairo, July 21, 1968, and August 2, 1968; Voice of Palestine (Cairo), August 9, 1968.

37. The PLO was given fifty seats, Fatah thirty-eight, PFLP ten, Independents two.

38. Voice of Fatah (Cairo), June 8, 1968.

39. Voice of Fatah (Cairo), July 17 and 19, 1968.

The PLO itself was seriously weakened by the mutiny of the PLA. Syria may have had a hand in shaping the PLA's attitude. In any event, the weakness of the PLO worked to the advantage of Fatah and Sa'iqa, which became increasingly cooperative toward each other in late 1968. The loser in this rapprochement was the PFLP, or what was left of it following internal splits dating from the middle of 1968.

In early January 1969, the PLO executive committee announced that the composition of the new congress had been agreed on and that the fifth session of the National Congress would be held in Cairo in February. Fatah received the largest number of seats, thirty-three, followed by Sa'iqa and the PFLP with twelve each. The PLA and PLF received only fifteen seats between them, and in reaction refused to participate, as did the PFLP. When the congress met in February, Fatah was able to turn its numerical advantage into a political victory. Fatah's official spokesman, Yasir Arafat, was elected chairman of the PLO. The eleven-man executive committee chosen by the congress included four members of Fatah, three Fatah sympathizers, and two Sa'iqa representatives and one Sa'iqa sympathizer, as well as a holdover from the old PLO executive committee, who was responsible for the Palestine National Fund.

EFFORTS AT UNIFICATION

Having succeeded in taking control of the PLO in February 1969, Fatah set about trying to bring some degree of unity to the badly fragmented commando movement. The persistent splits within the PFLP had erupted in open violence during January and February 1969, and Fatah helped serve as a mediator in settling the dispute by recognizing the PDFLP in late February. Fatah's major difficulties in trying to unify the Palestinian movement through diplomacy rather than the use of force were the controlling of the activities of splinter groups and the development of a working relationship with the strongly independent PFLP organization led by George Habash. In addition, the PLA was still not fully under PLO or Fatah authority.

In April 1969, the Palestine Armed Struggle Command (PASC) was formed as a loose coordinating body outside the framework of the PLO. Its purpose was to supervise the military activities of the fedayeen groups and to serve as a police force in Lebanon and Jordan. Fatah, Sa'iqa, the PLA, and the PDFLP were the initial members of the PASC. These four groups all enjoyed relatively good relations with Syria, and it was perhaps to weaken this Syria-oriented bloc that the Iraqi-sponsored Arab Liberation Front sought to join the PASC. Over Arafat's strong objections, the ALF was granted membership in June 1969.[40] In August, Za'rur's OAP also joined, to be followed shortly by two other minor groups, the PPSF of Abu Garbiyya and Jibril's PFLP-General Command.

In September 1969, another National Congress meeting was held, and was again boycotted by the PFLP. The members of the PASC, however, were all present and had been granted representation. Eight seats were allotted to the PDFLP, as well as one position on the executive committee. Other minor changes in the composition of the executive committee were made as well. Of the new participants, the PDFLP played an active role in pushing for debate on the meaning of the idea of a democratic Palestinian state. Their proposals, however, proved to be unacceptable to the majority of the congress.

Efforts to draw the PFLP into closer cooperation with the other members of the PLO continued during the fall of 1969. At one point it was announced that the PFLP had tried to join the PASC,[41] and this was followed shortly by a statement that the PDFLP had temporarily withdrawn its membership.[42] Finally, in February 1970, clashes with the Jordanian authorities led all of the recognized commando groups to form the Unified Command. For the first time since mid-1968, the PFLP agreed to cooperate with other groups. In addition, the AOLP of Sartawi and the tiny POLP agreed to join the PASC.

It remained for Fatah and the PLO to turn this paper unity into an effective organization of Palestinian commando movements. A common declaration of May 6 stated the terms of further unification.[43] All the members of the Unified Command signed the statement and pledged not to let the perennial problem of representation divide them.

The seventh National Congress meeting occurred in late May and early June 1970. The PFLP sent only one representative, despite the offer of eight seats.[44] All of the other members of the

40. Iraqi hostility toward Fatah in the spring of 1969 is related in *Jeune Afrique*, No. 517 (December 1, 1970), p. 45.

41. MENA Damascus to MENA Cairo, October 14, 1969; *Le Monde*, October 16, 1969.

42. *Le Monde*, December 20, 1969.

43. The text of the unity statement appears in *Fateh*, Vol. 2, No. 9 (May 29, 1970), p. 4, and in *al-Hadaf*, Vol. 1, No. 41 (May 9, 1970), p. 3. The text is signed by Fatah, PDFLP, PFLP, ALF, PPSF, AOLP, PLO executive committee, Sa'iqa, PLF, PLA, OAP, PFLP-GC, POLP.

44. The PFLP apparently insisted on equal treatment with Sa'iqa,

Unified Command attended. Among the accomplishments of the congress was the formation of a central committee of the Palestine Resistance movement, later called the central committee of the PLO, which consisted of twenty-seven members (see Figure 3). The central committee included the twelve members of the executive committee, a representative from each of the ten commando groups and the PLA, three independents, and the chairman of the Palestine National Congress. Shortly thereafter, following a major clash with Jordanian troops in June, a smaller general secretariat of the central committee was formed of six members, one each from Fatah, Sa'iqa, the PLO, the PFLP, the PDFLP, and the AOLP. Although the executive committee of the PLO continued to exist, for all practical purposes its authority had been transferred to the more representative central committee and the general secretariat.

At the seventh congress meeting, the issue of the PLA's autonomy was again discussed. Arafat succeeded in being named head of the PLA, a decision which set off a new crisis when an effort was undertaken to control the PLA by cutting off its funds. In July, Arafat ordered the dismissal of the chief of staff of the PLA, Colonel Uthman Haddad. Haddad, supported by the Syrian minister of defense, Hafiz al-Asad, refused to acknowledge the order, and it was with considerable difficulty that the PLO was able to enforce its decision.[45] Haddad remained, however, as head of the PLA's Hittin Brigade in Syria, and was eventually reappointed chief of staff.

A degree of unity had been reached by August 1970, with both the PFLP and the PLA accepting the authority of the central committee. The need for unity was particularly acute at that moment, for the UAR and Jordan had just announced their intentions of accepting a United States proposal of June 19 for a cease-fire and indirect negotiations with Israel. Two small commando groups, the AOLP and the OAP, had briefly broken ranks and defended the UAR position, but the other members of the central committee loudly rejected the idea of a peaceful settlement with Israel.[46]

---

namely fifteen seats in the congress. See MENA Cairo, May 30, 1970; see also *al-Hadaf*, Vol. 1, No. 44 (May 30, 1970), p. 3.

45. See *An-Nahar Arab Report*, Vol. 1, No. 19 (July 13, 1970), p. 3, and *An-Nahar Arab Report*, Vol. 1, No. 20 (July 20, 1970), pp. 3–4. Some elements of Sa'iqa seem to have supported Haddad. See MENA Damascus to MENA Cairo, July 12, 1970, and *Le Monde*, July 14, 1970.

46. See *Africasia*, No. 23 (September 28, 1970), p. 17; *Le Monde*, July 30, 1970. In reaction to criticism of his acceptance of the cease-fire, Nasser ordered that the PLO radio broadcasting from Cairo be shut down. It was not restored to service until late March 1971.

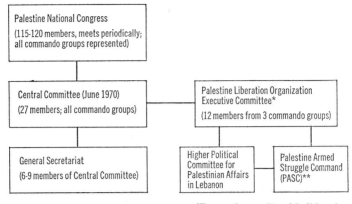

Palestine National Congress
(115-120 members, meets periodically;
all commando groups represented)

Central Committee (June 1970)
(27 members; all commando groups)

Palestine Liberation Organization Executive Committee*
(12 members from 3 commando groups)

General Secretariat
(6-9 members of Central Committee)

Higher Political Committee for Palestinian Affairs in Lebanon

Palestine Armed Struggle Command (PASC)**

*The executive committee of the PLO was included in the central committee after June 1970 and did not act as an independent body until after the central committee was disbanded and the executive committee reformed in July 1971.

**PASC was formed in 1969 to coordinate commando activities. PASC's functions were largely taken over by the central committee in June 1970.

Fig. 3. Organizational Structure of the Palestinian Resistance Movement in 1970

SUMMARY AND CONCLUSIONS

In their efforts to create viable political organizations based on the idea of Palestinian nationalism, Palestinians have always been confronted with massive obstacles. The nature of Palestinian society, with its deep traditional sources of distrust and division, frequently prevented effective unity.[47] In addition, the experience of engaging in the political life of other Arab countries during the 1950s and early 1960s had left many Palestinians with divergent ideological orientations which further split the political elite. For a brief moment, however, Palestinians were able to seize upon opportunities provided by the Arab defeat in the 1967 war to take the initiative in determining their collective fate.

The fedayeen were not the only expressions of Palestinian nationalism after 1967. Indeed, many traditional leaders on the occupied West Bank claimed to speak for sizable constituencies of Palestinians. In more than five years, however, West Bank leaders, whether traditional notables, mayors of the largest towns, or younger intellectuals and journalists, were unable to organize effective political groups. Instead, the organized expression of Palestinian aspirations consisted almost entirely of the Resistance movement.

No single Palestinian group could legitimately claim to speak for all Palestinians. The Palestinian Arabs inside Israel showed little evidence of overt support for the commandos.[48] In the Gaza Strip, however, anti-Israeli feeling ran strong and commando activities proved difficult to eliminate, indicating some popular support for the Resistance. On the West Bank, there were perhaps one hundred thousand politically aware Palestinians—most of the adult male population. While perhaps sympathetic to the commandos, this segment of Palestinian society was either linked to other leaders or kept from open expression of political sentiments by the fact of Israeli occupation. Also, Palestinians in the occupied territories generally saw the end of Israeli occupation as their primary objec-

47. The Egyptian scholar Muhammed Anis has attributed the lack of unity within the Resistance to both ideological splits and to the "traditional nature of Palestinian society and its inclination towards clannishness." *Al-Katib,* April 1970, pp. 2–8.

48. A survey conducted in the fall of 1967, however, indicated that younger, more modernized Israeli Arabs were *more,* not less, hostile to Israel. Y. Peres, "Modernization and Nationalism in the Identity of the Israeli Arab," *Middle East Journal,* Autumn 1970, pp. 479–492.

tive, and it was far from certain that commando activities could bring that goal any closer.[49]

Among the Palestinians residing outside of Palestine, the commandos enjoyed much greater support. A substantial majority of the three hundred thousand or more politically conscious Palestinians in Jordan, Lebanon, Syria, and elsewhere were, until September 1970, at a minimum sympathetic to the commandos, and many contributed funds to the various fedayeen groups. The manpower base for military recruitment probably did not exceed fifty to seventy-five thousand; of these, perhaps twenty thousand were full-time commandos by the fall of 1970 and another twenty thousand were members of the popular militia.

In brief, within the fragmented and dispersed Palestinian community, the commandos were able to organize a large part of the politically conscious population. While this fact did not ensure the success of the commandos in their effort to achieve Palestinian demands, it did suggest that thus far no Palestinian "silent majority" strongly opposed to commando activities and objectives had been able to organize effectively to present its own political demands.

Within the commando movement itself, however, serious organizational problems remained. Palestinian commando groups can best be distinguished in terms of size, autonomy, and ideology. In general, large and autonomous groups, such as Fatah and the PLO-PLA, have attained their status by diversifying sources of support, a strategy that is not conducive to a strong ideological orientation. An alternative strategy is to build a relatively large organization that is heavily dependent on a single source. Sa'iqa, which has pursued this approach, has little autonomy, but in return for following Syria's political line, it has generally been assured of adequate support.

Strongly ideological commando groups, such as the PFLP and the PDFLP, are either obliged to remain small and relatively powerless because of their desire to be independent, or they risk becoming the instrument of their major sponsors. Both the PFLP

49. Detailed reports of opinions of West Bank leaders appear in *Le Monde*, October 25–26, 1970; *New Middle East*, No. 26 (November 1970), pp. 6–7; and especially *Le Monde*, November 13, 1970. There seems to be little consensus among any of the major Palestinian leaders, according to these reports. Some prefer autonomy, others union with Jordan, while others would like to see a Palestinian state on both banks of the Jordan. Further information on West Bank opinion and leadership can be found in chapters 3 and 6.

and the PDFLP have thus far preferred considerable autonomy, even at the price of remaining relatively weak.[50] Other minor factions have been less able to acquire sufficient strength to resist becoming the spokesmen of their sponsors, or have found it necessary to offer themselves as allies to the larger groups.

As a result of the dependence of the fedayeen movements on outside support, unification has been difficult to achieve. The interests of individual Arab regimes have been a divisive force within the movement, as has the insistence of some of the smaller groups on articulating a rigorous ideological program that threatens to further embroil the commandos in the intricacies of inter-Arab factional politics.

Other sources of fragmentation have also been important within the Palestinian movement. Traditional social patterns within Palestinian society have placed a premium on the creation of numerous defensive alignments as a means of establishing a group-based bargaining posture. Palestinians frequently show a strong sense of individualism and are reluctant to accept the authority of existing institutions or organizations. Rather than join a unified movement, a committed Palestinian nationalist may first try to create his own following, and then negotiate with other political groups on a firmer basis. Coalition-building becomes a time-consuming process as each major power center within the society initially insists on forming an independent base from which it can deal with others on a more equal footing. Although outside pressures and threats occasionally succeed in bringing about temporary unity, it is just as likely that an outside enemy can play upon internal divisions to keep the Palestinians from forming effective organizations. Traditional sources of factionalism remain strong both in Palestinian society at large and within parts of the commando movement.

Finally, the Resistance movement has been unable to unify on the basis of an acceptable and potentially winning strategy. No single group has been able to demonstrate that it is capable of succeeding where others have failed. Promises of eventual victory

50. This comparative independence of both the PFLP and PDFLP from any Arab tutelage, and their strong commitment to developing a coherent ideology, have allowed these two organizations to play a role in Palestinian politics that greatly exceeds their numbers. At National Congress meetings, the PFLP and PDFLP are likely to come armed with resolutions and specific proposals, while Fatah, with more adherents and a less developed political line, often seems to resemble a debating society where nothing is ever decided.

may provide sufficient rewards for some, but the lack of tangible evidence that victory can soon be obtained contributes further to factionalism within the leadership and the rank and file. The events of September 1970 and their aftermath were doubtless the sharpest blow to the fedayeen and further hastened their decline as an organized political force.[51]

51. See chapter 6.

3
PALESTINIAN
POLITICAL LEADERSHIP

Palestinian political movements have suffered from inadequate resources and from the dispersion and division of Palestinian society. To overcome these weaknesses, a strong, unified political leadership would seem to be needed, but it has not been forthcoming. Instead, rivalries and disputes among self-appointed leaders have further compounded structural sources of dissension.

Conflict within the Palestinian political elite can be traced to at least three different factors, each responsible for distinct leadership problems. First, Palestinian Arab cultural values seem to predispose individuals toward suspicion, competition, strong emotions, and fluctuating loyalties in their political relationships. These values alone ensure a high level of tension in Palestinian political circles.

Second, historical circumstances in the 1950s and early 1960s led to the development of several Palestinian organizations, each of which, by the time of the June 1967 war, had reached a stage of development where it had a vested interest in protecting its organizational autonomy. The existence of these separate groups meant that unity, if it could be achieved at all, would result from the creation of a broad front under collective leadership, or by the absorption of the smaller units into the largest ones, or by the forceful elimination of one group by another.

Third, leaders of the various fedayeen groups found themselves divided on fundamental issues as a result of their social and national origins. Most fedayeen came from the Palestinian Sunni Muslim community, and tended to be narrowly nationalist in outlook. A significant minority, however, particularly among fedayeen leaders, either was not Palestinian by birth or was not from the dominant Sunni population. As a result of these differences in social background, non-Sunni Palestinians tended to give priority to issues of radical and secular change throughout the Arab world, not just in Palestine.

CULTURAL ATTITUDES TOWARD AUTHORITY

Two basic styles of leadership have been viewed favorably by Arabs. The first is that of the respected elder statesman who conscientiously consults with other notables and thereby reaches decisions reflecting the consensus of the group. In sharp contrast to the consultative pattern of decision-making, *shura,* is that of the strong charismatic leader, or *za'im,* who deals directly with the masses, over the heads of intermediaries. Distinctly lacking in these ideal types is the hard-working and efficient organization man who coerces, bribes, and otherwise induces his subordinates to follow his directives.

The idealization of both consultation and charisma in contrast to organizational effectiveness and hierarchy is rooted in a deep sense of individualism in Palestinian society.[1] This sentiment manifests itself not in nonconformist or innovative behavior, as one expects from individualism in the West, but rather in demands for equality and reciprocity in interpersonal relations.[2] At the heart of the matter is a strong feeling of personal honor in Arab culture. Among those of equal status, honor requires that respect be given. Only toward the acknowledged, undisputed leader, the *za'im,* can deference, even obsequiousness, be shown without loss of honor. The tyrannies of petty bureaucrats or the haughtiness of equals can, by contrast, easily become issues of honor leading to disputes.

Other cultural characteristics of Palestinian society compound the difficulty of creating effective leadership. A harsh critic of Arab society, Sadiq al-Azm, has argued that many Arabs have a "tribalist" mentality. By this he means that their primary concerns do not go beyond their own family. Thus loyalty to a political movement or to the nation is likely to take second place to more parochial attach-

1. For a general discussion of individualism in Arab society, see Morroe Berger, *The Arab World Today* (Garden City, N.Y.: Doubleday, 1962), pp. 274–275.

2. A similar set of values is present in Algerian political culture. See William B. Quandt, *Revolution and Political Leadership: Algeria 1954–1968* (Cambridge, Mass.: M.I.T. Press, 1969), chap. 13.

ments. Because of these more fundamental loyalties, leaders are reluctant to give up their independent bases of power and subordinate themselves to the interests of the larger group.[3]

Sadiq al-Azm goes on to condemn what he calls the *fahlawi* character of the Arabs. He describes the *fahlawi* as one who may be attracted to some great idea and initially shows much enthusiasm for it, but who, when faced with difficulties, frequently backs down and lapses into apathy. Revolutionary zeal is rarely sustained, and even more rarely transformed into appropriate social action. The *fahlawi* personality, then, is likely to enter the political arena when the tide seems to favor activism. Rather than accept existing structures of authority, the *fahlawi* will establish his own political network of friends and relatives. But when problems begin to arise, he is likely to abandon the cause rather than accept the discipline and regulations of the more effective organizations.[4]

Individualism, together with the characteristics of tribalism and the *fahlawi* personality described by Sadiq al-Azm, ensures an abundance of independent contenders for top positions of leadership. Lacking are the disciplined second-echelon leaders. A common remedy is to try to establish a framework of collective decision-making.

Although collective deliberation has been put forward as the preferred method of leadership, both within each major Palestinian group and in the coordinating bodies that unite them, it rarely works as well as its promoters hope. Several pressures tend to offset the fully egalitarian pattern adopted to cope with the overabundance of independent chiefs. First, large organizations seem to require some differentiation of functions in leadership if they are to be run efficiently. Specialists in fund raising, military operations, recruitment, public relations, propaganda, and internal organization should ideally complement each other in the performance of organizational tasks. Yet, inevitably, some functions bring more prestige, visibility, and power than others. Thus, some leaders become more influential than others. As this process takes place, prominent leaders are likely to come under attack from former colleagues for seeking to create a cult of personality and for making arbitrary and unilateral decisions. Threats of resignation, of bringing hidden disputes into the open, and of joining with a rival movement are likely to be heard from slighted leaders, but these fre-

3. See Sadiq al-Azm's major work, *Self-Criticism After the Defeat* (in Arabic) (Beirut: Dar at-Taliah, 1968), Part III. For an analysis of Sadiq al-Azm's writings, see Adel Daher, *Current Trends in Arab Intellectual Thought* (RM-5979-FF, The Rand Corporation, December 1969), p. 21ff.

4. Daher, *Current Trends*, p. 22.

quently end in temporary reconciliation and the reassertion of collective decision-making. On the other hand, an ambitious leader, by playing off rivals against one another or by drawing on the prestige of some powerful sponsor, may begin to develop a strong position as a *za'im,* above the factional struggles of his subordinates. Within the Palestinian Resistance movement, only Yasir Arafat and perhaps George Habash have at times come close to developing a position of strong, personal leadership, but even they have fallen far short of becoming undisputed spokesmen for the entire Palestinian community. Instead, factionalism and faltering efforts at committee rule have been dominant in Palestinian leadership circles. In large part, cultural values have been the basic cause of this generally high level of distrust and friction.

Career Patterns of Palestinian Leaders

In addition to cultural traits of competitiveness and disrespect for authority, the Palestinian commando movement has had to contend with the fact that a large number of Palestinians in the 1950s and early 1960s developed careers in politics in various parts of the Arab world. This meant that several distinctive groups of leaders, with established patterns of behavior and competing sets of credentials, were prepared to seize the opportunity provided by the Arab defeat in June 1967 to direct the forces of Palestinian nationalism. The abundance of vocal claimants to positions of leadership led to considerable bargaining, coalition-building, plotting, and maneuvering in Palestinian political circles after 1967, further compounding the problems arising from the lack of authority and unity that have long beset Palestinian society.

The formative years for most fedayeen leaders were those between Israel's creation in 1948 and the June war of 1967. This was a period of considerable uncertainty and instability in the Arab world as a whole, with numerous radical ideological movements casting about for ways to achieve unity, progress, and social justice. Arab nationalism came to incorporate the Palestinian problem, and individual Palestinians found themselves associated with groups as widely divergent in political orientation as the Muslim Brotherhood, the Syrian Social Nationalist party, the Ba'th Socialist party, and the Arab Nationalist movement.

Two Palestinian groups of particular importance took root in separate parts of the Arab world in the early 1950s. The first, organized by Yasir Arafat and his close associates, was located in Gaza, Cairo, and later Kuwait. It eventually became the core of Fatah's leadership. The second, associated with Dr. George Habash, consisted largely of students from the American University of Beirut and was organized primarily in Jordan, Syria, and Lebanon. Later, Habash's group also created a base among the relatively large and wealthy Palestinian population in Kuwait, as well as among followers in South Yemen. During the 1950s, however, Arafat's group had little contact with that of George Habash.

Yasir Arafat and Fatah's Core Leadership

Yasir Arafat, Fatah's most prominent leader, was born in 1928, probably in Jerusalem.[5] His family had links on his mother's side to the prominent Husayni clan, and it seems to have been through this relationship that Arafat as a young man began his career as a political activist. He became personal secretary to Abd al-Qadir al-Husayni, one of the few members of the Husayni family who fought with arms against the creation of the state of Israel.[6] The idea that only armed struggle could save Palestine for the Arabs was thus imparted to Arafat very early in his career.

By 1951, Arafat had moved from Gaza to Cairo, where he eventually became an engineering student at Cairo University. Already an effective political organizer, he became active in student politics. By 1955, he had made contact with a number of other Palestinian nationalists in Cairo and in Gaza, as well as with the conspiratorial methods of the Muslim Brotherhood. Arafat, along with two other young Palestinians from Gaza, Khalil al-Wazir and Salah Khalaf, were the founders of the political movement that later became known as Fatah.[7] In the spring of 1956 he was elected chairman of the Palestinian Student Union in Cairo. Later that same year he was a member of the official delegation sent by the General Union of Palestinian Students to attend the International Union of Students Conference in Prague. Accompanying Arafat to Prague were Salah Khalaf and Zuhayr al-Alami, both of whom later became members of the central committee of the Palestine Liberation Organization in 1970.

During the mid-1950s, Arafat, in addition to his studies and political activities, was given some training at the Egyptian Military Academy, particularly in the use of explosives. When the Israelis,

5. See the biographical sketch on Arafat in *Le Monde*, February 6, 1969.
6. Ehud Yaari, *Strike Terror: The Story of Fatah* (New York: Sabra Books, 1970), p. 12.
7. In later years, these three were known by the following code names: Yasir Arafat = Abu Ammar; Salah Khalaf = Abu Ayad; Khalil al-Wazir = Abu Jihad.

British, and French attacked Egypt in late October 1956, Arafat briefly fought in the Egyptian army with the rank of lieutenant. After the Suez war, Arafat left Egypt for Kuwait, where he established a contracting company and was employed by the Department of Public Works. Political activity remained in the forefront of Arafat's concern, however, and it was during these years in Kuwait that Fatah's core group expanded to include Faruq al-Qaddumi, Muhammad Yusif an-Najjar, Kamal Adwan, and Khalid al-Hassan.[8] By 1959, this group had found a means for articulating its political ideas in a publication entitled "Our Palestine." Having gained some recognition in Palestinian circles, Arafat was invited to attend the "Entity Congress" held in May 1964. By then he was actively involved in recruiting members for Fatah's military wing, al-Asifah, and others from Fatah's core leadership were busy raising funds and seeking Arab support for their impending armed campaign against Israel.

The remarkable fact about Fatah is that the seven key figures of 1957–1960 were still the undisputed leaders in 1971–1972.[9] To a large degree, Fatah's ability to dominate the Palestinian Resistance movement has been made possible by the unity and coherence of its leadership. Not surprisingly, Fatah leaders have been reluctant to disband their organization in favor of a broader national front that might fall under the control of rival groups.

George Habash and the Arab Nationalist Movement

In contrast to Fatah's leaders who had maintained their distinctive Palestinian organizational identity from the mid-1950s on, George Habash and his associates became active in a variety of Arab political movements during the 1950s. Habash was born in Lydda in 1926 of Greek Orthodox parents.[10] He received a medical

8. Later known as: Faruq al-Qaddumi = Abu Lutuf; Muhammad Yusif an-Najjar = Abu Yusif; Khalid al-Hassan = Abu Said.

9. Occasional challenges to Fatah's established leaders have been noted. Ania Francos, in *Jeune Afrique*, No. 512 (October 20, 1970), p. 44, discusses the generational differences in Fatah. See also *Jeune Afrique*, No. 525 (January 26, 1971), pp. 43–45. She identifies Salah Khalaf as one of Fatah's older generation with close ties to the younger cadres. See also *An-Nahar Arab Report*, Vol. 1, No. 3 (March 23, 1970), pp. 1–2; and Vol. 2, No. 3 (January 18, 1971), pp. 1–2. An article in *Fateh*, Vol. 1, No. 2 (October 15, 1969), p. 2, tends to play down Arafat's prominence within Fatah and reasserts the idea of collective leadership. The article claims that Arafat was named official spokesman in his absence by the other members of the central committee.

10. See Robert Anton Mertz, "Why George Habash Turned Marxist," *Mid East*, Vol. 10, No. 4 (August 1970,) pp. 33–36.

education at the American University of Beirut and also became involved in politics. By 1950, he was recognized as one of the prominent leaders of the Arab Nationalist movement (ANM), a relatively nonideological organization that called for Arab unity and justice in Palestine. Unlike its rival, the Ba'th Socialist party, the ANM did not initially include socialism as one of its major objectives.

During the 1950s, Habash turned to both Syria and Egypt for support. In 1957 he was expelled from Jordan on suspicion of working for Syrian intelligence, and shortly thereafter became an ardent supporter of President Nasser and the UAR. For several years, the ANM was seen as a Nasserist movement, and during the 1958–1961 period of Egyptian-Syrian union, the ANM remained loyal to Nasser. The more powerful Ba'th party, however, became disillusioned with Arab unity under Egyptian control and consequently was not grieved to see Syria break away from the UAR in September 1961. After Syrian secession, which was a serious blow to the hopes of the ANM, Habash was forced to flee to Lebanon, where he continued to organize the moderate, pro-Nasser faction of the ANM. Despite the prominence of intellectuals in its ranks, the ANM was unable to develop a coherent ideology, although the idea of socialism became widely accepted after Nasser's turn to the left in 1961.

As early as 1961, young ANM members began to challenge moderate leaders such as Habash, Wadi Haddad, Hani al-Hindi, and Ahmad al-Yamani. The left wing of the ANM, particularly strong in Lebanon, gained strength in early 1964 when, following the failure of unity talks with Syria and Iraq the previous year, Nasser announced that the Arabs were too weak to take military action to prevent Israel's diversion of Jordan River waters to the Negev. Even the moderate wing of the ANM was disillusioned with Nasser's stand, leaving initiative to the radicals to develop a more aggressive ideology based on the idea of class struggle and the need to replace the petit-bourgeois regimes of Syria and the UAR with more genuinely revolutionary ones. These ideas were voiced in the left-wing ANM publication, *al-Hurriyah*, under the editorship of a Lebanese Shi'ite, Muhsin Ibrahim.[11]

The Arab defeat in the Six-Day War facilitated the transformation of the ANM into an avowedly Marxist-Leninist organization. In part, the conversion to Marxism by the ANM leadership seemed to reflect a feeling that nationalism and socialism, as represented by Nasser and the Ba'th, had proved to be a weak basis for mobilizing the masses for the recovery of Palestine. Marxism at least had

11. *Ibid.*, p. 34.

the advantage of being relatively untested as the basis for a mass movement, and might attract considerable support provided it was not identified with the rather cautious Arab communist parties dependent on Moscow. For Habash, Haddad, Yamani, and their publicist, Ghassan Kanafani, later to become leaders of the PFLP, Marxism-Leninism provided a useful set of categories with which to criticize Arab regimes and other Palestinian movements, but the depth of their conversion to an internationalist, class-based view of the world was open to some question.

The left wing of the ANM, which tried to gain control of the PFLP during 1968 while Habash was in prison in Syria, was led by younger men such as Nayif Hawatmah, a Christian Transjordanian from the town of Salt; Billal al-Hassan, brother of Fatah leaders Khalid al-Hassan and Hani al-Hassan; Sami Dahi, a Syrian Christian; Salah Raf'at; and Muhsin Ibrahim.[12] Several of these leftist ANM leaders had been involved with the Vengeance Youth prior to the 1967 war, and they retained their organizational distinctiveness even after their formal merger into the PFLP. In 1968, however, after having succeeded in outvoting the Habash faction in successive PFLP meetings, but being unable to establish full control over the movement, the left wing split away to form the PDFLP under the leadership of Hawatmah in February 1969. The PDFLP was more firmly committed to the principles of Marxism-Leninism, particularly in their Cuban and Vietnamese applications, than any other fedayeen organization.[13]

The Palestine Liberation Organization

If Fatah, and eventually the ANM, succeeded in attracting the younger Palestinian activists to the doctrine of armed struggle, the older Palestinian militants, most of whom were established professional men, found in the Palestine Liberation Organization (PLO) an outlet for their political activities. The PLO leadership that was

12. In 1970, these PDFLP leaders, plus others on the central committee of the PDFLP, had an average age of about thirty. In comparison, the average age of PFLP and Fatah leaders was approximately forty.

13. When the PDFLP broke with Habash, Hawatmah took with him many of the best-trained and educated political leaders. As a result, the PFLP faced the problem of having to recruit and indoctrinate new men. The PFLP thus became one of the first commando groups to institute a formal program of training for second-echelon elites. Under Haytham Ayubi, the PFLP established a school for cadres which gave political instruction to approximately eighty recruits during successive four-month courses. See Gérard Chaliand, "Le Double Combat du F.P.L.P.," Le Monde Diplomatique, July 1970, pp. 6–7.

formed in 1964 represented those Palestinians from the older generation of politicians whose reputations as Palestinian nationalists
remained intact and who continued to insist on the need for a
distinctive "Palestinian entity."

Initially headed by Ahmad ash-Shuqayri, the PLO became the
channel of recruitment for many of the post-1967 Palestinian
leaders. Among these leaders were Yahya Hammuda, a lawyer with
one-time communist connections, who replaced Shuqayri at the
head of the PLO in 1968; Abd al-Majid Shuman, a respected banker
and financier; Hamid Abu Sittah, Abd al-Khaliq Yaghmur, and
Khalid al-Fahum; Wajih al-Madani, officer of the PLA forces in
Syria; and Bahjat Abu Garbiyya, former Ba'th party member in
Syria. These men all belonged to the 1964 PLO executive committee and succeeded in retaining positions of influence after 1967.
A number of Palestinian intellectuals also became associated with
the PLO in its early years, and some of these men continued to play
an active role in Palestinian politics after 1967. But despite the
talents of many members of the PLO, the younger generation of
Palestinians tended to view them as "armchair revolutionaries" or
bureaucrats instead of accepting their authority as representatives
of the Palestinian nationalist movement. Consequently, few of them
emerged as prominent leaders after 1967.

The Military Officers

Fatah, the ANM, and the PLO served as distinct training grounds
for political leaders before 1967. Other Palestinians, however, were
acquiring military experience, some as officers in the Syrian or
Jordanian armies. By the mid-1960s, several small groups of commandos had formed around these military leaders. Most prominent
was the Palestine Liberation Front (PLF), led by Ahmad Jibril, Ali
Bushnaq, Fadil Shukri Shruru, Ahmad Za'rur, and Tahir Dablan.
In late 1966, another military faction named *abtal al-awda* (Heroes
of the Return) was formed by anti-Shuqayri members of the PLO
(Shafiq al-Hut and PLA chief of staff Wajih al-Madani), as well as
by part of the Palestinian section of the ANM, led by Ahmad al-
Yamani.

These army officers had little in common other than their commitment to action, as opposed to the empty rhetoric of the PLO.
Their actions at times paralleled those of Fatah, but by the fall of
1966 suspicion was widespread that Syria was trying to use them as
a counterweight to Fatah. After the June 1967 war, the PLF and the
Heroes of the Return tried for several months to work with George
Habash as part of the PFLP, but by the end of 1968 Jibril, Za'rur,

and Dablan had all left the PFLP to form their own small commando units.

The Non-fedayeen Leadership

If the fedayeen and the establishment Palestinian nationalists of the PLO were badly divided as a result of their distinctive career patterns, the same was true of the non-fedayeen leaders. Intellectuals at the American University of Beirut were able to articulate ideas of Arab and Palestinian nationalism, but had little mass following. Other intellectuals were too dispersed to contribute effectively to the growth of a Palestinian movement.

Business and commercial leaders were especially prominent in Kuwait. Although they contributed heavily to the Palestinian movement, they did not take an active independent role in directing it. Several wealthy individuals, however, such as Abd al-Majid Shuman, assumed positions of responsibility in the PLO and Fatah.

The remaining potential source of leadership for the Palestinians consisted of prominent figures on the West Bank. After the annexation of the West Bank by Jordan in 1950, the militantly anti-Hashemite leaders, especially the Husayni family of Jerusalem, had fled into exile. The resulting void was filled by middle-class Palestinians, as well as a few traditional notables, who were willing to work within the Jordanian system. In the major municipalities of the West Bank, leaders with local followings emerged to become mayors, cabinet ministers, and ambassadors. After the Israeli occupation of 1967, many of these men remained on the West Bank, where they continued to carry some political weight within a limited constituency. Most important of these leaders were Shaykh Muhammad Ali al-Ja'bari, the aging traditional patriarch of Hebron; Hamdi Kan'an, Hikmat al-Masri, and, until his death in early 1971, Qadri Tuqan of Nablus; Aziz Shihadah of Ramallah; and Anwar Nusaybah and Anwar al-Khatib of Jerusalem. What distinguished these leaders was their reluctance to work together and the narrow, local base of support that they enjoyed. None could claim to represent all of the West Bank, let alone the entire Palestinian community. The Israeli occupation of the West Bank in June 1967 compounded their problems: if they became too active, they might be expelled by the Israelis to the East Bank, as many less well-known activists had been; if they appeared too moderate, they would be vulnerable to charges of collusion with the enemy. Most important, these men had for years worked with King Hussein and could no longer capitalize on those ties to assume positions of leadership among the Palestinians. For many of them, a restoration

of some form of Jordanian rule over the West Bank would provide
a surer opportunity of renewed political careers than would the
growth of Palestinian commando activities. Until the fall of 1970,
a dominant opinion among West Bank leaders was that once the
Israeli occupation had ended, then a new type of relationship to
the East Bank could be worked out which would allow considerable
autonomy for the Palestinians while preserving their links to the
Arab world.

Social Background and Political Orientation

Among the fedayeen leaders, a fundamentally different set of priorities distinguished the Palestinian nationalists from those who viewed
the Palestinian struggle as a means of bringing about radical social
change throughout the eastern Arab world. In large measure, this
distinction can be accounted for in terms of social origins and subsequent political involvement in inter-Arab politics.

Fatah has frequently been accused of being chauvinist or region-
alist because of its concentration on Palestinian affairs and its
general unwillingness to engage in inter-Arab quarrels. It has been
joined at various times in this orientation by the PLO and some of
the minor fedayeen groups such as the Action Organization for the
Liberation of Palestine, led by Dr. Isam as-Sartawi, and the Palestinian Popular Struggle Front of Bahjat Abu Garbiyya.

Fatah's concentration on Palestinan nationalism stems in part
from the makeup of its leadership. Nearly all of Fatah's leaders are
Sunni Muslim by religion and Palestinian Arab by birth. In these
respects, they represent the majority of Palestinian society. Fatah's
reluctance to press the theme of secularism is quite likely the result
of the continuing religious attachments of some of its leaders and
the obvious appeal of Islam as a political rallying point for the
masses of Palestinians, as well as the sensibilities of Fatah's reli-
giously oriented supporters, such as the rulers of Saudi Arabia and
Kuwait. The absence of secular Marxist thought among Fatah's
leaders and the narrowly Palestinian focus of their activities are
both consistent with their social backgrounds.

Other fedayeen leaders have been concerned with the consequences of the Palestinian struggle for the rest of the Arab world.
These same leaders are also likely to be advocates of secular and
radical social ideas. Their concerns, like those of Fatah's leaders,
can be partially accounted for by social origins. Prominent members of the PFLP, for example, are either non-Palestinian or non-
Muslim by birth. George Habash is a Greek Orthodox Palestinian;

Wadi Haddad is a Christian long active in the Syrian ANM; and Hani al-Hindi is a Syrian member of the ANM who participated in the unity talks of 1963. In the PDFLP, leadership also lies partly in the hands of non-Palestinians or non-Muslims. One-third of the members of the central committee of the PDFLP in 1970 were in this category. Nayif Hawatmah, the leader of the PDFLP, is a Christian Transjordanian, and his close associate, Sami Dahi, is a Syrian Christian. Other central committee members come from Iraq, Lebanon, and the Druze community in Syria. Similarly, a splinter group that broke away from the PFLP and took the name PFLP-General Command is led by two men, Ahmad Jibril and Ali Bushnaq, who have served as regular officers in the Syrian army.

The Syrian and Iraqi Ba'th have sponsored fedayeen groups that understandably concern themselves with issues that go beyond the liberation of Palestine. Sa'iqa, the Syrian-backed organization, has been led by members of the Jordanian branch of the Ba'th party, such as Dafi Jamani and Mahmud al-Ma'ita, by a Syrian Ba'thist, Zuhayr Muhsin, and by a former Syrian prime minister, Yusif Zu'ayyin, and has thus been more of a faithful instrument of Syrian policy than an exclusively Palestinian organization.

The Iraqi Ba'th, since 1966 a bitter rival of the regional Ba'th command in Damascus, has created the Arab Liberation Front and placed at its head a former secretary general of the Ba'th party, Munif ar-Razzaz, a Syrian who had long lived in Jordan and who followed the Iraqi Ba'th national command's political line after February 1966. Zayd Haydar, the ALF's other prominent leader, is best known as an ardent opponent of the Syrian Ba'th, not as a Palestinian nationalist.

Since many of these leaders are in fact less in tune with the main body of Palestinian nationalism, they have naturally sought to expand the scope of political activity to the surrounding Arab countries of Lebanon, Jordan, Syria, and Iraq. Also, because several leaders are from religious minorities, they have an interest in pressing for secular policies, particularly in their Marxist-Leninist form.

Added to the cultural values that foster competition in Palestinian society and the vested interests of established leaders, differences in social origin also contribute to the splits within the fedayeen movement. Those who by birth are least typical of the Palestinian community have often become the ardent advocates of secular social revolution in the Arab world, while the Palestinian Sunni majority has tended to focus more exclusively on Palestine. Yasir Arafat, a representative of this majority, has been distinctly more successful in rallying broad support than Christians such as

George Habash and Nayif Hawatmah. To some Palestinians, and to many Arabs, it is difficult to acknowledge the leadership of a man whose first name is George.

CONTINUITY AND DISCONTINUITY

Leadership of the Palestinian Resistance movement has come primarily from men active in politics for at least a decade prior to the 1967 war. The effect of the war was not to bring to the fore totally new leaders, but rather to allow a generation of relatively obscure Palestinian activists to emerge as visible spokesmen for a cause they had been pursuing during much of the previous two decades.

Within two of the major Palestinian groups, Fatah and the PFLP, the degree of continuity in top leadership positions has been impressive. Fatah's core leaders have all worked together since 1957–1958. The PFLP has been somewhat less dominated by a cohesive group of leaders, but George Habash has been able to maintain his prominent position, despite numerous challenges, since the late 1940s.[14]

Despite such continuity of leadership within some of the component parts of the Palestinian Resistance movement, the structure of the broader Palestinian institutions has changed radically since 1964. When the PLO was founded in 1964, it consisted of a large National Congress of over four hundred members and an executive committee of fifteen middle-aged nationalists. Of these fifteen men, six continued to occupy important positions within the framework of the PLO in 1968–1969. By that time, however, leadership was passing into the hands of the commandos. The smaller National Congress that met in mid-1968 was composed of fifty fedayeen representatives and fifty non-fedayeen. In subsequent years, this ratio continued to shift in favor of the commandos.

In February 1969, when Fatah succeeded in seizing control of the PLO, only two members of the old PLO executive committee were among the eleven-man body. Fatah was directly represented by Yasir Arafat, chairman and head of military affairs, as well as Khalid al-Hassan, Faruq al-Qaddumi, and Muhammad Yusif an-Najjar, all members of Fatah's central committee. In addition, Fatah seemed to have the support of Ibrahim Bakr, deputy chairman, Kamal Nasir, and Hamid Abu Sittah. Sa'iqa was directly represented by Ahmad ash-Shihabi, Yusif al-Barji, and enjoyed the support of Yasir Amr. Only the head of the Palestine National

14. Reports of opposition within the PFLP to Habash's leadership—growing out of his absence from Jordan during the September 1970 crisis—are evaluated in MENA Damascus to MENA Cairo, November 7, 1970.

Fund, Abd al-Majid Shuman, remained relatively independent of factional identifications, largely because of the technical nature of his job.

In September 1969, several changes were made in the executive committee. Ibrahim Bakr and Shuman were dropped, to be replaced by Billal al-Hassan of the PDFLP, Khalid Yashruti, who died in an accident four months later, and Husayn al-Khatib. The PFLP was still not represented in the PLO.

The next major change in the composition of the leadership of the Resistance movement came in June 1970, with the creation of the central committee. The central committee represented a compromise between the demand of the smaller groups for equal representation with Fatah and Sa'iqa and Fatah's insistence on proportional representation based on armed strength. In the end, the entire executive committee of twelve, in which Fatah and Sa'iqa were dominant, was included in the central committee, along with one representative from each of the ten organizations belonging to the Unified Command of February 1970, plus the head of the PLA, the chairman of the National Congress, and three independents. The twenty-seven members of this supreme executive body were as follows: [15]

PLO Executive Committee
   Yasir Arafat (Fatah)
   Yasir Amr (pro-Sa'iqa)
   Kamal Nasir (Independent)
   Khalid al-Hassan (Fatah)
   Faruq al-Qaddumi (Fatah)
   Hamid Abu Sittah (pro-Fatah)
   Muhammad Yusif an-Najjar (Fatah)
   Yusif al-Barji (Sa'iqa)
   Ahmad ash-Shihabi (Sa'iqa)
   Billal al-Hassan (PDFLP)
   Husayn al-Khatib (pro-Sa'iqa)
   Zuhayr al-Alami (head of the Palestine National Fund)
Independents
   Ibrahim Bakr
   Abd al-Khaliq Yaghmur
   Khalid al-Fahum

Chairman of the Palestine National Congress
   Yahya Hammuda
Commander of the PLA
   Abd ar-Razzaq Yahya
Representatives of the commando groups
   Salah Khalaf (Fatah)
   George Habash (PFLP)
   Dafi Jamani (Sa'iqa)
   Munif ar-Razzaz (ALF)
   Nayif Hawatmah (PDFLP)
   Ahmad Jibril (PFLP-GC)
   Isam as-Sartawi (AOLP)
   Ahmad Za'rur (OAP)
   Bahjat Abu Garbiyya (PPSF)
   Abd al-Fattah Yasr (?) (POLP)

15. The individual members of the central committee tended to vary slightly from one meeting to the next, since each fedayeen group was left free to designate its representatives.

From among these twenty-seven members, a smaller general secretariat was formed in June 1970. It consisted of Arafat, Kamal Nasir, George Habash, Dafi Jamani, Nayif Hawatmah, and Isam as-Sartawi. Thus the four major commando units—Fatah, PFLP, Sa'iqa, and PDFLP—were all represented by their leaders in the general secretariat. Fatah could probably also count on the support of Kamal Nasir and Sartawi in the event of disagreement with the other leaders.

CONCLUSION

The continuing rivalry within the leadership of the Resistance movement contributed to the decline of discipline during the summer of 1970. It also provided opportunities for ambitious leaders such as Habash and Hawatmah to try to reverse their sinking fortunes by pushing for a direct confrontation with the Jordanian regime. Fatah, reluctantly or perhaps even willingly, might then be dragged into a conflict which the smaller groups hoped to set off but were incapable of winning on their own. The familiar pattern of overbidding in Arab politics, made possible by inter-Arab conflicts, was therefore repeated on a Palestinian scale in late summer 1970. In inter-Arab politics, the result of such overbidding in 1967 had been defeat at the hand of Israel. In September 1970, the result was a major setback for the Palestinians by King Hussein's Jordanian forces.[16]

16. The September 1970 crisis and its aftermath are dealt with in chapter 6.

4
IDEOLOGY
AND OBJECTIVES

In view of the organizational fragmentation and lack of unity among Palestinian leaders, consensus among Palestinians on current policies and long-term objectives should not be expected. Indeed, it would be an error to assume that carefully formulated programs and consistent ideological analysis can exist within a society that is physically divided and undergoing very rapid social change. In addition, the momentum of the movement of armed struggle, with its successes and setbacks, has led to continual reformulations of objectives, as well as of tactics and strategy, on the part of Palestinian leaders and intellectuals. Finally, stated positions do not always correspond to privately held views. For most Palestinians, a range of minimum and maximum goals is under consideration at any given time, and circumstances beyond the control of individuals largely determine which means seem appropriate to which ends. Ideology, rather than hindering such flexibility, is often available to justify apparent inconsistencies.

If priorities frequently become the object of dispute among Palestinians, several broad areas of agreement nevertheless exist. First, Palestinians would generally agree that there must be some form of redress for the injustices they associate with the creation of Israel at their expense. The means of "restoring Palestinian rights" are a subject of debate, but the feelings of injustice and resentment run very deep. Palestinians are most in agreement in their analysis of the origins of the conflict that has pitted them against Israel and Zionism.

In recent years, and particularly since 1967, some segments of Palestinian society have agreed on the necessity of armed struggle under Palestinian leadership as the means of obtaining some or all nationalist objectives. Palestinians living under Israeli rule, for whom the primary goal has been to end the occupation, have been less attracted to the idea of armed struggle than the Palestinians in Jordan, Syria, Lebanon, and elsewhere. Nonetheless, the belief in the need for Palestinian, as distinct from Arab, action is relatively widespread.

Beyond these general areas of agreement, Palestinians remain divided over issues such as the nature of the future Palestinian state they hope to live in. Disagreements also exist over the issue of whether armed struggle should be directed exclusively toward Palestinian national objectives, or whether it should be part of a broader revolutionary process in the Arab world as a whole. On both of these issues, distinct opinions have been articulated by individuals who have frequently been labeled "rightists" or "leftists," "nationalists" or "internationalists," and "moderates" or "extremists." The labels, however, are often misleading, for those who are most extreme in their attitudes toward Jews are often the least prone to advocate revolution in the Arab world. By contrast, the self-styled Marxist-Leninists have generally made the most thorough effort to understand the nature of both Palestinian and Israeli society, and have been largely responsible for shifting the level of debate over Israel from that of military conflict toward the political context in which Jewish and Palestinian communities might coexist within some type of political structure. But while the quality of political and social analysis on the part of the "left" is frequently of high quality and lacks the apologetic nature of other writings, the conclusions drawn are often dogmatic and require capabilities well beyond those available to the Marxist-Leninist groups. Some of these differences in approach can be seen in the treatment of the problem of the place of the Palestinian revolution within the Arab world and the nature of the envisaged democratic, nonsectarian state.

PALESTINIAN OR ARAB REVOLUTION?

In the Arab political lexicon, the term "regionalism" (*iqlimiyya*) has carried a highly charged negative connotation. It refers to the belief that narrowly defined state interests should take precedence

over broader Arab nationalist interests. As Palestinians have begun
to speak out in defense of their distinctive problems, they, like the
Lebanese, the Syrian nationalists, and Iraq's Prime Minister Qasim
in an earlier period, have been accused of the sin of regionalism.

The unresolved tensions between state nationalism (*wataniyya*)
and Arab nationalism (*al-qawmiyya al-arabiyya*) have been described by Hisham Sharabi: "National awareness inevitably brought
in its train the polarization between a narrow, 'local' nationalism
and a larger, all encompassing nationalism. This dichotomy is reflected today—both politically and psychologically—in the insurmountable contradictions in every Arab nation-state between the
reality of national sovereignty and the idea of greater Arab unity." [1]

Fatah, as the largest of the Palestinian organizations, has been
particularly vulnerable to the charge of placing Palestinian interests
above those of the Arab nation at large.[2] To defend itself from this
accusation, Fatah has adopted a position midway between regionalism and Arab nationalism. Fatah has clearly stated that the Arab
regimes, during their period of custodianship over the Palestinian
problem, proved themselves incapable of dealing effectively with
Israel. In the words of a Fatah representative, "The Arab countries
have their specific problems, their own interests which condition
their thinking and determine their action." [3]

Despite Fatah's determination to remain independent of any
Arab regime, the Palestinian movement has relied on the Arab
countries for aid, arms, and territory from which to operate. The
Palestinians cannot cut themselves off from the Arab world, and
yet they have been determined not to leave the initiative concerning
their problems in the hands of non-Palestinians. The strategy
initially adopted by Fatah was to insist that Arab and Palestinian
objectives were compatible. Fatah only asked for assistance and
protection, and in return would contribute to the struggle against
Israeli occupation of Arab lands. In the early period of fedayeen
activity, it was common to find references to the goal of recovering
the territories lost in the 1967 war. Armed struggle could serve as a

1. Hisham Sharabi, *Arab Intellectuals and the West: The Formative
Years, 1875–1914* (Baltimore: Johns Hopkins Press, 1970), p. 119.

2. The suspicion that Palestinians after 1967 were placing their own
interests above Arab nationalist interests was given credence by the
conscious change in terminology chosen by the Palestinian National Congress from 1964 to 1968 to express the word "national." In 1964, the word
used was *qawmi* (nationalism in the broad sense); in 1968, the word *watani*
(state nationalism) was used.

3. Gilbert Denoyan, *El Fath Parle: Les Palestiniens contre Israel* (Paris:
Editions Albin Michel, 1970), p. 21.

complement to diplomatic initiatives. For example, in May 1968, Arafat was quoted as saying: "Since we do not interfere in the internal affairs of the Arab countries, where we have no ambitions, since we have in common with them and with the Arab people the objective of ending the Israeli occupation, we see no reason for a conflict between us." [4]

By 1969, Fatah was referring more frequently to the theme of the liberation of Palestine rather than using the more ambiguous phrase "ending Israeli occupation." Following the setback of September 1970, however, Fatah again modified its stance, stating through the central committee that "the Palestinian revolution is not opposed to elimination of the consequences of the June Israeli aggression, nor does it object to recovery by the Arab states of their territory occupied by the enemy as long as this does not undermine the rights of the Palestinian people or the Palestinian revolution." [5]

Initially, during its period of rapid growth, Fatah made serious efforts to avoid clashes with established Arab regimes. To keep from threatening the governments of Lebanon and Jordan, Fatah consciously refrained from taking a strong revolutionary line. Instead, national independence was the primary objective of Fatah, and only after attaining that goal would Palestinians turn to the issues of social and economic revolution and Arab unity.

The ambiguity of Fatah's position toward the Arab countries was obvious, however, as Fatah insisted on full autonomy and at the same time asked for aid and supported Arab unity. The charge of regionalism, pushed most insistently by the Iraqis,[6] was countered by the claim that the regional battle was only a part, and perhaps even a precondition, of the larger struggle for Arab liberation.[7]

Fatah spokesman Hani al-Hassan expressed Fatah's views toward the rest of the Arab world when he stated:

> We in Fatah have learned that the Arab nation will not embark on the course of struggle and cannot change its conditions unless it practices revolutionary mutiny. . . . Revolutionary struggle as we view it is the only way for the recreation of the Arab nation, the reformation of its soul, and the reactivation of the Arab

4. *Jeune Afrique,* No. 383 (May 6–12, 1968), p. 494.

5. *New York Times,* January 21, 1971, p. 5.

6. See "Guerrilla Activity and the Danger of Regionalism," *al-Ahrar,* December 19, 1969.

7. Jalal as-Sayyid, "The Palestinian Revolution between Nationalism (*qawmiyya*) and Regionalism (*iqlimiyya*)," *al-Katib,* April 1970, pp. 45–49; see also Naji Alush, *The Palestinian Revolution: Its Dimensions and Issues* (in Arabic) (Beirut: Dar at-Taliah, 1970).

masses. . . . Naturally, we in the Palestine revolution aspire to the day we will begin our social revolution, but it is stupid to insist that we wage both revolutions together, because if we do we will lose both.[8]

Hani al-Hassan goes on to say that Fatah is not a movement of the right or left, but rather one of "the new progressives—the movement which has gone beyond the Arab right and the Arab left." While reiterating Fatah's lack of interest in seizing power in Jordan, he asserts that if the choice for Fatah becomes that of liquidation or seizing power, Fatah will not hesitate to seize power. Also, if there is a peaceful settlement, he warns, the slogan of noninterference in Arab affairs will be dropped.[9]

While avoiding the untenable position of total devotion to Palestinian interests and lack of concern for the rest of the Arab world, Fatah has nonetheless remained essentially a nationalist movement. Fatah's objective is clearly the creation of a Palestinian state, although the social, economic, and even territorial makeup of that state are left undefined. Devotion to Arab nationalism is proclaimed, but Fatah shows little willingness to turn over the Palestine problem to any Arab regime. Instead, Fatah, until 1970, sought to build up its strength without having to confront the armed forces of Jordan, Lebanon, or Syria.[10]

To maintain this independent posture, Fatah has been obliged to appear as a relatively moderate, nonideological movement. The alternative would be to accept confrontation with the Lebanese and Jordanian regimes as inevitable and to enlist Syrian and Iraqi support for a military showdown. To adopt this strategy, however, Fatah would jeopardize its own autonomy and might very well be abandoned in the midst of battle, as was the case in September 1970. Despite much talk of the need for a stronger ideological line

8. *Ar-Rai al-Aam,* April 23, 1970, pp. 1–8.   9. *Ibid.*

10. This ambiguous stance toward other Arab countries is well illustrated by the following quote: "Many [in 1968] . . . made the serious mistake of linking the Palestinian nature of the revolution to the area which imperialism called Palestine. We, in Fatah, view Palestine in terms of national, not geographic, dimensions. While we insist that it would be a mistake to appropriate the Palestinian identity . . . , we also stress that it is clear that the plan to destroy Zionism, indeed the main lines of any strategy of revolution, depends on the measure of clarity with which we can answer the following question: How can we exploit the demographic and topographic status of the Arab people, at least those who figure in the Zionist expansionist design, to launch a popular war based on the enlightened, organized and armed masses?" *Fateh,* April 17, 1970, pp. 10–11.

and for revolution in the Arab world, Fatah cannot afford to alter its essentially nonideological nationalist posture without losing its unique position of wide support throughout the Arab world. The alternative to Fatah as a broad-based national movement would seem to be a Syrian-backed—or Iraqi-backed—organization, such as Sa'iqa, or a small, but ideologically rigorous movement like the PFLP or PDFLP.

The PFLP and the PDFLP have generally taken a different stance toward the Arab regimes as well as toward the issue of regionalism. Both groups argue that the Palestinians alone are not capable of defeating Israel and the forces allied with her.[11] Nor do they believe that the existing Arab regimes are capable of pursuing the struggle with success. In their analysis of the obstacles facing the Palestinian revolution, both of these "leftist" movements frequently demonstrate more insight than the less ideological spokesmen for Fatah or the PLO.

Both the PFLP and the PDFLP appreciate the limits of armed struggle in the absence of fundamental social and political changes in the Arab world. George Habash of the PFLP, however, stresses that armed struggle can help to mobilize and educate the masses, and accuses his rival, Nayif Hawatmah of the PDFLP, of following a strategy of first building a political movement, then educating the people, then fighting.[12] The two groups nonetheless agree that the Palestinians cannot achieve their objectives until social and political revolutions have occurred in most of the Arab world. The slogan of noninterference in the affairs of the Arab countries is rejected by both Habash and Hawatmah and their followers.[13] The regimes in Lebanon, Jordan, and Saudi Arabia are all branded as reactionary, and both the PFLP and the PDFLP have made no secret of their belief that they should eventually be overthrown. These groups also have often been critical of the so-called progressive regimes in Syria, Iraq, Algeria, and the UAR, all of which they see as dominated by the "petite-bourgeoisie." [14]

The PFLP and the PDFLP argue that the liberation of Palestine will follow the success of revolution in the rest of the Arab world. Over a period of twenty or thirty years, armed struggle will transform the Arab world, and then the forces of the liberated Arab

11. The PFLP identifies the enemies of the Palestinians as Israel, world Zionism, imperialism, and Arab reaction.

12. *Jeune Afrique*, March 24, 1969, pp. 50–53.

13. *The Palestinian Resistance Movement in Its Present Reality* (in Arabic) (Beirut: Dar at-Taliah, 1969), pp. 72–79.

14. *Action*, June 8, 1970, p. 5.

nation will be engaged on the side of the Palestinians. When Palestine is finally liberated, it will become part of a larger socialist unified Arab nation ruled by a Marxist-Leninist party. In reply to Fatah's less ambitious strategy, the PFLP replies that "the Palestinian revolution will become an Arab revolution before it reaches the stage, many years from now, of building the state." [15]

The irony of the PFLP-PDFLP viewpoint is that in some ways it is more realistic concerning the balance of forces than Fatah's, and yet the conclusions drawn are far beyond the capabilities of the relatively small and poorly financed radical fedayeen groups. Indeed, their militancy ensures that these groups will remain small, since no existing Arab regime can fully agree with their objectives. By contrast, Fatah, with much greater resources and capabilities, is more modest in its goals, and yet less self-critical and more apologetic in its propaganda than either the PFLP or the PDFLP. Like many radical movements, the PFLP and the PDFLP may count less for their armed strength than for the few well-argued and courageous ideas that they have managed to introduce into the political arena.

THE DEMOCRATIC, NONSECTARIAN STATE

One of the most controversial ideas advanced by Palestinians since 1967 has been that of a democratic, nonsectarian state of Palestine in which Jews, Muslims, and Christians would enjoy equal rights. At first glance, such a slogan would not appear to be a subject of great controversy, particularly since the prospects for its realization in the near future are virtually nonexistent. Nonetheless, one finds that Israelis have gone to considerable lengths to discredit the motives of those who advance the idea, while Palestinians have been firm in arguing that a new and more humane approach to the conflict with Israel is emerging, especially among younger Palestinian Arabs.

To understand the debate over the Palestinian proposal for a democratic, nonsectarian state, it is necessary to recognize that, since 1967, the immediate problems of mere survival have been greater for the fedayeen than the need to define long-range objectives in consistent and convincing detail. As a result, no authoritative document or set of statements can be taken as representing Palestinian thinking with respect to the nature of the envisaged democratic state. Individuals and groups have given quite different interpretations to the slogan of a democratic, nonsectarian state, depend-

15. *Al-Hadaf*, Vol. 1, No. 16 (November 8, 1969), p. 12.

4019 121 338 947

DAVID M LIVINGSTON

ID 9480-995-964
CAPRICORN BOOKS
MILL VALLEY

02/28/74*BAC

P U R C H A	M A N	N E O	M N B E A R M E	

DATE	DEPT.	SALES NO.	INITIALS	SEND

QUAN. CLASS	DESCRIPTION	AUTHORIZATION CODE	UNIT COST	AMOUNT
1	Book			2 95

4-13-73

TAKE

| | TAX | 15 |
| TOTAL | | 3 10 |

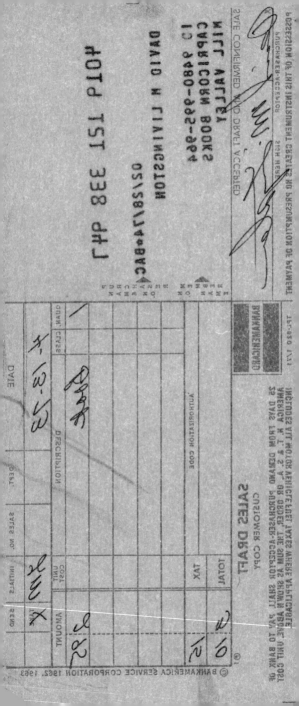

ing on time and on whether the topic is publicly or privately debated. The issue has remained remote, theoretical, and abstract for most Palestinians, and yet it is an important element in trying to understand the dynamics of the Palestinian movement.

The current generation of Palestinian leaders generally supports the idea of a democratic, nonsectarian Palestinian state as the ultimate goal of their efforts, not because they believe they will soon attain their stated objective, but rather because it demonstrates their desire to break with the sterile slogans of the old PLO. Under Shuqayri, the PLO was not particularly active, but violent rhetoric compensated for its passivity. While never having the capabilities to do so, the old-guard Palestinian leadership spoke of destroying the state of Israel and of expelling any remaining Jews to their countries of origins. In the National Charter of 1964, the PLO implied that only those inhabitants of Israel who had come prior to 1948 could become citizens in a future Palestinian state. In 1968, the PLO, still under the influence of the older generation of leaders, altered article 6 of the charter to read: "Jews living in Palestine until the beginning of the Zionist invasion are considered Palestinians."

As Israel's former chief of army intelligence, Yehoshafat Harkabi, has pointed out, the Palestine National Congress of 1968 elsewhere referred to the date of the Zionist invasion as 1917.[16] From this fact, Harkabi draws the conclusion that the more recent definition of citizenship within the future democratic Palestinian state is even more restrictive than the 1964 version. Consequently, Harkabi argues, as he has done consistently since 1967, that there is no basis for accommodation between Israeli and Palestinian demands. In fact, the Palestinian goal of dismantling the state of Israel implies a desire to commit genocide toward all Israeli Jews. In his view, "politicide" entails genocide.[17]

Despite Harkabi's insistence on the importance of article 6 of the Palestinian National Charter, it is obvious that the charter is not an adequate expression of the complexity of the debate over the issue of the democratic state. Several significant schools of

16. Yehoshafat Harkabi, "Three Articles on the Arab Slogan of a Democratic State" (mimeo), 1970. The full text of the charter, constitution, and resolutions of the PLO can be found in *International Documents on Palestine, 1968* (Beirut: The Institute for Palestine Studies, 1971), pp. 393ff.

17. Yehoshafat Harkabi, *Fedayeen Action and Arab Strategy*, Adelphi Papers, No. 53 (London: Institute for Strategic Studies), December 1968; and his longer study, *Arab Attitudes to Israel* (New York: Hart Publishing Company, 1972).

thought can be identified that explicitly reject the earlier PLO line of 1964 and 1968. In the rapidly changing Palestinian context, a document drafted in 1968 by PLO leaders chosen in 1964 is unlikely to reflect the opinions of the leaders of the 1970s, even if the charter is supposedly still in force.

Most Palestinian fedayeen leaders would probably agree that little attention has been paid thus far to the nature of a future Palestinian state. They would publicly insist that binationalism or a two-state federation in Palestine is unacceptable, but that within a democratic, nonsectarian Palestinian state, those Jews who wished to live as Palestinian citizens with full rights would be allowed to do so. Some of the Palestinian leaders who have devoted more thought to the issue would go further and talk of national rights for Jews within a Palestinian state, without defining precisely what this entails. Since the issue has been controversial, some quotations from Palestinian leaders may help to reflect the diversity and uncertainty that surround the topic of the future state. Certainly there are few signs of the kind of consensus Harkabi implies on a program of explusion of Jews from the future Palestine.

George Habash, in an interview shortly before the September 1970 conflict, acknowledged the relative unimportance that has been attached to the issue of the democratic state. "The nature of the future Palestinian state doesn't seem to me to be in urgent need of definition. . . . We now have problems that are more important to resolve, since we have no lack of difficulties in our current stage of development." [18]

Earlier, Arafat was quoted as defining a peace founded on justice as "the restitution of Palestine to its legitimate inhabitants. The Jews can live in an Arab state of Palestine like the Arabs have lived in the state of Israel since 1948." [19] Other Fatah spokesmen have indicated that "all those who wish to remain in Palestine as Jewish Palestinian citizens equal to Christian and Muslim Palestinians can stay with us. The others, if they want to leave, will have the right to leave." [20] Later, in December 1970, Arafat was cited as calling for a "democratic, non-Zionist, secular state where we would all live in peace and equality as we did for thousands of years. If the Zionists would accept this principle, we could share power on a democratic basis. We would not insist on having an Arab majority." [21]

18. Quoted by Gérard Chaliand in "Le Double Combat du F.P.L.P.," *Le Monde Diplomatique,* July 1970, p. 7.
19. *Jeune Afrique,* No. 383, May 6–12, 1968, p. 49.
20. Denoyan, *El Fath Parle,* p. 212.
21. *Time,* December 21, 1970. A few days after this interview appeared, Arafat was in Saudi Arabia, where he was asked about his acceptance of a

As these quotes indicate, Fatah has established a position that essentially rejects the interpretation that only Jews living in Palestine before some specific date would be allowed citizenship in a Palestinian state. Instead, any Israeli who was willing to live in such a state would be accepted. Fatah has asserted that "the revolution rejects the thesis according to which only the Jews living in Palestine before 1948 or before 1914 and their descendents will be acceptable. After all, Dayan and Allon, who were born in Palestine before 1948, are racist Zionists who cannot pretend to Palestinian citizenship, whereas some newly arrived Jews may be anti-Zionist and contribute to creating the new Palestine." [22] Fatah has further argued that "all Jewish Palestinians—at present Israelis—have the same rights provided of course they reject Zionist racist chauvinism and fully accept to live as Palestinians in the new Palestine. . . . It is the belief of the revolution that all present Israeli Jews will change their attitudes and will subscribe to the new Palestine, once they are aware of its ideology." [23]

While Fatah has clearly stated that the terms of the Palestinian charter do not reflect its position on future citizenship in a Palestinian state, its leaders have insisted upon the necessity of a unified independent state of Palestine with some links to the Arab world.[24] Since Israelis would certainly reject such political arrangements, all debates on the future Palestinian state inevitably have an air of unreality about them. Only occasionally do Palestinian statements suggest a somewhat more unconventional and intriguing approach to the conflicting claims of Arab and Jewish sovereignty in Palestine. A very small fraction of the Palestinian movement, the PDFLP of Nayif Hawatmah, has on several occasions pressed for an open debate on the issue of relations with Israelis, and has even gone so far as to mention *national* rights for Jews in Palestine. The suggestion has been made that the PDFLP would accept some form of federal or two-state arrangement, although the PDFLP has itself denied such intentions. Nonetheless, the PDFLP has introduced a new theme by acknowledging that the Israelis constitute a national

---

secular state in which the Jews might form a majority. He denied having ever made such a statement, limiting himself to support for a democratic state in which Jews, Christians, and Muslims would enjoy equal rights. See MENA Damascus to MENA Cairo, December 25, 1970.

22. *Jeune Afrique*, March 3, 1970, p. 61.

23. Quoted in *Arab News and Views*, February 1969, pp. 4–5.

24. Fatah leaders have publicly called for an amendment to the Palestinian National Charter to lift the restrictive qualifications on Jews eligible for Palestinian citizenship. *Fateh*, Vol. II, No. 2 (January 19, 1970), p. 10. The issue was debated and referred to a committee at the June 1970 meeting of the National Congress.

society in the process of formation. Thus far, the PDFLP has not accepted the idea of a separate Jewish state in Palestine, but the logic of its position might eventually lead some to such a conclusion. In fact, other fedayeen groups have attacked the PDFLP precisely on these grounds.

In September 1969, the PDFLP presented its views on a democratic state of Palestine to the National Congress meeting in Cairo. There it argued that in a popular democratic Palestine, "both Arabs and Jews shall live without discrimination, and will be granted the right to develop and promote their respective national (*watani*) culture." Further on it is asserted that the democratic state "will include Arabs and Jews enjoying equal national rights and duties." [25]

Elsewhere the PDFLP has referred to Israel as a "complete society" and has called for equal rights for Arabs and *Israelis* in a democratic state.[26] For this reference to Israelis instead of Jews, the PFLP has sharply criticized the PDFLP, arguing that even the PDFLP had earlier held that Judaism was only a religion, not the basis for a people with a distinctive nationality.[27]

The PDFLP's ambiguous position of recognizing national rights for Israeli Jews, while insisting on a unitary state, is reflected in the following statement of a minor PDFLP spokesman:

> We believe that the Israeli Jews are a national (as distinct from religious) community in Palestine who have national (as distinct from religious) rights, the right to develop their own culture and heritage with complete freedom. In a liberated Palestine, their national rights will be fully respected, and all the citizens, of whatever ethnic (as distinct from religious) group will be absolutely equal in all duties and rights. Here. . . , I want to correct a misunderstanding of the PDFLP position. We have never accepted the idea of a bi-national state of Palestine.[28]

Significant opposition to the positions on the democratic state as sketched by Fatah and the PDFLP has come from the more strongly Arab nationalist fedayeen organizations. The Iraqi ALF has entirely rejected the idea of a Palestinian democratic state, arguing that there should be no separate solution to the Palestinian

25. *The Palestinian Resistance Movement in Its Present Reality*, pp. 166–167. In an interview in *Jeune Afrique*, No. 429 (March 24–30, 1969), p. 53, Hawatmah also talks of "political rights" for Jews in Palestine.

26. *Al-Hurriyah*, No. 518 (June 8, 1970), p. 4. See also Maxime Rodinson, in *Le Monde Diplomatique*, July 1970, p. 9; and Gérard Chaliand, *La Résistance Palestinienne* (Paris: Editions du Seuil, 1970), p. 157.

27. *Al-Hadaf*, Vol. I, No. 39 (April 25, 1970), p. 12.

28. *Militant*, August 7, 1970.

problem. The Syrian-backed Sa'iqa has also gone on record with the statement that "neither the Palestinians alone nor any part of the Resistance movement are entitled to determine on their own a solution for the fate of Palestine after victory." [29] Many Palestinians, as well as their Arab supporters, judge it premature to discuss the issue at all. Given these views, can one say that there has been any change in Palestinian thinking toward Israel, Zionism, and Jews? For some individuals, if not for all Palestinians, the answer is clearly yes.

One of the most forthright Palestinian statements, including self-criticism and a sense of continuing evolution in Palestinian thought, appeared in a publication entitled "The Palestinian Revolution and the Jews." The writer admits that in the past many Palestinians were unable to distinguish between their bitterness toward Israel and their feelings toward Jews. With the beginning of the Palestinian armed movement after 1967, however, a more serious effort has been made to understand Israeli society:

A new attitude was being formed toward the enemy. Distinctions between Jew and Zionist started to have meaning. Realization that revenge was not a sufficient course for a liberation war led to further examination of the final objectives of the revolution. . . . The first step in the creation of a democratic, non-sectarian Palestine has been made by the Palestinian revolutionaries. A change of attitude through relearning is taking place. The long-exiled and persecuted Palestinians are redefining their objectives and are finding the goal of creating a new Palestine that encompasses them and the present Jewish settlers a very desirable one.[30]

In other public expressions, Fatah representatives have given voice to a relatively moderate view of possible political arrangements in Palestine. For example, it is not uncommon to hear that the Palestinians "are asking the Jews to build with us a country where we could live together, where our two communities would interact and mutually adjust to each other's idiosyncrasies." [31] In private conversations, Palestinian leaders are willing to consider a variety of political arrangements that might satisfy the requirements of the two major claimants to sovereignty in Palestine, namely, the Israelis and the Palestinian Arabs. While admitting

29. *Al-Anwar*, March 20, 1970. This statement was made in a debate on the theme of a democratic Palestinian state among representatives of the PLO, Fatah, Sa'iqa, the ALF, the PDFLP, and the PFLP.

30. "The Palestine Revolution and the Jews" (mimeo) (New York: Palestine Liberation Organization, 1969), pp. 3–4.

31. *Newsweek*, April 27, 1970, pp. 50ff.

that little thought had been devoted to the topic, Palestinian leaders in the spring of 1970 were willing to consider political arrangements similar to the Swiss canton system, Czech federalism, and virtually any form of loosely knit political system of a federal nature.[32]

Israelis would, of course, not find these arrangements acceptable, but the fact that Palestinians have been willing to consider them seriously indicates that there may be considerable flexibility in their position regarding a future political settlement in which both major communities in Palestine would find an outlet for their distinct national sentiments.

The lack of a clearly articulated Palestinian position regarding long-term objectives is related to the problems of divisiveness that have plagued the Resistance movement. Nonetheless, some signs exist that individual Palestinians, including important leaders, have substantially altered their views toward Israel over the past few years.[33] Also, the population of the West Bank, while unlikely to feel warm sentiments toward the Israeli occupiers, has nonetheless been able to have direct contact with Israeli society and thereby to see the degree of cohesiveness and strength that mark Israel as a modern nation-state.[34] Combined with a greater willingness to acknowledge that Israelis constitute a national society and the renunciation of any intentions of expelling Israelis from Palestine, these changing attitudes may in time lead to serious consideration of the means by which Israeli Jews and Palestinian Arabs might coexist as national societies inside Palestine.[35]

32. Author's interviews with Palestinian leaders in Beirut and Amman, spring 1970. An evaluation of later Palestinian thinking, based on interviews in September 1971, is found in chapter 6.

33. Hisham Sharabi discusses the debate over the future Palestinian state in *Palestine Guerrillas: Their Credibility and Effectiveness,* Supplementary Papers for the Center for Strategic and International Studies, Georgetown University, 1970, pp. 34–35. See also articles by Clovis Maqsud, in *al-Ahram,* September 14, 1969, p. 5, and in *Mid East,* June 1970, pp. 7–10.

34. An Israeli Christian Arab, Atallah Mansour, has argued that increased contact with Israel has bred a greater sense of realism among Palestinians, but that the vast majority of them would refuse to live in a binational state for fear that it would be dominated by the Jewish population. "Palestine: The Search for a New Golden Age," *New York Review of Books,* Vol. 17, No. 5 (October 7, 1971), p. 21.

35. There has been some ambiguity as to the geographic confines of Palestine in the minds of fedayeen leaders. A PFLP spokesman excluded Jordan east of the river (Transjordan) from his definition, whereas Fatah has stressed at times that Transjordan is a part of Palestine. See *New Middle East,* No. 24 (September 1970), p. 35, for the PFLP view expressed by Ghassan Kanafani. *Fateh,* Vol. 2, No. 2, p. 10, quotes a Fatah leader as saying, "What you call Transjordan is actually Palestine." The

Thus far, neither the Palestinians nor the Israelis have addressed themselves adequately to this issue. Until the Palestinians become convinced that a clear position on their part may influence the prospects for a Palestinian state, they will be unlikely to go beyond the few tentative steps toward an accommodating posture that have already appeared. To dismiss these modest developments as meaningless is premature and intellectually unfounded. The real issue is whether the changes in attitude already apparent in the younger generation of Palestinians can lead to a viable political bargaining position that could capitalize on the widespread interest in finding an acceptable solution to one of the key issues in the Arab-Israeli dispute.

THE SOCIAL CONTENT OF PALESTINIAN THOUGHT

Fatah, as the most broadly based fedayeen organization, has avoided defining the social content of the Palestinian society it is seeking to create. While progressive in nature, this society has not been described in class terms. As a sympathetic Egyptian Marxist has noted: "The commando movement is essentially a national front that combines the extreme left with the extreme right under the unity of one cover. . . . It is meaningless to bring up discussion of an ideological line at the present time. It will crystallize from the active struggle for liberation. . . . Fatah has stated clearly that Palestine will belong to its liberators, be they Marxists or bourgeois." [36]

In order to specify the social content of the revolution, Fatah argues, it is necessary first to unite people, land, and state. After liberation, the type of social and political institutions appropriate to Palestinian society can be decided on. Until then, such debates become divisive and counterproductive. While some individuals in Fatah have adhered to a stronger ideological line, the core leadership has defended the nonideological posture of Fatah. Despite demands from Fatah's younger members for greater ideological clarity, there have been no signs of a turning to the left in Fatah's official positions concerning social and political issues.[37]

---

unity of the East and West Banks of the Jordan River became a major theme in spring 1971.

36. Muhammad Anis, in *al-Jumhuriyah*, May 15, 1969.

37. Fatah's social views are presented in "From the Principles of Fatah," *Hisad al-Asifah*, September 1969, pp. 11–12; "The Revolution and Social Content," *Fatah* (weekly), No. 4 (May 13, 1969), p. 5; Naji Alush, *The Palestinian Revolution: Its Dimensions and Issues* (Beirut: Dar at-Taliah, 1970), pp. 55–72; and *Fatah* (daily), July 20, 1970, p. 3, on the role of labor unions during the armed struggle.

In contrast to Fatah, both the PFLP and the PDFLP have been deeply concerned with the social content of the Palestinian revolution. Habash, as a recent convert to Marxism-Leninism, relies heavily on class analysis to define the nature and goals of the Palestinian movement. In general, the PFLP argues that armed struggle and social revolution in the Arab world must proceed simultaneously, under the leadership of the revolutionary classes, in which he includes the petite bourgeoisie. Habash, however, has been notably reluctant to talk about the future democratic state of Palestine, judging such discussion premature and unnecessary. He has nevertheless made it clear that the word "democratic" must be understood in its class meaning as the dictatorship of the proletariat and in the context of Arab unity.[38] A representative statement of the PFLP social and political thinking claims:

> The future state of Palestine after the liberation will be run according to Marxist-Leninist principles. There will be a Marxist-Leninist party, and the PFLP will be the leader of the revolution. This fight for the liberation of Palestine will take another 20 to 30 years, and after victory everything will be different. Not only will Palestine be free from Zionism, but Lebanon and Jordan will will be free from reaction, and Syria and Iraq from the petite bourgeoisie. They will be transformed in a truly socialist sense and united. Palestine will be a part of a Marxist-Leninist Arabia.[39]

The PDFLP, led by Nayif Hawatmah, has agreed with the PFLP on the need for a strong ideological posture. While generally viewed as the most "leftist" of the commando groups, the PDFLP has been more flexible than the PFLP in its use of Marxist-Leninist analysis and has generally been willing to cooperate with the other more moderate groups such as Fatah.

On several specific issues, the PDFLP has disagreed with Habash. In particular, Hawatmah has stressed the primary need for social revolution in the Arab world as a precondition for effective armed struggle in Palestine. Unlike the PFLP, the PDFLP argues that the leadership of the revolution can be entrusted only to the revolution-

38. See "Palestine: Toward a Democratic Solution," *al-Hadaf*, Vol. 2, No. 75 (November 14, 1970), pp. 10–11. The idea of democracy as "one man, one vote" is explicitly rejected by the PFLP.

39. DPA (Hamburg), January 18, 1970. See also *Action*, June 8, 1970, p. 5; *Al-Hadaf*, Vol. 1, No. 16 (November 8, 1969), pp. 11–12; *Al-Hadaf*, Vol. 1, No. 39 (April 25, 1970), pp. 11–12; "Palestine: Toward a Democratic Solution," *al-Hadaf*, Vol. 2, No. 75 (November 14, 1970), pp. 10–11.

ary class (workers, peasants, refugees), not to the petite bourgeoisie.[40] This esoteric issue of the role of the middle class and intellectuals has been of considerable importance in the debate between the rival Marxist-Leninist groups.[41]

The need for a strong ideological definition on the part of the Palestinian leadership was argued by Nayif Hawatmah late in 1970: "The resistance movement is indeed in a crisis and this crisis is not new. Its roots are in the ideological and political structure of the resistance, a structure which has not made it possible for the movement to become organized on either the political or military level in such a way as to enable it at any moment to define the precise strategy to be adopted in the face of the reactionary Jordanian regime." [42]

It has been asserted that radicalization of the Palestinian movement, and particularly of Fatah, would contribute to the unity and determination of the commando groups. Following the September 1970 crisis, several observers believed that the fedayeen were in fact moving more to the left. If this were to occur, the Palestinians would immediately run the risk of full-scale confrontations with established governments, such as occurred in Jordan in July 1971.[43] At the same time, support from most Arab regimes would decline, exposing the Palestinians even more to the superior forces of the Jordanian or Lebanese authorities. Radicalization is thus more likely to weaken and divide the fedayeen movement than to unite it.[44] For that reason, Fatah, at least, will probably publicly adhere to its relatively nonideological social and political philosophy, while perhaps encouraging the development of a clandestine organization capable of pursuing more extreme objectives.

40. *On the Crisis of the Palestinian Resistance Movement* (in Arabic) (Beirut: Dar at-Taliah, 1969), pp. 49–68; see also *The Palestinian Resistance Movement in Its Present Reality* (in Arabic), pp. 28–44.

41. See "On the Role of the Petite Bourgeoisie in the Literature of the PDFLP," *al-Hadaf*, Vol. 1, No. 39 (April 25, 1970), pp. 10ff.

42. *L'Orient*, December 20, 1970, p. 11.

43. For more detail on the July 1971 clash, see chapter 6. Following the September 1970 crisis, the PFLP has called openly for the overthrow of King Hussein of Jordan; indeed, it was for this purpose that unity of the Resistance movement was deemed necessary. "The Unity of the Resistance Groups . . . for What Purpose?" *al-Hadaf*, Vol. 2, No. 76 (November 21, 1970), pp. 6–7.

44. Clovis Maqsud has developed the argument of the need for a "national left" consisting of part of Fatah, the PFLP, and the PDFLP to give the fedayeen a new lease on life and to combat the resurgence of Islamic populism. See *al-Ahram*, September 10, 1971, p. 9.

PROMOTING SOCIAL CHANGE

Beyond the intellectual debates over the class nature of Palestinian society, the major commando groups have become involved in a variety of social and educational programs. Fatah, for example, has gone to considerable lengths to set up schools for refugee children and to provide social services such as health care to the refugees. In the Fatah camps, boys and girls together are taught the goals of the Palestinian movement, a version of Palestinian history, simple physical training, and the symbols of Palestinian nationalism. The ideas of secular nationalism, equality between the sexes, and self-reliance are all instilled at a very early age and may well prove to be among the most revolutionary consequences of Palestinian actions since 1967.

The more radical groups, such as the PDFLP, have tried, with their modest resources, to engage in political and social action with the poor Jordanian and Palestinian peasantry.[45] While the results have not been dramatic, such behavior on the part of any political movement in the Middle East represents a major break with the past.

As a result of concrete actions among the refugees and peasantry, the Palestinian movements may do more to bring genuine social change than all of the ideological debates in the pages of al-Hadaf, al-Hurriyah, and Fatah. The change has obviously been slow, but by 1969–1970 the Palestinian commando movement was beginning to perform many of the functions of a government, including the provision of major social services, the maintenance of order, and the resolution of conflicts. These efforts were most strongly felt only in the refugee camps of Jordan, Syria, and South Lebanon, and their consequences cannot yet be judged.[46] Nonetheless, the generation of Palestinians reaching political consciousness in the 1980s is quite likely to carry with it some of the lessons taught by the commando groups in the 1970s. Primary among these lessons will be the idea of a progressive Palestinian nationalism.

45. Gérard Chaliand, *La Résistance Palestinienne* (Paris: Editions du Seuil, 1970), pp. 104–136.

46. Arafat, in an interview published in Algiers, stated that "our revolution has been able to transform our people from downcast refugees into aroused fighters. This in itself is not unimportant; we consider it to be one of the greatest achievements of our revolution." *Al-Mujahid*, December 28, 1969, pp. 16–17. The loss of control over the refugee camps in Jordan after September 1970 weakened the ability of the fedayeen to pursue their social objectives as well as to recruit new members.

Summary and Conclusions

A survey of the ideologies of the major Palestinian groups suggests that ideology has not been of much importance in the recent development of Palestinian nationalism. The largest commando groups have been consistently opposed to the idea of carefully defining a social and political program in ideological terms. In fact, this relative abstinence from ideological debate has been partly responsible for Fatah's success in gaining a broad following compared with that of the smaller and more radical PFLP and PDFLP.

To assume that the commandos can be classified along a "left–right" spectrum is more misleading than it is helpful. Differences in objectives and priorities do appear, but they do not follow this dichotomy in any consistent fashion. Instead, one should distinguish the narrowly Palestinian nationalist movements (Fatah, most of the smaller groups, and some members of the PFLP), which insist on concentrating on armed struggle in Palestine, from the more internationalist, Pan-Arab movements (PDFLP, ALF, Sa'iqa, part of the PFLP), which call for revolution in the Arab world as the precondition for the liberation of Palestine.

The radicals, in terms of calling for profound revolutionary change, are the most willing to talk of the vague notion of national rights for Jews in Palestine. On this issue, the old-guard PLO leadership has been much more extreme in its views, calling for the expulsion of most of the present Israeli population from Palestine.

In addition to expressing more tolerant views of Israeli society, the Palestinian "left" has been more genuinely self-critical and aware of the limitations of armed struggle. While the PFLP and PDFLP are unlikely to dominate the Palestinian movement, they have had an impact on Palestinian thinking that goes well beyond their numerical strength. At least part of their influence has weighed on the side of a progressive, secular version of nationalism in contrast to the vague formulations of the PLO. Fatah itself has appropriated some ideas from its more radical rivals, but has recognized the pitfalls of adopting a strongly ideological posture in a context where Palestinians are inevitably dependent on the goodwill and tolerance of regimes of many different ideological orientations. The desire for autonomy on the part of the main body of Palestinian leadership, and the need to avoid costly clashes with Arab armed forces, have thus far set distinct limits on ideological developments within the Palestinian movement. As long as the Palestinians hope to remain a potentially independent actor in the Middle East, they will continue to adhere to a relatively nonideological style. If, however, they are weakened and driven underground, radical movements may become more prominent in Palestinian political life.

5
MILITARY STRATEGY
AND CAPABILITIES OF
THE FEDAYEEN

The failure of conventional Arab armies to defeat Israel in 1967 led many Palestinians to question their former reliance on Arab unity as well as the possibilities of succeeding in a war requiring the mastery of advanced technology and weaponry. Dim prospects of military success, however, did not lead to the conclusion that peace with Israel was the only viable alternative. Instead, the idea of pursuing the confrontation by means of popular armed struggle became widely accepted among Palestinians. Fatah, of course, had argued for this strategy since 1965, and consequently gained considerable prestige for its early recognition that the efforts of regular Arab armies would not suffice to restore Palestinian rights.

Despite the widespread acceptance of the need for armed commando actions against Israel, there was no consensus among Palestinians as to what were the appropriate tactics or the real goals to be pursued. At one level, armed struggle might serve to mobilize the Palestinian population on behalf of nationalist objectives and at the same time raise the salience of the Palestinian issue in the international community as a whole. Relying on the popularity they had won in Arab circles as a result of their activism, the fedayeen might also hope to prevent Arab regimes from concluding a peace with Israel at the expense of the Palestinians. A more ambitious objective was at times described as that of bringing about changes within Israel that would make an eventual accommodation possible. Israelis, it was argued, could be forced to recognize the validity of Palestinian grievances.[1] The burden of continuing warfare, heavy defense spending, and costly casualties would also eventually serve to convince the Israelis to accept political arrangements in which Palestinian demands were granted. More ambitious still was the goal of continuing the battle with Israel until changes had occurred in the Arab world that would increase the chances of a successful armed confrontation with Israel. This latter prospect not only threatened Israel, but also brought into question the survival of regimes in Jordan and Lebanon, as well as in Iraq, Syria, and Egypt.

EXPLICIT DOCTRINES OF ARMED STRUGGLE

The Palestinians have not produced an original theory of guerrilla warfare. Instead, they have borrowed ideas from other contexts and have sought to adapt them to the unusual circumstances in which they are obliged to operate. Unlike some guerrilla movements, the Palestinian Resistance has not been able to conduct armed actions from secure internal bases. For this reason, the Palestinians have faced major obstacles in establishing territory from which to launch raids against Israel. They have had to rely on the tolerance and protection of the established authorities of Lebanon, Syria, and Jordan in order to carry out their fight against Israel. In addition to the constant danger of clashes with these Arab regimes, the Palestinians face an enemy with impressive resources, a high level of motivation, and proven military capabilities. Confronted with these obstacles, Palestinians have produced several answers to the problem of appropriate use of force in such an unfavorable context.

Fatah has generally argued that political action and armed struggle are inseparable. During the early phase of armed action, decisive battles with the enemy must be avoided. Guerrilla bands alone cannot hope to confront Israel effectively. Instead, efforts must be made to establish secure bases and to build popular support. This period of "birth, growth, and sinking roots" is recognized as one of weakness. With time, however, the unorganized and apathetic masses can be transformed into a popular army, and at that stage the Palestinians can begin to engage in decisive battles. Needless to say, the second stage has not been reached, for it requires years of political

1. Nabil Sha'ath, "Palestine of Tomorrow," *Fateh*, Vol. 3, No. 1 (March 23, 1971), p. 9.

education and training.[2] During this first stage, the Palestinians must avoid large battles not only with the Israelis but also with the Arab regimes. Given these constraints, the most appropriate forms of armed action against Israel involve commando acts of sabotage, the planting of mines, and the firing of mortars and rockets against Israeli positions. Generalized acts of terrorism, particularly against objectives outside of Israel, have been strongly condemned by Fatah.

In contrast to Fatah's cautious strategy of armed struggle, the more radical fedayeen groups, especially the PFLP, have at times favored acts of terror on an international scale and the use of force against Arab regimes that place restrictions on Palestinian actions. The PFLP and its offshoot, the PFLP-General Command, have specialized in attacks on Israel and international airlines en route to or from Israel. In the summer of 1968, Ahmad Jibril's group, which later became the PFLP-General Command, was responsible for hijacking an Israeli plane to Algiers. The same group was later suspected of blowing up a Swissair flight to Israel in February 1970 that resulted in the death of fifteen Israelis and over thirty non-Israelis. The PFLP led by George Habash has also succeeded in hijacking planes, the first en route to Damascus in September 1969. A year later, the PFLP again resorted to this tactic out of fear that the Arab states were preparing to make peace with Israel and in an effort to weaken the Jordanian regime. The spectacular hijacking of three planes to Jordan and one to Cairo was the opening move in what came to be the Jordanian civil war of September 1970. Several other attacks on Israeli planes and airline offices in Europe were also carried out by smaller fedayeen groups during 1969. In most cases, a major objective of these attacks was to bring attention to the Palestinian cause, even over the protests of those Arabs and Palestinians who argue that terrorism and hijackings are counterproductive. A second object, especially in September 1970, was to force the Resistance movement into battle with the Jordanian regime.

The PFLP has called for revolution in the entire Arab world as a prelude to the liberation of Palestine. This will ultimately require armed actions against the Jordanian regime, and the PFLP has tried to draw the other commando groups into confrontations with the Jordanian army.[3] Fatah has resented this tactic, and sought to avoid

2. *Political and Armed Struggle*, Palestine National Liberation Movement, Fateh, 1969; "Fateh's Armed Struggle: Theory and Application," *Fateh*, April 17, 1970, pp. 10–12.

3. The PFLP's military strategy of uniting all Palestinian fighting or-

the clashes of February, June, and perhaps even September 1970. The PDFLP of Nayif Hawatmah has also been somewhat skeptical of the PFLP call for immediate confrontations with the Jordanian regime. The differing viewpoints of the two radical groups on this issue have to do with timing more than with long-range objectives. The PDFLP during 1969 and early 1970 seemed to believe that direct clashes with the Jordanian army might lead to Hussein's overthrow, but that Fatah, not the PDFLP, would come to power as a nonrevolutionary movement. Fatah would then be likely to turn against the PFLP and the PDFLP in order to maintain its dominant position. Thus, until the revolutionary forces held the balance of power, the PDFLP favored the avoidance of a showdown with any Arab regime. Nonetheless, the PDFLP appears to have abandoned this careful strategy in late August 1970 and to have accepted the inevitability of conflict with King Hussein's forces. By early September, the PDFLP had launched the slogan "All power to the Resistance."

In contrast to the vague notions of popular war developed by Fatah, the PFLP, and the PDFLP, part of the PLO and its conventional armed forces, the PLA, have continued to view the conflict with Israel in conventional military terms. The PLA did establish a commando unit, the PLF, in 1968, which was particularly active in Gaza, but most of the PLA forces stationed in Egypt, Syria, and Iraq have received training for regular warfare. The Syrian-based units have generally shown the greatest independence of the PLO, and like traditional armies elsewhere, they have tended to look down on guerrilla and commando actions. This attitude has frequently been echoed by other Arab leaders, such as Colonel Mu'ammar al-Qadhafi of Libya. Qadhafi jeopardized his reputation as defender of the Palestinian cause when he dismissed the idea of popular war against Israel as fanciful and told the fedayeen to join with the Arab armies to fight Israel.[4] At other times, both President Nasser and al-Ahram's editor, Muhammad Hasanayn Haykal, have echoed similar sentiments.[5]

---

ganizations to overthrow the Jordanian regime has been outlined in the following issues of al-Hadaf: November 2, 1970, pp. 6–7; November 28, 1970; December 5, 12, and 19, 1970. The PDFLP's doctrine of people's war is outlined in The Palestinian Resistance Movement in Its Present Reality (in Arabic) (Beirut: Dar at-Taliah, 1969), Part II, "The Palestinian Resistance and the Arab Situation," pp. 69–113.

4. Qadhafi's first critical remarks on the fedayeen occurred in his speech broadcast on April 8, 1970, over the Bayda Domestic Radio Service.

5. Fatah has replied to their criticisms in Fatah, August 9, 1970, referring to Haykal's column in al-Ahram, August 7, 1970. Haykal is accused of

In brief, three alternative uses of force have been considered by Palestinians in their current struggle with Israel. Fatah has viewed armed struggle as part of a political effort to establish its representativeness, to mobilize the Palestinian population, to induce changes in Israeli attitudes toward Palestinians, and, finally, to create a strong base from which, one day, negotiations with Israelis might take place. The PFLP and the PDFLP have viewed popular war as a means of bringing revolutionary change to the Arab world as a prelude to a united Arab confrontation with Israel sometime in the distant future. Finally, the PLA and various Arab regimes have argued that Palestinian armed actions should complement those of regular Arab armies as part of a conventional war against Israel.

The PFLP and the PDFLP are, in some ways, the most realistic in their views relative to the current limitations on the use of force. Their belief that Arab society must be radically transformed before it will be able to make use of advanced technology and weaponry against Israel is certainly easy to accept after the 1967 war. But the weakness of this radical position is that it threatens existing Arab regimes and fails to provide a coherent strategy based on existing capabilities for attaining the revolutionary changes that seem to be required. As a result, it seems likely that the contest for an appropriate form of Palestinian armed struggle against Israel will be between Fatah and the PLA. The problem for Fatah will be to develop a political-diplomatic bargaining position that stands some chance of being accepted if Fatah succeeds in establishing its authority over the Palestinian population. In the absence of such a political platform, Fatah's use of armed struggle may well lead to defeat at the hands of either the Israelis or the Arab regimes, particularly if Fatah veers toward the PFLP position of overthrowing the regime in Jordan or Lebanon as a precondition for fighting Israel. Alternatively, Fatah will be obliged to abandon its goal of Palestinian autonomy and to accept the PLA position that conventional armed actions in a Pan-Arab context are the appropriate forms of military struggle. As a last resort, the fedayeen may "go underground," avoiding major clashes with either the Arab regimes or Israel, while trying to create a small dedicated group capable of occasional spectacular acts of violence. This clandestine group would then hope to reassert its authority if and when international circumstances provide opportunities. By 1972, the PLO was calling for the "Pan-Arabization" of the battle, while generally maintain-

---

saying that the Palestinians are incapable of liberating their homeland by themselves.

ing a low posture in Lebanon and Syria in hope of better days. In addition, a small, disciplined group of terrorists named Black September was engaged in anti-Israeli and anti-Jordanian actions.

MILITARY CAPABILITIES

The military potential of the fedayeen is severely limited by a lack of manpower, arms, and funds, as well as territory in which to operate freely. Combined with the lack of overt popular support on the West Bank, these constraints have obliged the fedayeen to resort to commando actions rather than guerrilla warfare as their primary mode of operation. Although they are able to inflict casualties on the Israeli population by these means, they have not succeeded in establishing themselves in force in areas under Israeli occupation or in engaging Israeli units in large battles.

The size and distribution of the Palestinian population limits the number of armed men that the fedayeen can mobilize. At their peak strength in the fall of 1970, the fedayeen may have had 20,000 men under arms and another 20,000 trained as militia units.[6] With a maximum effort at mobilization, they cannot expect to exceed fifty thousand armed and trained men.

The commando organizations have recruited heavily in the refugee camps, as well as among educated Palestinians living abroad. Since the educated Palestinians tend to engage primarily in political activities, most fedayeen come from the relatively poor sectors of society. Part of the training provided new recruits involves basic education in addition to the use of light arms. Lacking a military tradition, the Palestinians have had to create an armed force under very unfavorable circumstances.

To sustain a large military force, the fedayeen have sought secure bases in Jordan, Syria, and Lebanon. Some officer training has been provided by the Algerians and the Syrians, but most fedayeen have received their introduction to the use of arms at camps scattered along the cease-fire lines. Some of the fedayeen organizations pay their recruits a minimal salary and provide help for their families, while the more radical PFLP and PDFLP rely less on material incentives to motivate their members.[7]

6. A publication of the PLO Research Center, entitled *Black September* (Beirut, 1971), p. 59, gives the following figures on Palestinian armed strength in September 1970: fedayeen, 5,000; PLA, 3,500; militia, 8,500. The PLA was organized into one infantry brigade and one armored brigade with fifty T-34 tanks and twenty-five armored cars.

7. Gérard Chaliand, *La Résistance Palestinienne* (Paris: Editions du Seuil, 1970), pp. 104–136.

The acquisition of arms has presented the fedayeen with problems. Arab regimes have provided light arms from their own inventories, but often with political conditions attached. Arms from the Soviet Union have not been particularly forthcoming, although some Soviet weapons have been channeled to the PLO for eventual distribution to the PLA and other organizations. China has also provided small arms, particularly to Fatah.[8] Finally, the Palestinians have been able to buy some articles in the world arms market.

In carrying out military operations, the fedayeen have relied most heavily on rockets, mortars, land mines, grenades, machine guns, and the Soviet-made AK-47 rifle. Except for some units of the PLA, the fedayeen have not been able to obtain heavy artillery or tanks. The lack of both heavy armor and air power contributed to the defeat of the fedayeen at the hands of the Jordanian army in September 1970.

On the Israeli front, the fedayeen have found it difficult to carry out operations across the Jordan River because of Israeli security measures, including an electronic fence. As infiltration across the Jordan River became increasingly difficult in 1969, the fedayeen shifted their efforts and began to stage raids into Israel from southern Lebanon. Also, cross-border shelling with rockets and mortars became a favorite fedayeen tactic.[9] At the same time, clashes with Lebanese and Jordanian authorities became more frequent.

Within the Gaza Strip, fedayeen military activity consisted primarily of throwing grenades at both Israeli police and suspected Arab collaborators. During 1969, the first instances of political assassinations of Palestinians by the fedayeen were beginning to occur in the occupied territories. Occasional bomb explosions within Israel proper indicated that the fedayeen were able to carry out sporadic acts of violence even under careful Israeli control. In a few instances, Israeli Arabs were implicated in these armed actions.

While the level of their military activity against Israel remained

8. In one instance, when the Algerians sent heavy arms of Chinese origin to Fatah, Syrian authorities refused to allow Fatah to take delivery. See the *New York Times,* July 7, 1971.

9. A report of fedayeen activities in early 1971 stated that bases along the Jordan River had considerable autonomy in deciding on operations. The most common type of action was that of firing across the cease-fire lines. Penetration of the West Bank was considerably more difficult, requiring at least ten days' preparation. Each base therefore limited itself to a few such raids per month. *Jeune Afrique,* No. 526 (February 2, 1971), pp. 3-4.

limited to sabotage and small-unit commando raids, the fedayeen did periodically engage in larger battles with the armed forces of Lebanon or Jordan. In both the spring and the fall of 1969, Lebanon was the scene of clashes between the army and the commandos. The Cairo agreement of October 1969 put a temporary end to the conflict and shifted the scene of fedayeen activity back to Jordan. There, in February 1970, during Arafat's absence in Moscow, fighting erupted between the Jordanian army and the fedayeen. Arafat returned in time to negotiate an end to the shooting, but many Jordanians and Palestinians seem to have drawn the conclusion that an armed showdown was inevitable. Fedayeen forces began to leave their bases along the Jordan River for the larger towns of north Jordan and Amman.

In June 1970, the PFLP capitalized on the outbreak of renewed fighting in Amman by holding a large number of Westerners hostage in two Amman hotels, thereby directly challenging King Hussein's authority. Fatah once again tried to bring the fighting to an end, and an agreement was finally reached in which King Hussein dismissed two Jordanian officers who were strongly anti-fedayeen, his uncle, Sharif Nasir, and his cousin, Zayd Bin Shakir. Conciliation was not successful, however, and the radical wing of the fedayeen tried to continue the pressure on the Jordanian regime. By late August, fighting between fedayeen and the Jordanian army had become a daily occurrence and Bin Shakir had returned to a position of influence as deputy chief of staff. The "hawks" on both sides were beginning to seize the initiative from the "doves."

CASUALTIES: ISRAELI AND PALESTINIAN [10]

In the first three and one-half years following the June 1967 war, more Israelis died from hostile action than during the war itself. Of the total Israeli casualties during that period, about one-half were the result of fedayeen attacks, while the remainder were primarily attributable to Egyptian shelling along the Suez Canal. Reliable numbers on casualties are often difficult to obtain, and different methods of accounting yield varying results. Most of the available figures come from Israeli sources, but where possible they have been

10. The following estimates of casualties and incidents have been derived from numerous sources, including: Ehud Yaari, *Strike Terror: The Story of Fatah* (New York: Sabra Books, 1970); *Ma'arakhot,* Vol 55, No. 204 (January–February 1970), pp. 3–23; official Israeli aggregate figures published at regular intervals; analysis of daily press reports for certain periods.

cross-checked with press reports, Arab accounts, and totals from other sources. In general, however, it seems safe to say that between June 1967 and January 1971, over three hundred Israelis died and over fifteen hundred were wounded as a result of fedayeen attacks.

During the second half of 1967, fedayeen activities resulted in approximately five Israeli fatalities per month. In subsequent years, this rate increased to seven per month in 1968, nine per month in 1969, and eleven per month in 1970.[11] For each fatality, five or six Israelis were wounded. Military casualties generally exceeded civilian ones by a four-to-one ratio.

The number of incidents that produced these casualties rose at a more rapid rate than the casualties themselves. In 1968, fewer than one hundred fedayeen actions per month took place. By 1969, over two hundred per month were occurring, and during the spring of 1970 the rate had exceeded three hundred per month.[12] Of these incidents, about three-fourths consisted of mortar and rocket shellings of Israeli positions; 15 percent were acts of sabotage; and about 10 percent involved planted land mines.

Israeli and Palestinian figures are at times strikingly different, but some sources yield comparable results. For example, one Israeli account cites twenty-five hundred fedayeen incidents in 1969, and a Palestinian source mentions thirty-four hundred. The areas in which these incidents supposedly occurred are nearly identical in the two accounts. The Jordan valley was the most active region, with about 70 percent of all incidents. Gaza was next with between 10 and 15 percent, followed by the Golan Heights with under 10 percent. Incidents on the West Bank and inside Israel also accounted for less than 10 percent.[13]

Of the various commando groups, Fatah has been responsible for over one-half of all operations. Sa'iqa, the PLF, and the PFLP account for about 8 percent each. The remaining 25 percent either are impossible to identify by source or were carried out by smaller groups.

Fedayeen activity has not been steadily increasing since 1967.

11. Hisham Sharabi, *Palestine Guerrillas: Their Credibility and Effectiveness* (Washington, D.C.: Supplementary Papers, Center for Strategic and International Studies, 1970), argues that Israeli figures on military fatalities are underreported. His study of fatalities during June 1969 suggests that instead of the official figure of twelve fatalities due to guerrilla action, at least twice that number would be a more accurate figure.

12. During February and March 1971, Israel reported about seventy-five incidents per month.

13. Yaari, *Strike Terror*, pp. 366–370; *Al-Bilad*, June 30, 1970, quoting PASC figures.

Instead, a cycle of activity can be discerned in 1968, 1969, and 1970. From November to February, during the rainy winter months, fedayeen activity was generally relatively light. From March to June, there was an increase in armed actions, which continued at a steady rate during the hot summer months. During September and October, fedayeen attacks again were likely to increase until the onset of winter. The civil war of September 1970 disrupted this pattern of activity, which explains the relative calm along Israel's borders during most of 1971 and 1972.[14]

The greatest number of casualties suffered by Israel as a result of fedayeen actions occurred in March 1968, February 1970, and May 1970. In March 1968, Israeli troops crossed the Jordan River to destroy a fedayeen base at the Jordanian town of Karameh. Fighting ensued and the Jordanian army intervened alongside the fedayeen. The results of this joint Jordanian-Palestinian effort against Israeli forces were twenty-six Israeli dead and seventy wounded. Nearly two years later, during February 1970, fedayeen attacks resulted in twenty Israeli deaths, fifteen in the explosion of a Swissair plane. In May 1970, Israeli losses, due to fedayeen actions as well as fighting on the Syrian front, again exceeded twenty in a single month. Generally, however, fatalities have been kept well below these rates.

The Palestinians have sustained relatively heavy losses in their attacks on Israel. By the end of 1970, Israel claimed to have killed over eighteen hundred fedayeen and held another twenty-five hundred Palestinians in prison.[15] Fedayeen losses were in proportion to their activity: Fatah members suffered over one-half of all fatalities, and the PLF, PFLP, and Sa'iqa accounted for a little less than 10 percent each.

While casualties resulting from the Israeli-Palestinian conflict have not reached such proportions that either side has felt compelled to end the struggle, the losses have been deeply felt in the small Israeli and Palestinian populations. Ten Israeli or Palestinian fatalities per month are equivalent to about one thousand American fatalities, given respective population sizes. As in the United

14. Israeli sources acknowledged that fedayeen actions in February, March, and April 1971 had killed seven Israelis and wounded forty-four. (*The Jerusalem Post*, May 4, 1971.) Official figures for all of 1971 are as follows: 679 hostile actions, one-half of which occurred in Gaza. These resulted in nineteen Israeli soldiers and ten civilians killed (Jerusalem Domestic Service, January 2, 1972). In the first six months of 1972, approximately thirty Israelis were killed by fedayeen actions, including the terrorist attack at Lod Airport carried out by three Japanese on May 31.

15. *Le Monde*, January 7, 1971, p. 4.

States with respect to the Vietnam war, casualties that may be tolerable in military terms can nonetheless have far-reaching political and social consequences. The continuation of fedayeen attacks on Israel has had the ambiguous effect of obliging the Israelis to take the Palestinians seriously and at the same time inhibiting an accommodation between the two peoples inhabiting Palestine.

Although armed action against Israel was the ostensible mission of the fedayeen, fighting with the established governments of Lebanon and especially Jordan has involved the Palestinians in the most serious combat to date. Hostilities occurred in Lebanon on a limited scale during 1969, then shifted to Jordan in early 1970. Clashes in February and June provided forewarning of the much more serious crisis that erupted in September 1970. The war between the fedayeen and the Jordanian army marked the high point of Palestinian military activity, after which the political and military potential of the Palestinians rapidly declined. For this reason, the September civil war deserves special attention.

6

THE SEPTEMBER 1970 CRISIS AND ITS AFTERMATH

The rapid growth of the Palestinian commando movement during 1969 and the first half of 1970 was not accompanied by corresponding organizational developments capable of disciplining and directing the forces of Palestinian nationalism. Lacking effective decision-making and control structures, fedayeen leaders were unable to deal with the threat posed to the Resistance movement by President Nasser's acceptance of a United States-sponsored peace initiative and cease-fire in the summer of 1970. While strongly opposing any settlement of the conflict with Israel based on the so-called Rogers plan, the fedayeen were not agreed upon appropriate means to thwart these peace efforts. Having lost the support of Egypt—reflected most clearly in the suspension of fedayeen radio broadcasts from Cairo—part of the PLO leadership recognized the potential danger to the Resistance movement of confronting the regime in Jordan by force. At the same time, fears were expressed in Palestinian circles that King Hussein, with Nasser's tacit approval, would now move to control and, if possible, to destroy the autonomy of the commandos in Jordan.

THE MOUNTING CRISIS

Throughout 1970, the fedayeen had been encouraged to press their advantages in Jordan by the weak and hesitant policies of the Jordanian governments led by Bahjat at-Talhuni and Abd al-

124

Mun'im ar-Rifa'i. Witnessing the rapid erosion of the authority of the Jordanian state during the summer, the militant Palestinians seem to have concluded that the well-equipped and disciplined Jordanian army would hesitate to crack down on the commandos in the event of a full-scale challenge to Hussein's rule.

Toward the end of August 1970, several fedayeen organizations had apparently reached the conclusion that the time had come for a direct attack on the Jordanian regime. Fatah, while perhaps agreeing with the objective of deposing Hussein and bringing to power a more sympathetic Jordanian government, was doubtless concerned that the most extreme commando groups, such as the PFLP and the PDFLP, might try to force a confrontation before Fatah was fully prepared to fight. The available evidence suggests that both the PFLP led by Habash and the PDFLP led by Hawatmah were planning to do precisely what Fatah feared, thereby forcing Fatah at least to prepare for the contingency of toppling the Jordanian regime. At their annual meeting held on August 21–24, PDFLP representatives seem to have decided on immediate actions against Hussein's government. The slogan "All power to the Resistance" began to appear, and open calls for Hussein's overthrow were heard. The Resistance movement as a whole began to speak of the need for a "national authority" in Amman.

As the sense of crisis spread throughout Jordan, the Palestine National Congress met in emergency session in Amman on August 27–28. The only published result of this meeting was a total rejection of plans for a peaceful settlement with Israel. The question of moving against the regime in Amman must also have been raised, at least by the PDFLP, but it is not clear that Fatah was willing to push the issue to the breaking point so soon.[1] Jordanian authorities later claimed, however, to have found documents indicating that Fatah, along with the more radical organizations, had decided to attempt a coup d'état during September.

Whatever Fatah's plans regarding Hussein may have been in early September, they were quickly bypassed by events as the PFLP executed its own program to bring down the Jordanian regime, to embarrass Fatah, and to stall the movement toward a peace settlement with Israel. On September 6, the PFLP carried out the spectacular hijackings of three international airplanes, two of which were flown to an airstrip in the Jordanian desert, where their pas-

---

1. Nayif Hawatmah subsequently asserted that a resolution was passed at the emergency session of the congress calling for a national democratic government in Jordan and the transformation of Jordan into a revolutionary base. *Africasia*, No. 37 (March 29–April 11, 1971), p. 12.

sengers were held as hostages. The third plane, a Pan American 747, was flown to Cairo, where it was blown up minutes after the passengers had disembarked. Three days later another plane was also hijacked to Jordan.

The central committee of the PLO responded to these provocative acts by suspending the PFLP, but this did little to prevent the deterioration of the situation inside Jordan. Small-scale clashes between fedayeen and the Jordanian army were daily occurrences and were only temporarily halted by rapidly negotiated cease-fires. By mid-September, the fedayeen had seized control of several strategic positions in Jordan, including the oil refinery at Zarqa. A general strike had been called and plans were under way for a campaign of civil disobedience. Hussein at this point faced the choice of relinquishing authority or of allowing his angry and frustrated army to take action. On September 15, he named a military government. For twenty-four hours negotiations with the fedayeen went on, until finally Arafat refused further discussions with Prime Minister Dawud. The following day, the conciliatory Jordanian chief of staff, Mashur Haditha, was dismissed and Field Marshal Habis al-Majali was named commander in chief. That same day Yasir Arafat was given full military powers as head of the Palestinian revolutionary forces.[2]

ARMED CONFLICT

Fighting broke out the following day between the Jordanian army and the fedayeen. Both sides were acutely aware of the crucial role that might be played by the armed forces of other Arab countries. Iraq had earlier promised to turn over to the Resistance movement its armed force of twelve thousand men in Jordan. To prevent Iraqi action, the Jordanians moved one full division to block the movement of the Iraqis toward Amman. On September 17–18, Iraqi forces began to withdraw from their fixed positions near Zarqa to Mafraq.

The following day, September 19, tanks from Syria entered the fighting in full strength. The PLA Hittin Brigade stationed in Syria was known to possess approximately fifty old Soviet T-34 tanks, but the invasion force was substantially larger than anything the Palestinians could muster and included new Soviet T-54s. At this point, Salah Jadid and his supporters seem to have made the decision to intervene in the fighting in Jordan, using the Syrian

2. The PFLP was also restored to full membership in the central committee.

Twenty-eighth Brigade. This may have been done over the opposition of the minister of defense, Hafiz al-Asad. Jadid's purposes in sending support to the Palestinians must have included a desire to embarrass his rivals, the Iraqis and Asad, as well as to bring about Hussein's overthrow. In any event, between one hundred and two hundred Syrian tanks, marked as units of the PLA, entered Jordan and in some cases moved into positions recently evacuated by Iraqi forces.[3]

In the midst of the crisis, both the United States and Israel staged elaborate military maneuvers and dropped hints that they might intervene if the Syrians threatened to take Amman. Because of presumed Soviet backing for the Syrian intervention, the local conflict quickly took on the proportions of a confrontation between the superpowers. Close consultations between the United States and Israel seem to have led to a contingency plan whereby Israel would intervene against the Syrian tanks, and the United States would protect Israel from retaliation. The plan broke down when Israel insisted on combined ground and air action.[4] King Hussein wanted no part of an Israeli invasion of Jordan, and instead of inviting outside support on these terms, he committed his own small air force between September 21 and 23. The counterattack proved to be effective. Significantly, Syria's air force, under the control of Asad, did not participate in the fighting, perhaps as a result of clear Soviet disapproval of Syria's involvement in the civil war. Badly defeated by the Jordanian forces, the Syrian tanks began to withdraw from Jordan on September 23–24, leaving a large number of vehicles destroyed or captured by Jordanian forces.[5] Having refrained from direct intervention in the conflict,

3. Estimates of the number of tanks involved in the Syrian intervention vary from a maximum of three hundred reported by Jordanian and Israeli sources, to the more modest figure of sixty mentioned by some United States and Arab observers. The Syrian decision to intervene may have been related to the fact that the Jordanian commander of the second infantry division in the north had fled during the first day of fighting, leaving his troops leaderless.

4. The fullest account of U.S.–Israeli plans is contained in the *New York Times*, October 8, 1970. The crisis is also discussed in William B. Quandt, "The Middle East Conflict in U.S. Strategy, 1970–71," *Journal of Palestine Studies*, Vol. 1, No. 1 (Autumn 1971).

5. Spokesman for the PLO, Kamal Nasir acknowledged some Syrian support. In *Le Monde*, September 27–28, 1970, he is quoted as saying, "Among the Arab states surrounding Israel, we must mention Syria as having given us assistance which we consider the minimum possible. Given the circumstances, she could not do more." Some information on the Syrian-Jordanian battle can be found in Neville Brown, "Jordanian Civil War," *Military Review*, Vol. 51, No. 9 (September 1971), pp. 38–48.

the United States now moved rapidly to rearm Jordan and to bolster King Hussein's authority.

During the fighting, Fatah had called on Egypt for support and had refused offers of a cease-fire. Egypt, as well as other Arab countries, did in fact actively press Jordan to end the fighting short of extermination of the fedayeen. Contributing to this pressure was Nasser's decision to transfer the Ain Jallut Brigade of the PLA from Egypt to Syria. On September 25, after ten days of fighting, the fedayeen had been placed on the defensive throughout Jordan, and with no Arab support in sight, they agreed to a cease-fire. Drawing on his prestige as leader of the Arab world, Nasser convened a meeting of Arab leaders in Cairo to which King Hussein and Arafat were summoned. An agreement was signed ending the civil war on September 27. The fedayeen, while not entirely crushed, had received a severe setback from which they would not recover rapidly. Nasser's death the following day further weakened the Resistance movement by removing a potentially valuable supporter.

THE AFTERMATH OF THE CIVIL WAR

The effects of the brief war on the Palestinian movement were somewhat ambiguous in their long-term significance. The persistent tensions between Palestinians and the Jordanian regime were intensified, thereby undermining, at least temporarily, King Hussein's claim to speak on behalf of the Palestinians. The fedayeen, however, had been weakened and disorganized by the fighting, which cut deeply into their popular appeal. During the conflict, large quantities of fedayeen arms had been captured, and heavy casualties had been sustained.[6]

In the months following the war, the fedayeen tried to avoid further clashes with the Jordanian army so that they might reorganize and strengthen their own battered forces. In mid-October an agreement was reached with the Jordanian government concerning future relations between the two parties. With the danger of

6. Estimates of casualties during the September fighting vary greatly. The Red Cross estimated that about 3,000 were killed and 10,000 wounded. Arafat later stated that only 900 fedayeen had been killed, but claimed civilian casualties in the range of 20,000. Some Jordanian authorities insist that only 1,000 armed men were killed, one-half of whom were Jordanian soldiers, and that very few civilians were killed or wounded. In an interview with the author on September 8, 1971, the Jordanian minister of information stated that the September 1970 fighting had produced about 2,000 to 2,500 fatalities and 5,000 to 6,000 wounded.

renewed fighting temporarily reduced, organizational and leadership problems again assumed critical importance.

A significant result of the brief civil war was the disappearance of the smallest commando groups as autonomous parts of the Palestinian movement.[7] Several fedayeen units, such as the Iraqi ALF, the AOLP, the OAP, the PPSF, and the POLP, virtually disappeared or were incorporated into Fatah.[8]

The remaining organizations of some importance were Fatah, the PLA-PLF, Sa'iqa, and the PFLP. Nayif Hawatmah of the PDFLP remained a prominent figure, but his organization had virtually collapsed. The same was largely true for Ahmad Jibril of the PFLP-General Command. Within each of the major groups, the experience of the Jordanian war produced conflict within the leadership, as political setbacks generally do.[9] Recognized leaders in Fatah were challenged by the younger generation of activists at a congress held in late November. The core leadership of Fatah, however, despite its own divisions, formed a united front to ward off this threat and succeeded in retaining control of the movement.[10] Similar challenges were dealt with effectively within the PFLP and the PDFLP, although it seemed as if both groups were less assertive and self-confident in the fall of 1970 and early in 1971 than they had been earlier. Sa'iqa, the Syrian-backed organization, underwent major internal changes, which reflected in large part political develop-

7. Salah Khalaf, of Fatah, speaking in Kuwait, mentioned the error of having tolerated the minor groups. At first Fatah welcomed them, but "we later found that whenever we met we spoke like representatives of the Arab countries. . . . Every Arab regime created an organization so that it would have a voice in the revolution and to keep up with what was happening within the Resistance." *Ar-Rai al-Aam*, January 10, 1971, p. 2. See also *Le Monde*, December 4, 1970, p. 6, where Eric Rouleau quotes a Fatah leader as saying that "the central committee of the Resistance, far from being an organ of coordination and decision, became a kind of parliament in which all the conflicts and all the intrigues of the Arab world were reflected."

8. On January 9, 1971, Salah Khalaf claimed that the AOLP had been dissolved. He mentioned, however, that Fatah would not use force to bring about unity. *Al-Anwar*, January 10, 1971, p. 7. See also SANA Damascus, November 15, 1970, for a report that AOLP units were joining Fatah. At the ninth National Congress, Fatah claimed to have fully absorbed the PPSF, OAP, and AOLP. MENA Damascus to MENA Cairo, July 11, 1971.

9. Arafat's own self-criticism and his analysis of the September crisis appear in an interview with Eric Rouleau, *Le Monde*, November 12, 1970.

10. *An-Nahar Arab Report*, Vol. 2, No. 3 (January 18, 1971), pp. 3-4; *Jeune Afrique*, No. 512 (October 20, 1970), pp. 43ff; *Jeune Afrique*, No. 525 (January 26, 1971), pp. 43-45.

ments in Syria. Yusif Zu'ayyin and Dafi Jamani were ousted as leaders of Sa'iqa, to be replaced first by Mahmud al-Ma'ita, then by Zuhayr Muhsin.[11] Initially, there was some indication that Syria might be willing to see Sa'iqa become an autonomous Palestinian organization, but by January 1971 Asad was again carefully controlling Sa'iqa's activities. The Iraqi-backed group, the ALF, was seriously weakened when its leader, Munif ar-Razzaz, resigned over the issue of Iraq's refusal to intervene in the September fighting.[12] Within the PLO itself, several changes occurred in the composition of the executive committee and the central committee.[13]

By December 1970, the major fedayeen groups had sufficiently overcome their own internal divisions, so that they were able to face the question of reorganizing the Palestinian Resistance movement in light of the new balance of forces. Fatah seemed insistent on creating a unified front under its own leadership.[14] For a brief period, George Habash of the PFLP appeared to be willing to accept Fatah's lead.[15] A full-scale meeting of the National Congress was announced for December and then postponed until late February 1971. The central committee was periodically reported to be discussing unity, but in fact it rarely met in full session.

In the absence of an effective central committee after September 1970, the general secretariat was reshaped to reflect Fatah's determination to dominate the Resistance movement. The new general secretariat, formed in early December 1970, consisted of Arafat, Salah Khalaf, and Kamal Adwan, all of Fatah; Ibrahim Bakr, the new official spokesman of the PLO; Hamid Abu Sittah of the PLO; and Bahjat Abu Garbiyya of the PPSF. Of the six active members,

11. MENA Damascus to MENA Cairo, November 23, 1970. By early 1971, Jamani was again briefly active in Sa'iqa's leadership until his expulsion in July 1971.

12. *Africasia*, No. 29 (December 7–20, 1970), p. 47.

13. Kamal Nasir was temporarily replaced as official spokesman of the PLO by Ibrahim Bakr. Other minor changes were less noticeable because of the diminished role of the central committee after the September crisis.

14. Fatah Radio (clandestine), November 30, 1970, broadcast a call for unity in the following terms: ". . . the revolutionary camp [the Palestinian Resistance] lacks up to this very moment a unified command capable of giving guidance and issuing orders. The fact is that there are several armies, not one army, of the Palestinian revolution, and ten organizations, not one organization, for the revolution."

15. The Chinese reportedly advised Habash during his trip to Asia in September 1970 to cooperate with Fatah. *Christian Science Monitor*, November 14, 1970; *An-Nahar Arab Report*, Vol. 1, No. 28 (September 14, 1970), p. 2; *Africasia*, No. 28 (December 7, 1970), pp. 10–11.

Arafat was the only one who had belonged to the secretariat of June 1970.[16]

While Fatah was trying to gain control over the commando movement during the fall of 1970, the Jordanian regime was attempting to complete the unfinished business of establishing its authority throughout the country and of removing the fedayeen from populated areas. In mid-December, the Jordanian army drove the fedayeen from the town of Jarash. Jordan hoped to be able to undertake these actions without incurring the hostility of the UAR and without risking the suspension of Kuwaiti aid.[17]

Without firm backing from the UAR, Fatah could not afford further confrontations with the Jordanian army. The risk that incidents might result from the behavior of the smaller fedayeen groups encouraged Fatah to try to consolidate its control over the Resistance movement, and at the same time to seek to regain Cairo's favor.

As Fatah moved to assert its authority, the PLA, Sa'iqa, the PFLP, and the PDFLP joined together to protest Fatah's unilateral actions.[18] Syria, under the rule of Hafiz al-Asad since mid-November 1970, began to play an active role in fedayeen politics in January. After renewed clashes between the Jordanian army and the commandos, Syria offered to mediate the conflict. A cease-fire was reached in mid-January, as well as an agreement to disarm the militia forces of the Resistance movement. During the January 1971 fighting, Fatah leader Muhammad Yusif an-Najjar had openly called for Hussein's overthrow,[19] but several days later Fatah

16. *Al-Muharrir*, November 13, 1970, p. 4, mentions that an executive bureau of five members was leading the Resistance movement. By mid-December, however, a six-man secretariat had been formed. *New York Times*, December 13, 1970. Other sources indicate that Habash, Hawatmah, and Dafi Jamani of Sa'iqa were also nominal members of the general secretariat of December 1970, as they had been earlier in June. They did not, however, seem to participate actively. Agence France Presse, December 29, 1970, correctly named all nine members of the general secretariat.

17. Libya ended its payments to Jordan after the September events, and Kuwait had also briefly suspended its aid. Kuwait again cut off aid in mid-January 1971 and had not restored it by late-1972.

18. The possibility of an alliance among Sa'iqa, PFLP, and the PDFLP against Fatah was suggested in *An-Nahar Arab Report*, Vol. 2, No. 3 (January 18, 1971), p. 3. *Le Monde*, January 6, 1971, p. 3, reported that Sa'iqa, PFLP, and PDFLP had released a joint statement protesting "unilateral acts" and "dictatorial methods," presumably by Fatah. See also, INA Baghdad, January 18, 1971.

19. *New York Times*, January 12, 1971.

spokesman Kamal Adwan threatened instead to use force against the PFLP if it continued to provoke clashes with the Jordanian army.[20] Fatah seemed to be trying to isolate the Iraqi-supported PFLP while avoiding an open clash with Syria. In late January, Arafat traveled to Algeria to talk with Asad, who was there on an official visit.[21]

Arafat's strategy of trying to unify the Resistance movement under Fatah's leadership entailed not only preventing a Syrian-backed anti-Fatah front from forming, but also improving ties with Egypt. To this end, Fatah made a tactical concession during late January by agreeing that Egypt's pursuit of a peaceful settlement did not conflict with the objectives of the Palestinians to recover their full rights.[22]

While Fatah's relations with Egypt took a turn for the better in January 1971, Syria remained somewhat hostile. Perhaps with encouragement from Syria, new challenges were directed at Arafat from two quarters early in February.[23] First, much to Arafat's displeasure, the chairman of the National Congress, Yahya Hammuda, announced that a regular session of the congress would be held at the end of the month.[24] Second, the commander of the PLA, Abd ar-Razzaq Yahya, hinted that all fedayeen forces should be placed under the authority of the PLA. Later in the month, Yahya openly called for Arafat's dismissal as head of the PLO and for major reforms in organization and leadership.[25] Fundamental choices now lay

20. Kamal Adwan accused the PFLP on January 16, 1971, of providing pretexts for the Jordanian army to attack the Palestinian commandos. *Le Monde,* January 19, 1971, p. 7; *New York Times,* January 18, 1971. Adwan's threat to use force came after a call by the PFLP for King Hussein's overthrow.

21. In October 1970, Fatah leader Muhammad Yusif an-Najjar stated that at one time Syria had adopted a proper attitude toward the Resistance, but that this was no longer true. *Révolution Africaine,* November 20–26, 1970.

22. On January 20, 1971, *al-Ahram* announced in Cairo that the Palestinian Resistance had agreed to the idea of a peaceful settlement. The PFLP and the PDFLP immediately denied such intentions, whereas Fatah's official response was less categorical in its rejection of a political solution. The Arab states were free to try to recover their territory by any means, Fatah asserted, provided that Palestinian rights were not affected. *Le Monde,* January 22, 1971; *Christian Science Monitor,* January 23, 1971. PLO central committee member Ibrahim Bakr elaborated on the view that the acceptance of a political settlement by the Arab states was not necessarily contrary to Palestinian interests. *An-Nahar,* January 28, 1971, p. 10.

23. *Washington Post,* February 21, 1971.

24. *Le Monde,* February 20, 1971, p. 4.

25. Both Yahya Hammuda, chairman of the Palestine National Con-

before fedayeen leaders, and the impending National Congress appeared to be the forum in which problems of leadership, strategy, and organization would be thrashed out.

THE EIGHTH NATIONAL CONGRESS

Prior to the convening of the eighth National Congress at the end of February 1971, widespread debate and self-criticism were taking place within the commando movement. Fatah leaders in particular were critical of the tolerance formerly given to the small fedayeen groups that had acted as instruments of various Arab states' policies. Salah Khalaf of Fatah also attacked the "bourgeois" structures of the PLO, the overemphasis on publicity, and the misjudgment of the true strength of the commando movement.[26] Arafat went so far as to call for a return to clandestinity as the remaining alternative open to the fedayeen, a theme that had been advanced several months earlier by Khalaf.[27] Consistent with this line of thought, as well as with political realities, Fatah offices were closed in Lebanon and Jordan during January, and the daily newspaper, *Fatah,* ceased publication.

Fatah leaders were also heard to criticize the Resistance movement for its failure to develop a viable political-negotiating strategy. With most Arab states openly favoring a political solution of the conflict with Israel, the Palestinians ran the risk of being isolated and deprived of any role in the postsettlement arrangements. During December and January, voices were raised in favor of accepting the idea of a political settlement, and considerable interest seemed to be focusing on the possibility of a Palestine state, at least as a first step toward satisfying Palestinian national aspirations.[28] Rumors

gress, and General Abd ar-Razzaq Yahya, commander in chief of the PLA, called for the merger of fedayeen organizations into the PLA. DPA Cairo, February 9, 1971. Later in the month, reports were circulated that Yahya was calling for Arafat's dismissal as head of the PLO.

26. *Le Monde,* January 5, 1971, p. 5.

27. See *al-Anwar,* January 1, 1971, p. 8, for Arafat's statement. *Jeune Afrique,* No. 512 (October 20, 1970), p. 44, quotes Salah Khalaf of Fatah as saying, "We must return to the true Fatah line, that of pre-1967. Then we had a strategy; we knew we were in contradiction with all the Arab regimes. Our secret, clandestine movement was a revolutionary impetus in the region. After 1967, we became an enormous movement, too open to infiltration from elements tied to this or that Arab regime."

28. See *Le Monde,* January 22, 1971, p. 2, for Fatah's official statement on a political settlement. In a series of articles published in *Le Monde,* December 1–4, 1970, Eric Rouleau critically assesses the prospects for the Palestinian movement after the September crisis. He quotes Fatah leaders

were circulating, contrary to reality, that the United States was in
favor of a Palestinian state on the West Bank and Gaza.

Fatah came in for its share of criticism from other commando
organizations. The PLA's commander, General Yahya, expressed the
scorn of a professional military man for the ineffective military operations of the fedayeen. More trenchant still were the attacks by
the PFLP on the basic policies of Fatah. George Habash, in his first
published interview after the September crisis, argued that the main
error of the Resistance forces had been to believe in the possibility
of coexisting with the regime in Jordan. Habash also criticized the
narrowly Palestinian focus of the Resistance movement, claiming
that this orientation had alienated many Jordanians, including
those in the army who might otherwise have sided with an anti-
Hussein coalition. Habash put forward a slogan that was to be
heard frequently in later months: the unity of the Palestinian and
Jordanian masses.[29]

Palestinian leaders were well aware of the weaknesses of the
fedayeen movement after the September crisis, but, as usual, there
was little agreement on the proper remedies.[30] During February,
debate centered on the question of calling for a Palestinian state
and the steps needed to unify the Resistance forces. On February 14,
a pro-Egyptian Beirut newspaper reported that two members of the
general secretariat of the PLO, Ibrahim Bakr and Kamal Adwan,
favored the creation of a Palestinian state on the West Bank and
Gaza.[31] A few days later, Arafat reportedly met with Soviet representatives in Jordan, who urged him to accept a Palestinian state as

---

as saying their main concern is survival. When queried on their attitude
toward a political settlement, these leaders replied that if Israel gives back
the occupied territory, they will take the risk of considering the U.N.
resolution of November 22, 1967. See also William Touhy's article in the
Washington Post, December 17, 1970.

29. *An-Nahar*, January 17, 1971, p. 9. Similar sentiments concerning
Palestinian chauvinism were attributed to Salah Khalaf; see *Le Monde*,
January 5, 1971.

30. In the article entitled "Les Palestiniens font leur autocritique,"
Jeune Afrique, No. 512 (October 20, 1970), p. 44, Ania Francos quotes
Salah Khalaf of Fatah as saying, "Ours is an impossible revolution. When
we were in China, Abu Ammar and I, we were shown a computer. Abu
Ammar maliciously suggested that we take it with us. We could feed it all
of our problems, all of our contradictions, and it would tell us the solution. I answered that we didn't want the computer to explode. And, if it
didn't explode, it would merely spit out a little card with the words—
mush mumkin—not possible, an insoluble problem."

31. *Al-Anwar*, February 14, 1971, p. 6. By the fall of 1971, Bakr had left
the ranks of the PLO and was in private law practice in Amman.

part of a political settlement.[32] At meetings of the central committee held in Damascus, Salah Khalaf presented the position of several West Bank Palestinians who had approached him with a plea to accept a Palestinian state. They argued that coexistence with King Hussein's regime was no longer possible and that the Palestinians should take what they could get as part of a settlement.[33]

The idea of a Palestinian state on the West Bank and Gaza was apparently of less interest to fedayeen leaders than were the various plans for unification of the Resistance movement that had been prepared in anticipation of the meeting of the National Congress. The most detailed of these plans was put forward by a group from the PLO Planning Center in Beirut under the leadership of Dr. Yusif as-Sayigh. Presented to a meeting of the central committee on February 8, 1971, the plan called for a more rational decision-making structure in the PLO, for a clearer statement of objectives in a revised National Charter, and for continued autonomy of various groups within a broad front similar to the Vietnamese National Liberation Front. The PFLP seemed to be in favor of the plan, but Fatah was rather noncommital, viewing it as the abstract product of intellectuals rather than as a structure for leading the diverse forces of Palestinian nationalism.

As debate over unity continued, the PLA called for the disbanding of the central committee in favor of a more limited executive committee. This change would reduce the voice of the minor fedayeen groups and augment that of the supporters of the PLA.[34] Fatah opposed this move and, under pressure from various sources, finally came forward with its own plan for unity on the eve of the congress.[35]

The eighth Palestine National Congress met in Cairo from February 28 to March 5, 1971, its longest session to date. Several important developments took place at the congress.[36] For example, the rapprochment between the Resistance movement and Egypt

32. *Africasia*, No. 35 (March 1–14, 1971), pp. 30–31.

33. *Le Monde* (English edition), February 24, 1971. Khalaf was reporting the ideas of Dawud Husayn, Abd al-Hamid as-Sayigh, and Abd al-Majid Shuman. Shuman had formerly been head of the Palestine National Fund and a member of the PLO executive committee.

34. *Al-Ahram*, February 16, 1971.

35. MENA Cairo, February 27, 1971. The "Arafat Plan," as it was adopted by the congress, was published in *Fateh* (English edition), Vol. 3, No. 1 (March 23, 1971), pp. 14–16.

36. Accounts of the congress are given in *Africasia*, No. 36 (March 15–28, 1971), pp. 32–35, and in *Jeune Afrique*, No. 532 (March 16, 1971), pp. 39–43.

was symbolized in President Anwar as-Sadat's opening speech. His theme was, predictably, the complementary nature of Egypt's search for a political solution to the conflict with Israel and the armed struggle of the Palestinians to attain their rights.[37]

Instead of opening for discussion the potentially dangerous topic of a Palestinian state, the leaders of the congress picked up the PFLP-PDFLP theme of unity of the Jordanian and Palestinian peoples. The political program adopted by the congress stated: "what links Jordan to Palestine are national ties and a national unity moulded by history, culture and language since time immemorial. . . . The Palestinian Revolution which brandished the slogan of the liberation of Palestine did not intend to differentiate between the eastern bank and the western bank of the River [Jordan]."[38] To accentuate the theme of Jordanian-Palestinian unity and to broaden the base of the Resistance movement, a Popular Palestinian Congress was held in Cairo along with the National Congress. Large numbers of West Bank figures, former Jordanian cabinet ministers, and long-time Jordanian national leaders, such as Sulayman an-Nabulsi, attended the Popular Congress.[39] The result of this meeting was a public rejection of all plans for a Palestinian state and an emphasis on unity of the Jordanian and Palestinian peoples. The basis for this new-found unity seemed most clearly to lie in common opposition to King Hussein.

Arafat's plan for unification of the Resistance movement was debated at the congress and finally accepted. The practical result of this move was to avoid immediate decisions on leadership and organization in favor of a general program of reorganization. Arafat's plan called for the creation of an enlarged National Congress of 150 members, a new central committee, and a political bureau. The model seemed to be that of the Vietnamese National Liberation Front. New members for the congress were to be selected over the next few months, and the expanded organization was to meet by June 30, 1971. At that time, further decisions would be made on the leadership of the Resistance. These plans apparently satisfied the PLA, which had earlier been critical of Arafat, and a significant

37. *New York Times,* March 1, 1971.

38. *Fateh,* Vol. 3, No. 1 (March 23, 1971), p. 4.

39. Prior to the Popular Congress, a number of non-fedayeen Palestinians and Jordanians met together in Beirut. These included Qadri Tuqan, who died of a heart attack on February 26; Hikmat al-Masri; Nablus mayor Rashid an-Nimr; former Jordanian premiers Abd al-Mun'im ar-Rifa'i and Sulayman an-Nabulsi; and a former deputy premier, Akif al-Fayiz. MENA Damascus to MENA Cairo, February 10, 1971.

result of the eighth congress was a temporary reconciliation of Fatah and the PLA.

The more serious and divisive issues discussed at the congress involved representation of the communist fedayeen organization, al-Ansar, and the problem of finances. The former was resolved in favor of including one member of al-Ansar, Faiq Warrad, in the congress, over the protest of some of Fatah's top leaders.[40] The question of finances was more serious, since the financial report given by Dr. Zuhayr al-Alami indicated that the National Fund was nearly empty. Since the September crisis, the Palestinians had been obliged to pay the costs of the PLA brigades in Syria, whereas previously the host governments covered these expenses. In view of this hopeless situation, Alami offered his resignation.[41] Other members of the PLO executive committee whose resignations were also rumored included Yasir Amr, Hamid Abu Sittah, and Ibrahim Bakr.[42]

JORDAN AND THE PALESTINIANS

In the months following the eighth National Congress, Fatah continued to strengthen its ties to Cairo as insurance against Jordanian hostility. For Egypt this relationship was a convenient answer to those Arab regimes, especially the Iraqis, who were accusing Egypt of having abandoned the Palestinian cause because of its desire for a political settlement.

By the end of March, Fatah was allowed to broadcast again from Cairo. Relations between Egypt and Jordan were strained, as the Jordanians feared that Egypt might be considering a separate peace with Israel under the guise of President Sadat's proposal for an interim agreement on reopening the Suez Canal. In this context, King Hussein ordered further measures against the Resistance movement. First, the town of Irbid was brought fully under control of the Jordanian army on March 26. The next critical turning point came with the Jordanian demand that the fedayeen leave Amman with all their weapons. A skillful campaign of intimidation went on for several days, replete with Jordanian threats to send the army

40. In accordance with Soviet policy in the Middle East, al-Ansar was not totally opposed to a peaceful settlement. See Faiq Warrad's article in *al-Akhbar,* March 14, 1971, p. 3.

41. Alami's resignation became effective during the spring. Kamal Nasir was quoted as saying it had been accepted. MENA Damascus to MENA Cairo, March 11, 1971; *New York Times,* March 9, 1971.

42. MENA Cairo, March 6, 1971.

into Amman to drive the commandos out by force. The choice between acquiescing and fighting faced the fedayeen once again. After some hesitation, the fedayeen began to evacuate the city.[43] In the following days, the Jordanian army found enough light arms hidden in Amman to equip a full division.

Folowing the evacuation of Amman, the Resistance forces in Jordan were limited to a small forested area between Jarash and Ajlun, far from densely populated areas. Opportunities for fedayeen action were not much better in Lebanon, as authorities there limited movement of armed men in the south.[44] Syria also seemed to be adopting a less supportive stand: first it received an official visit from Jordanian Crown Prince Hassan in March, then called on the fedayeen to be "realistic" in early April,[45] and finally sent General Mustafa at-Tlas to Amman to help mediate the clashes with the Resistance. Even Iraq, the most militant of the Arab countries in providing verbal backing of the fedayeen, took the step of fully withdrawing its armed forces in Jordan during the spring of 1971. Fatah, obviously feeling threatened from many quarters, responded by calling openly for the overthrow of the Jordanian "puppet separatist authority." [46] The PDFLP, perhaps also fearing Syria's moderation under Egyptian influence, turned to Iraq for support and seemed satisfied with the results.[47]

Early in May 1971, Fatah again began to call for "national rule" in Jordan. While denying that it wanted to seize power, Fatah insisted on the need for "a favorable atmosphere for continuing the march along our course. . . . We demand a national rule in Jordan, because, on the one hand Jordan is a geographical-historical extension of the occupied Palestine homeland, and, on the other, because of its masses Jordan is the base and springboard for any effective move against the occupation enemy and forces." [48]

Against this background of continuing challenges to Jordanian authority, King Hussein and his closest advisers, Prime Minister Wasfi at-Tal, Crown Prince Hassan, and General Zayd Bin Shakir, moved to eliminate the remaining Palestinian forces in Jordan.

43. The decision to evacuate Amman was apparently taken by Salah Khalaf, central committee representative in Amman. Arafat was reported to have opposed the move. MENA Damascus to MENA Cairo, April 22, 1971; Amman Domestic Service, April 17, 1971.

44. *An-Nahar Arab Report,* Vol. 2, No. 15 (April 12, 1971).

45. Damascus Domestic Service, April 5, 1971.

46. Voice of Fatah (Cairo), April 15, 1971.

47. INA Baghdad, March 19, 1971.

48. Voice of Fatah (Cairo), May 7, 1971.

This decision, which had been foreshadowed by the evacuation of Amman in April, was facilitated by a number of recent developments. Iraqi troops had left Jordan, and the Syrians had moderated their hostility to Hussein.[49] The constraint formerly imposed on Jordanian policy by close coordination with Cairo had faded, especially after President Sadat's proposal for an interim settlement. An element of urgency was added to the plan to liquidate the fedayeen by the occasional incidents of violence that inevitably occurred in the areas near Ajlun and Jarash. On May 16, the Jordanian government announced that it had discovered secret fedayeen plans to assassinate various individuals who were judged to be hostile to the Palestinians. This accusation amounted to a declaration of war on the fedayeen.

In early June 1971, amid persistent rumors that the PLO was considering the formation of a government-in-exile, King Hussein directed Prime Minister Tal to "deal conclusively and without hesitation with the plotters who want to establish a separate Palestiniq state and destroy the unity of the Jordanian and Palestinian people." [50]

During June, the Jordanian army moved into positions surrounding the fedayeen in the Ajlun forest. Incidents occurred from time to time, but a final showdown did not take place immediately. Instead, the PLO focused its attention on internal organization in preparation for the scheduled ninth National Congress in the second week of July.[51] The newly named congress consisted of 155 delegates, 85 of whom represented commando groups, with the remainder drawn from unions, popular organizations, and independents.[52] Khalid al-Fahum presided over the congress as chairman. Some progress toward formal unification and rationalization of the PLO's organizational structure took place amidst the most significant leadership reshuffle since Fatah's takeover of the PLO in February

49. The Syrians went so far as to seize a shipment of heavy arms sent from Algeria to Fatah by way of the Syrian port of Lataqiyah.

50. *New York Times*, June 3, 1967.

51. The convening of the congress was somewhat delayed because of a crisis in Sa'iqa which resulted in the ousting of Dafi Jamani, Yusif al-Barji, and Husayn al-Khatib, all of whom had been on the central committee.

52. Several prominent individuals refused to participate, including Yahya Hammuda, Abd al-Muhsin Qattan, Nimr al-Masri, and Abd al-Khaliq Yaghmur. MENA Cairo, July 7, 1971. The eighty-five fedayeen representatives consisted of thirty-three from Fatah, twelve from Sa'iqa, twelve from the PLA, twelve from the PFLP, eight from the PDFLP, four from the PFLP-GC, and four from other groups.

1969. The new executive committee, which replaced the central committee and the general secretariat, consisted of the following leaders: [53]

* Yasir Arafat, chairman (Fatah)
* Khalid al-Hassan (Fatah)
* Faruq al-Qaddumi (Fatah)
* Muhammad Yusif an-Najjar (Fatah)
  Salah Raf'at (PDFLP)
  Zuhayr Muhsin (Sa'iqa)
  Sami Attari (Sa'iqa)
  Taysir Qubba'ah (PFLP)
  Ahmad al-Marashli (ALF)

* Bahjat Abu Garbiyya (PPSF-Fatah)
* Hamid Abu Sittah (independent—pro-Fatah)
* Kamal Nasir (independent—pro-Fatah)
  Salah Muhammad Salah (representative of popular organizations—pro-PFLP)

In addition to these thirteen members of the executive committee, the PLA commander in chief, Abd ar-Razzaq Yahya, and the new National Fund director, Yusif as-Sayigh, were to participate in committee meetings. The composition of the new leadership demonstrated both the continuing dominance of Fatah's core leadership and the willingness of the PFLP for the first time to participate, however reluctantly, in the formal institutions of the PLO.

As the ninth National Congress was finishing its deliberations in Cairo, the Jordanian army began to implement its plan for eliminating the remaining fedayeen presence in the Ajlun-Jarash area.[54] After several days of sharp fighting, Prime Minister Tal announced that over two thousand fedayeen had been arrested and that the Cairo and Amman agreements regulating the relations of the fedayeen and the Jordanian government were no longer binding.

After the Ajlun-Jarash defeat, the fedayeen ceased to exist as a political or military force in Jordan. Several thousand remained in Lebanon and Syria, upon whose continued goodwill they had become heavily dependent. The Jordanians seemed delighted to be back in full control of the country, and a strong sentiment of defiant East Bank Jordanian nationalism was apparent in government circles. The confident and aggressive Jordanian policies of subsequent months reestablished King Hussein's authority throughout

53. Asterisk denotes previous membership on executive committee or central committee.

54. The attack took place while King Hussein was in Morocco congratulating King Hassan on having survived a coup attempt. It also preempted a planned meeting of several Arab heads of state which was intended to work out a new Jordanian-PLO *modus vivendi.*

the country, but at the price of alienating virtually all of Jordan's neighbors and isolating Hussein in the Arab world. Algeria, Libya, Syria, and Iraq all broke or suspended diplomatic relations with Amman, and the latter two closed their borders and airspace to Jordanian traffic. Kuwait refused to renew its subsidy to Amman, which meant that Jordan was heavily dependent on the remaining Saudi Arabian grant of £18 million sterling and American military and economic aid.[55]

Despite their decline as a military factor in the Middle East after September 1970 and July 1971, the fedayeen retained a residual capacity to threaten Jordan's economic well-being by means of Syrian, Iraqi, and Kuwaiti pressures. To keep this capability, the fedayeen had to remain on good terms with Syria and Egypt and to avoid overt dissension that would further weaken the already crippled Palestinian movement. To avoid clashes with the regimes in Lebanon and Syria, the PLO decided to become a "clandestine" movement, which seemed to mean primarily that military actions and public relations would not be undertaken in host countries. By shedding its bureaucratic superstructure, the PLO might also remove some of the least militant and most easily penetrated parts of the movement, retaining a small but committed body of leaders who were attracted less by publicity than by action. In order to avoid a lapse into total obscurity, however, the fedayeen continued to carry out occasional acts of violence, especially in Gaza and Jordan, and at times in Israel proper. Some of these operations were the work of a newly formed secret group called Black September. Unlike most fedayeen organizations, Black September shunned publicity, appeared to be tightly disciplined, and concentrated on spectacular acts of terrorism. Initially its members consisted of dissident members of Fatah who were close to Abu Ali Ayad, a leader of Fatah's armed forces in north Jordan until his death in mid-1971. After the expulsion of the fedayeen from Jordan, Black September became a genuinely clandestine band of several hundred guerrillas dedicated to the use of terror and assassination against Israelis and Jordanians.

Several sources of tension were apparent within the PLO late in 1971. One issue that caused considerable division in the leadership was the effort by Egypt and Saudi Arabia to mediate the dispute between Jordan and the PLO. Part of Fatah's leadership, as well as Sa'iqa and the PLA, seemed to favor going through the

55. Kuwaiti and Libyan aid to Jordan, suspended after September 1970, had amounted to 27 million pounds under the Khartoum agreements of August 1967.

motions of talking with Hussein's representatives, at least as a means of retaining Saudi support and financial assistance. The PFLP, the PDFLP, and several others on the executive committee opposed the mediation effort.[56] Arafat's apparent willingness to compromise, which had long been the key to his success, was beginning to alienate some of the younger and more militant fedayeen, and the failure of the mediation effort may have increased discontent with Arafat's leadership. Salah Khalaf, long considered the second most important man in Fatah, and reportedly closer in his ideas to the PFLP than to Arafat, succeeded in winning the largest number of votes at the Fatah congress held in Damascus in September. The possibility of a split within Fatah and a new alignment of the militant wings of Fatah, the PFLP, and the PDFLP was being discussed, but faced the obvious problems of likely Syrian, Egyptian, Libyan, and Saudi hostility.[57]

In addition to the possibility of a split in Fatah, the periodic problems of relations with the PLA arose again in the fall of 1971. The commander in chief of the PLA, Brigadier General Yahya, had called for Arafat's ouster in February 1971 and had refused to cooperate in organizing the ninth National Congress in July.[58] In addition to opposing Arafat, Yahya was a bitter rival of the Syrian-supported chief of staff, Uthman Haddad. Following the murder of an aide to Yahya, an action attributed to Haddad, the dispute within the PLA flared up. Then, after an unexplained assassination attempt against Arafat, both Yahya and Haddad were dismissed from their positions in the PLA, to be replaced by Brigadier General Misbah al-Budayri, who had been Yahya's predecessor as commander in chief.[59]

56. See MENA Damascus to MENA Cairo, September 8, 1971.

57. *Ath-Thawrah* (Baghdad), September 24, 1971, inaccurately reported that Salah Khalaf had left Fatah after a dispute with Arafat. The split between Arafat and Khalaf is also reported in *Le Monde*, October 9, 1971. See also *An-Nahar Arab Report*, Vol. 2, No. 43 (October 25, 1971), p. 1; and Abdallah Schleifer's interview with Khalaf in *Jeune Afrique*, No. 563 (October 19, 1971), pp. 24–26.

58. *Le Monde*, June 20, 1971.

59. *New York Times*, September 29, 1971; *An-Nahar Arab Report*, Vol. 2, No. 40 (October 4, 1971). Two brigades of the PLA left Syria in the fall of 1971. The Ain Jallut Brigade returned to Egypt and the Qadissiya Brigade to Iraq. *Le Monde*, October 9, 1971. In an effort to control the PLA, the executive committee of the PLO gave Zuhayr Muhsin authority to ban political activity by the PLA (see *al-Ahram*, October 24, 1971). The new head of the PLA, al-Budayri, reportedly decided to transform the PLA into commando units, since fighting a classical war with Israel was an impossibility. See *al-Hayat* [Beirut], November 1, 1971.

Despite the disarray within the ranks of the PLO, Palestinians retained a capability, however modest, to influence the course of events in the Middle East. On November 28, 1971, at a time when serious efforts were being made to overcome divisions within the Arab camp, four Palestinians assassinated Jordan's prime minister, Wasfi at-Tal, in Cairo. The assassins, claiming membership in the previously unknown Black September group, appeared to have some links to Fatah. The effect of Tal's assassination was to end any immediate prospects of reconciliation between Jordan and the fedayeen. In addition, the Black September group and its tactics began to attract attention and support, leading part of the Fatah leadership to try to reassert control over this clandestine movement. Those who were most in sympathy with the Black September group and who eventually seem to have gained influence over it were the reputed leftists within Fatah, Salah Khalaf and Khalil al-Wazir.

Unable to return to Jordan, the fedayeen became increasingly dependent on bases in Syria and in the Arqub region of southeastern Lebanon. Perhaps fearing expulsion from Lebanon on the pattern of the previous year's events in Jordan, the guerrillas sought to minimize frictions with the host government, while nonetheless using Lebanese territory to stage raids into Israel. In February 1972, the fedayeen succeeded in inflicting comparatively heavy casualties within Israel, and in predictable fashion Israel responded with the largest military operations to date against Lebanon. After several days of attacks within Lebanon, the Israeli army withdrew. Shortly thereafter, the Lebanese army entered the Arqub area to insure that further fedayeen raids would not result in more Israeli attacks. The following June the Israelis staged air attacks on Lebanese villages following a renewal of fedayeen activity. Heavy civilian casualties were sustained, creating a new crisis between Lebanon and the Resistance movement. The result was an agreement by the major fedayeen groups to suspend operations from Lebanon and to withdraw from the border areas. This agreement lasted through the summer, until September 5, when Black September, in another of its terrorist operations, kidnapped and then executed eleven members of the Israeli Olympic team in Munich. While dissociating themselves from Black September, PLO leaders nonetheless claimed that the Munich killings served the Palestinian cause. Israeli opinion was outraged and demanded vengeance, so that once again, in mid-September 1972, Lebanon was the target of harsh Israeli attacks. As in the past, the Lebanese government moved to control fedayeen activities across its borders, but the effectiveness of these measures remained in doubt. In any event, the latest in the cycle of attacks and retaliation left the fedayeen more heavily dependent on Syria than before, but also managed to revive the guerrilla mystique briefly at a time when the fortunes of the Resistance movement were otherwise at an all-time low.

Added to these external pressures, internal factionalism led to the split of the most influential of the radical fedayeen groups, the PFLP. In mid-March, following Habash's reelection as secretary-general, part of the PFLP, consisting of the self-designated left wing, broke away to form the Popular Revolutionary Front for the Liberation of Palestine (PRFLP). Accusing Habash of having opposed national unity and of having carried out the hijacking of a plane to Aden the previous month, despite a policy decision dating from November 1970 disapproving such actions, the PRFLP seemed willing to work with Fatah inside a broad front.[60]

Fatah was likely to be the prime beneficiary of any split within the PFLP. In March 1972, unity of the fedayeen movement seemed more urgent than ever, as King Hussein launched a new initiative promising eventual autonomy to a Palestinian state on the West Bank within a United Arab Kingdom of which he would be the head.[61] While eliciting little immediate favorable response, the king's proposal, plus impending elections for municipal offices on the West Bank, threatened the PLO's claim to represent the Palestinian people. In light of these challenges, the fedayeen once again convened a National Congress in Cairo from April 6 to 10. The Hussein Plan and elections on the West Bank figured prominently in the deliberations, but no action other than ritual denunciation of these "plots" was forthcoming. Questions of leadership and organization were also addressed, and a draft unification plan of sorts was adopted which recommended political and military unity within a national front in which each group would retain its organizational

60. See *Le Monde*, March 9 and March 12–13, 1972; also, *An-Nahar Arab Report*, Vol. 3, No. 12 (March 20, 1972), pp. 2–3. *An-Nahar*, March 8, 1972, carries a report on the PRFLP based on its "secret constitution."

61. Jordan also resumed paying salaries to West Bank officials, a practice that had been suspended in July 1971. The "Hussein Plan" came in a speech on March 15, 1972, reprinted in *New Middle East*, May 1972. Among those analyzing the Hussein Plan, the Egyptian journalist Ahmad Baha ad-Din has concluded that the proposal should be seen as a step toward declaring Jordan's independence within the old Transjordan borders. This would effectively absolve Jordan of further responsibility for the "liberation of Palestine." *Al-Ahram*, March 26, 1972. One consequence of the Hussein Plan was that Egypt used it as a pretext to break diplomatic relations with Jordan.

and ideological independence.[62] Under pressure from nonfedayeen Palestinian leaders, a follow-up unification committee was formed, which indicated that the need for unity within the ranks of the Resistance was becoming widely recognized. By late-1972, however, the only step toward unity that had been taken was in the field of information, and even there the process was incomplete. Inevitably, it seemed, the quest for an effective and cohesive Resistance movement would go on, but its realization would always lie in the future, to be implemented by the next National Congress. Meanwhile, on the West Bank and elsewhere, Palestinians were obliged to cope with their own problems outside the framework of the increasingly ineffective Resistance.

Developments on the West Bank

With the weakening of the fedayeen, the failure of progress toward a negotiated Arab-Israeli settlement, and King Hussein's harsh actions against Palestinians on the East Bank, West Bank Palestinian opinion began to budge perceptibly in mid-1971 from its uncommitted position of previous years. West Bankers, who had long hoped for the end of the Israeli occupation, came to realize that outside forces could do little to bring this about. While continuing to hope for a political settlement, West Bank Palestinians also seemed to realize that the occupation would not end soon.[63] Palestinians had long held ambiguous feelings toward the Hashemites, but some ties to Jordan seemed essential as a means of avoiding isolation from the Arab world and Israeli dominance. But when the Jordanian army crushed the fedayeen, many West Bank leaders expressed a strong distaste for returning to Jordanian rule.

In May 1971, reports circulated that the Jordanians had drawn up arrest warrants for West Bank personalities, including Hamdi Kan'an, Hikmat al-Masri, and the political writer for *al-Quds,* Muhammad Abu Shilbayah.[64] That same month, a group of Palestinians on the West Bank addressed a memorandum to U.S. Secretary of State Rogers calling for an end to the Israeli presence and a

62. MENA Cairo, April 10, 1972. The emphasis on "Pan-Arabization" of the struggle for Palestine received particular emphasis at the congress, along with the theme of unity.

63. Hamdi Kan'an, former mayor of Nablus, expressed this view in *al-Quds,* May 17, 1971.

64. *New York Times,* May 5, 1971.

referendum to determine Palestinian desires prior to the return of the West Bank to Jordan.[65]

After the events at Ajlun and Jarash in July, West Bank spokesmen attacked King Hussein's regime more bitterly than ever. Jamil Hamad, editor of a new weekly newspaper, *al-Bashir*, published in Bethlehem, spoke of the "overwhelming animosity with which Jordanian rule is viewed on the West Bank." [66] Demands for the right to hold political discussions and petitions for local elections were received by the Israelis from West Bank leaders. Shlomo Hillel, Israel's minister of police, was attacked for saying that political organization could not take place under an occupation regime. *Al-Quds* argued that Germans and Japanese, despite the post-World War II occupation, had been allowed to engage in political activity, including elections, which eventually permitted the establishment of fully sovereign national governments.[67]

If West Bank opinion was gradually shifting toward ideas of Palestinian autonomy and eventual independence, the issue of leadership was still an open question. The fedayeen seemed weak and without much support in most of the West Bank. The authority of the traditional leaders of the market towns on the West Bank was being eroded as the result of a complex social and economic process of modernization. The major market towns of Ramallah, Nablus, Jenin, Jericho, and Hebron were losing some of their original functions as transportation and employment patterns changed. The mediator role between villager and government that had been filled by the town notables in the past was being slowly altered. Young intellectuals and independent personalities were beginning to make their voices heard, albeit softly.[68] It should be emphasized, however, that these voices had virtually no effect on Palestinians living outside the West Bank.

The facts of full employment on the West Bank and of forty thousand Palestinian Arabs working in Israel helped to lighten the burden of the occupation and to render less urgent a settlement that

65. Text in *New Middle East,* No. 33 (June 1971).

66. *New Middle East,* No. 35 (August 1971), pp. 66ff.

67. Atallah Mansour, "Palestine: The Search for a New Golden Age," *New York Review of Books,* Vol. 27, No. 5 (October 7, 1971), p. 24; and author's interview with Muhammad Abu Shilbayah, September 17, 1971, in Jerusalem. Abu Shilbayah's book, *No Peace Without a Free Palestinian State* (in Arabic), aroused controversy for its criticisms of both Hussein and the fedayeen. See the *New York Times,* November 14, 1971.

68. *Al-Quds, al-Bashir,* sometimes *New Middle East,* and more recently *al-Anba,* are good sources for information on the thinking of the new generation of West Bank spokesmen.

would restore Jordanian rule to the area. Summer visits from Palestinians on the East Bank also reduced the feeling of isolation. In addition, the relatively freewheeling Israeli political process may have sparked a desire for open political life among the Palestinians on the West Bank.

The dilemma for the West Bank Palestinians is to cope with the Israeli occupation without being branded as traitors by the rest of the Arab world. Local elections and limited autonomy have been feasible goals for West Bank Palestinians to pursue even in the absence of an overall Arab-Israeli settlement. The issue of a Palestinian state, however, is more complex, not only because of Israeli hostility to the idea, but also because of probable Arab reaction. Prior to a peace settlement, efforts by Palestinians to form a state of their own on the West Bank would be condemned by Egypt, Jordan, and Syria, at the very least, as leading to an Israeli-dominated puppet regime. On the other hand, as part of a settlement, a Palestinian state may stand little chance of success because of Jordanian and Israeli opposition. The best that the Palestinians can hope for in a peace settlement will probably be transitional arrangements prior to Jordanian reoccupation that will allow them some measure of self-determination.

Without prospects for a settlement, West Bank political leaders such as Hamdi Kan'an spoke out, calling for the right to engage in political activity and to hold municipal elections. In early 1972, Israel responded by authorizing elections under Jordanian law, but without permitting open political campaigning prior to the elections. Under the law governing elections, only property-owning males were eligible voters, or about 10 percent of the West Bank population. Nonetheless, the elections did provide some opportunity to judge new political forces among the Palestinians living under Israeli occupation. On March 28 elections were held in the northern part of the West Bank. In the town of Nablus the election took place in an atmosphere of Israeli coercion after the leading candidate had withdrawn, thereby threatening the success of the experiment in Israeli eyes. Despite this incident, participation was high, perhaps partly because of the practice of stamping the identity cards of voters. On May 2, elections were held in the rest of the West Bank, and again participation exceeded 85 percent of the eligible voters. The latter election brought a large number of new faces to public office, including several young professionals who defeated more traditional incumbents.

While far from a complete or accurate gauge of public opinion on the West Bank, the elections did demonstrate that the threats of the Resistance did not stop candidates from running for office, and that in a test of strength the Israeli authorities could exact cooperation more easily than the commandos.[69] In addition, the election results suggest the gradual emergence of a new political class of young professionals who are attached neither to Amman nor to the fedayeen, nor to the traditionally powerful families. If the occupation continues indefinitely, it is these men who can be expected to raise their voices for political rights for Palestinians living under Israeli rule.

69. The elections are analyzed well in *Le Monde Diplomatique*, April 1972.

7
CONCLUSION

From 1968 to 1972, Palestinians became important political actors in the Arab-Israeli conflict. The organizational embodiment of Palestinian nationalism became the various Resistance movements that formed after the 1967 war. Judged by their stated goals of eliminating Zionist institutions in Palestine by means of popular armed struggle or through revolution in the Arab world, the fedayeen have been notably unsuccessful. Their vulnerability to superior Arab and Israeli military forces has been repeatedly demonstrated. Nonetheless, in their few years of existence, the fedayeen have been responsible for several potentially significant changes. In terms of these less frequently acknowledged accomplishments, the Palestinian movement has been surprisingly successful, particularly in view of its limited resources.

Accomplishments

The single most impressive success of the Palestinian commandos in recent years has been to raise the issue of Palestinian national claims to the center of the Arab-Israeli conflict. In the Middle East, in Europe, at the United Nations,[1] and in the United States, recognition of the need for some role for Palestinians in any eventual

1. U.N. Resolution 242 of November 1967 made virtually no reference to the Palestinians, whereas subsequent General Assembly resolutions after 1969 stressed "the inalienable rights of the people of Palestine" and recognized that "the people of Palestine are entitled to equal rights and self-determination, in accordance with the Charter of the United Nations."

peaceful settlement involving Israel and the Arab world has increased dramatically in recent years. By insisting on the right to speak on their own behalf, Palestinian nationalists have sought to forestall a political solution to the Arab-Israeli conflict that would be at their expense. Even the Jordanian regime, which stands to lose the most from the creation of a Palestinian state, has acknowledged Palestinian rights to self-determination following an eventual settlement with Israel. Although the idea that the Palestinians hold the key to a peaceful Middle East may be nothing more than wishful thinking, it has nonetheless gained unprecedented acceptance in recent years. That this is true is a major accomplishment of the Palestinian commandos.

Whether or not the Palestinians eventually succeed in creating a Palestinian state, the post-1967 Resistance movement will have left its mark on Arab nationalist development. Since the early twentieth century, Arab nationalism in the sense of integral Arab unity has held a strong attraction for many Arabs. But because reality has never matched the desired ideal, ambivalence and uncertainty have prevailed in virtually all Arab countries. The Palestinians themselves were attracted in large numbers to Arab nationalism as a solution to their homelessness in the 1950s, but the 1967 defeat revealed the fallacy of relying on non-Palestinians to lead the battle against Israel. For most Palestinian nationalists, the conclusion drawn from the repeated failures of unified Arab action was that Palestinian leadership should henceforth pursue Palestinian interests without interference from any Arab regime. As this position was rationalized and developed, it became a strong argument in favor of state nationalism as a legitimate basis for political organization. The events of September 1970 further confirmed the Palestinian belief that they could not count on the support of other Arab regimes.[2]

While some Arab nationalists have denounced the Palestinians for their exclusiveness, a number of Arab regimes, including Egypt and Algeria, have supported the idea that Palestinians should become primarily responsible for their own problems. In view of these developments, Arab nationalism, rather than requiring Arab intervention in the Palestine issue, can be seen as a call for cooperation and solidarity on issues of common Arab concern, while leaving the sovereignty of each Arab state unquestioned. If this interpretation becomes widely accepted in the Arab world, Arab nationalism will have served as a transitional ideology facilitating

2. Hisham Sharabi, "Palestine Resistance: Crisis and Reassessment," *Middle East News Letter,* January 1971.

the passage from the traditional Islamic community to the modern Arab nation-states.[3] While some signs of changing attitudes toward Arab nationalism have been visible for many years, the Palestinian Resistance movement has greatly accelerated the trend toward state nationalism by demonstrating the weakness of Arab unity and by insisting on Palestinian autonomy.

In addition to legitimizing a less global concept of Arab nationalism, the Palestinian commando movement has served to accelerate the pace of social change in the Palestinian community. These modernizing consequences of fedayeen activities are most visible among the younger generation, many of whom have received training and instruction from the various Palestinian groups. The content of this education has generally been progressive, stressing such simple ideas as secularism, equality between men and women, and commitment to the nationalist cause. Traditional social habits are gradually being eroded, and conscious efforts are being made to instill ideas of self-reliance, activism, and progress among a population that has long been neglected, embittered, and apathetic. An increase in Palestinian self-confidence has been one of the major results of fedayeen actions.

Finally, a modest intellectual trend toward possible reconciliation with Israel's Jewish population can be noted in the attitudes of many Palestinians.[4] Compared with an earlier generation of Palestinians, some of the current spokesmen for the fedayeen, as well as many independent Palestinian intellectuals, especially on the West Bank, are willing to talk about political accommodations in which both Jewish and Arab communities would be able to express their distinctive cultures within the area of Palestine. The range of possible political solutions to reach this end has hardly been explored, but even at this early stage one can find some Palestinians talking of Israelis as a nation and of national rights for Jews in Palestine. As yet, this intellectual transformation has not resulted in a widespread belief that self-determination for both Jews and Arabs in Palestine will require the existence of two distinct political entities, but such an eventual conclusion cannot be excluded. What already exists as individual opinion may become a bargaining position for some Palestinian organization in the future.

3. For similar conclusions, see Richard H. Pfaff, "The Function of Arab Nationalism," *Comparative Politics*, Vol. 2, No. 2 (January 1970), p. 167.
4. Israeli views of the Palestinians have also been undergoing significant changes. See Abraham S. Becker, *Israel and the Palestinian Occupied Territories: Military-Political Issues in the Debate,* R-882, Santa Monica, California: The Rand Corporation, December 1971.

ENDURING PROBLEMS AND FUTURE PROSPECTS

While the Palestinians have been somewhat successful in gaining recognition of their central position in the conflict with Israel and have also managed to bring about some social and attitudinal changes within Palestinian society, immense difficulties remain for the Resistance movement. Despite a deep desire for autonomy, most Palestinian groups have been dependent, to varying degrees, on Arab regimes. Combined with traditional sources of divisiveness in Palestinian society, dependency on outside sources for arms, funds, territory, and protection has prevented unification of the Palestinian movement. Lack of unity has resulted in military weakness as well as in a poorly developed negotiating position. Quarrels within the Palestinian leadership have both reflected and accentuated the divisions and weaknesses of the Resistance movement. As the fedayeen have declined as a military and political force, West Bank Palestinians have begun to explore the possibilities of working out their own arrangements with the Israelis, thereby further weakening a unified Palestinian position.

As the largest organized expression of Palestinian nationalism, Fatah, along with its supporters in the PLO and in intellectual circles, will face difficult choices in the future. Until 1971, Fatah was able to pursue a comparatively moderate course of engaging in armed struggle to establish its claim to representativeness, to mobilize the Palestinian masses, and to unify the ranks of the fedayeen. By 1970, partial success in these terms had been achieved, and precisely for that reason the Palestinian movement became something of a threat to existing Arab regimes, especially in Jordan.

The crisis of September 1970 was a decisive turning point for the Resistance movement, and in its aftermath several courses of action seemed open to Fatah. First, Fatah could accept the revolutionary logic of the PFLP and PDFLP that the regimes in Jordan and Lebanon must be overthrown if the Palestinian Resistance is to survive. To follow this route, however, would result in costly confrontations with Arab armed forces and in a likely loss of support from most Arab regimes, and would oblige the Resistance movement to operate clandestinely. The Jordanian liquidation of the fedayeen in July 1971 increased the incentive to adopt this strategy, but made its realization vastly more difficult.

Second, the argument put forth by the PLA and some Arab regimes that commando actions and guerrilla warfare cannot succeed against Israel could gain currency among the Palestinians. In that case, the PLO might become a government-in-exile with conventional armed forces at its disposal in countries such as Syria or Iraq. Armed actions against Israel would then be part of a comprehensive Arab strategy rather than an expression of Palestinian nationalism. In this case, Palestinian autonomy would once again be subordinated to the interests of various Arab regimes, and this would be justified as the "Pan-Arabization" of the battle.[5]

Each of the alternatives available to the Palestinians in late 1972 had some obvious drawback. Going underground and seeking to overthrow the Jordanian or Lebanese governments would ensure that the Resistance movement would remain small, conspiratorial, and very vulnerable to superior force. Becoming a conventional army would run the risk of losing the autonomy that Palestinians fought to attain after 1967. A third alternative, that of forging a broadly based political movement capable of developing a viable military-diplomatic position, would require the greatest amount of discipline and leadership. Revolutionary forces would undoubtedly try to outbid the proponents of such an intermediate posture. Consequently, the path that might ensure that some Palestinian demands would be reflected in any future political arrangements in the area seemed likely to be bypassed, leaving the Palestinians in the political limbo so familiar to them since 1948.

5. One Arab observer writing in mid-1972 foresaw such a development and argued that Pan-Arabization of the Palestinian struggle would simply be a pretext for the "progressive" Arab regimes to regain control over the Resistance movement, thereby weakening its revolutionary potential. Samir Frangié, *Le Monde Diplomatique,* June 1972, p. 5.

PART III
THE PALESTINIAN RESISTANCE
AND
INTER-ARAB POLITICS

BY

FUAD JABBER

I

THE RESISTANCE MOVEMENT
BEFORE THE SIX-DAY WAR

The aftermath of the 1967 Arab-Israeli war witnessed the sudden growth of Palestinian armed resistance in the Middle East. This, however, should not obscure the fact that attempts by Palestinians to regain the initiative in the struggle to assert their claims to Palestine considerably antedate the conflict of June 1967. In fact, Syrian-sponsored raids by Palestinian commandos into northern Israel were the immediate cause for the crisis that triggered the Six-Day War. The defeat of Arab conventional armies provided the burgeoning Resistance movement with the opportunity to move to the forefront of the Arab effort against Israel and thereby restore the Palestinian dimension to the conflict, which had been all but lost in the course of the previous two decades. From a historical perspective, this may perhaps turn out to be the most significant and lasting accomplishment of the Resistance movement.

From 1961 onwards, there arose among some Palestinians the distinct conviction that the Arab governments, if left to themselves, could not be relied on to bring about the desired confrontation with Israel in the foreseeable future, if ever, and it was therefore the responsibility of Palestinians to take the lead in seeking a redress of their grievances. An awareness of this necessity had been present since the 1950s—witness the creation of the Palestine Liberation Movement (Fatah) in 1957–1958. But it was the secession of Syria from the United Arab Republic in September 1961 that presaged the indefinite postponement of the final showdown with Israel, for which Arab unity had been posited as the essential prerequisite, if the matter was to be left in the hands of the existing regimes. In addition, the period 1961–1962 saw the fulfillment of the Algerian fight for independence, in which Fatah read a vindication of its own faith in a popular war of national liberation as the correct mode of struggle. Following the Syrian secession, the regime of Egypt's President Nasser substituted the slogan "unity of purpose" for "unity of ranks," [1] but even this more limited goal, which seemed to be within reach in the period of Arab "summitry" (1964–1966), was to prove elusive with the renewal of inter-Arab political warfare in mid-1966 and the indefinite postponement of the fourth summit conference. "With the collapse of the last hope for united Arab action . . . the Palestinian realized that . . . it was incumbent upon himself to strive to create a tense situation that would revive his cause in all fields of action and turn the potential Israeli danger into an active and imminent threat." [2]

The modalities of interaction that have developed between the different fedayeen groups and the Arab governments since June 1967 were to a considerable degree established in their main lines prior to the postwar upsurge of the Resistance. This crucial but still obscure period has not been adequately studied thus far. This interaction can be explained in its most basic form in terms of the interplay between *dependence* (of commando groups on Arab regimes) and *popular support* (by Arab populations for the commandos) in a matrix of *inter-Arab politics* characterized by an extremely intricate web of issues, ideologies, and personalities. Widespread popular support accrued to the Resistance mainly in the aftermath of the 1967 conflict, providing it with the leverage it needed to counterbalance the effects of its unavoidable dependence on one or more Arab governments for protection and material aid as well as political assistance. In the period 1964–1967, by contrast, the incipient movement had no comparable counterweight and was therefore compelled to allow itself to be manipulated in the context of the inter-Arab political game in exchange for the opportunity to engage in the struggle for liberation. This symbiotic relationship is best exemplified in the Fatah-Syria connection, and to a lesser extent in the case of the Palestine Liberation Organization (PLO), set up in May 1964. Since the PLO was basically a political body created for the purpose of preserving the Palestinian entity from

1. See Nasser's speech of February 22, 1962, *al-Ahram* (Cairo), February 23, 1962.

2. *Filastin* (biweekly supplement of the Beirut daily *al-Muharrir*), No. 58 (January 26, 1967), p. 6.

extinction, and not a military organization (though later it developed a military arm, the Palestine Liberation Army, and a commando force), the analysis in this chapter will focus primarily on Fatah, which remains to this date by far the most important Resistance group.

THE EMERGENCE OF THE FEDAYEEN

The Arab-Israeli dispute remained relatively dormant for over half a decade following the withdrawal of Israeli forces from Sinai in March 1957 and the stationing of United Nations troops on the Egyptian-Israeli borders. Regional inter-Arab issues—such as the Iraqi revolution of 1958 and the subsequent feud of the Qasim regime with Nasser, the Lebanese civil war of the same year, the union of Syria and Egypt and its dissolution three frustrating years later, the Egyptian and Saudi involvement in Yemen, and the increasing division along ideological lines between "conservative" and "revolutionary-progressive" regimes—were keeping Arab capitals more than busy. By the end of 1963, when the Israeli problem again came to the fore with the dispute over the diversion of the Jordan River waters, the Arab camp was rent by more crosscutting internal divisions and squabbles than at any time in the past.[3]

While the Arab governments were thus endlessly bickering among themselves and furthering their own interests—more often than not allegedly on behalf of the "sacred" cause of Palestine—the young Palestinian activists in Kuwait and other Gulf states who formed the nucleus of Fatah had gradually come to the conclusion that the time factor decidedly was not on the Arab side. They saw two particular developments as ominous indicators that Israel was on the way to becoming a permanent fact of life: the impending completion of the project for the utilization of the Jordan River waters in the Negev desert, and Israeli nuclear activities. The settling of the Negev was seen as permitting the Israelis to absorb several million more immigrants, increasing Israel's wealth and power, and dispersing its population. The presence or potential threat of atomic weapons would provide a "standing argument for the defeatists." Both developments threatened to "turn the existing status quo into a permanent reality." These two factors were constantly emphasized in Palestinian political literature up to the 1967 war,

3. For a description of the overall Arab political scene in this period, see Malcolm H. Kerr, *The Arab Cold War: Gamal 'Abd al-Nasir and His Rivals, 1958–1970* (New York: Oxford University Press for the Royal Institute of International Affairs, 3rd ed., 1971), pp. 96–105.

and served as focal points for analyses purporting to demonstrate the necessity for immediate action and the dangers of further temporization. Arab conventional military superiority over, or at least parity with, Israel was generally assumed; hence Fatah saw its role as one of activating tension along the borders and causing armed confrontations in the expectation that this would embroil the Arab countries in an all-out decisive war of liberation.[4]

Fatah's military arm, al-Asifah (the Storm), launched its commando operations in early 1965 with a strike of symbolic significance aimed at the Israeli national water-carrier. Al-Asifah was set up throughout 1964, and some of its members may have undergone training in Algeria, which Fatah leader Arafat visited in 1963. The Algerians are reported to have offered assistance to the Palestinians on condition that it would be limited to activities undertaken inside Israel.[5] The main source of aid, however, was the Syrian Ba'th regime, which had come to power after the coup of March 8, 1963, against the "secessionists." Though little was revealed about the relationship between Fatah and Damascus before June 1967—probably so as not to substantiate Israel's charges of Syrian responsibility for commando activities inside its borders—it appears that the Syrians initiated contacts with Fatah leaders in 1964. By April of that year, the Amin al-Hafiz regime had come to realize that the Palestine Liberation Organization, which the January 1964 Arab summit meeting had resolved to create in order to safeguard the "Palestinian entity" and give new momentum to the political-diplomatic battle against Israel, was actually to be under Cairo's effective control. Coupled with the fact that the newly established Unified Military Command was to be headed by an Egyptian, General Ali Ali Amir, and that the summit meeting had agreed, over Hafiz's objections, on forsaking as premature any individual or joint action that could lead to war with Israel, this meant that the Ba'th had been neatly outmaneuvered by its main competitor for the favor of the Arab masses—Nasser—and had lost to him the initiative in pro-Palestine action: a complete reversal of the situation before the summit meeting.

The gravity of the circumstances from the viewpoint of the

4. See the Fatah series of pamphlets entitled "Revolutionary Lessons and Experiences," especially *From the Fundamentals of Fedayeen Action* (reprint August 1967); the Fatah Memorandum to the third Arab Summit conference, *al-Ba'th* (Damascus), September 10, 1965; and most biweekly issues of *Filastin*, particularly those of December 30, 1965, February 24 and March 14, 1966.

5. *Jeune Afrique* (Paris), January 13–19, 1969, p. 43.

Syrians was considerable. Following the disappointing unity talks of March–April 1963 in Cairo with Egypt and Iraq, which had provided the Ba'thists with a disquieting measure of Nasser's dislike and distrust of them,[6] the Syrian and Egyptian regimes had increasingly drifted apart, and the virulent propaganda war that followed was accompanied by the gradual political isolation of Damascus, which became more acute following the November 13, 1963, ouster of the Ba'th regime in Iraq by the pro-Nasser Abd as-Salam Arif. The partial rapprochement of the first summit did not break the Syrian isolation, and it deprived Damascus of its main weapon against Cairo, namely, Nasser's neglect of the Palestinian question to which his involvement in the Yemen and his awareness of the realities of the Arab-Israeli equation had prudently led him. Ever since 1948, devotion to the struggle against the Zionist state—even if only verbal—has been the touchstone of true "Arabism," nationalist fervor and revolutionary progressivism, the supreme virtues which are supposedly a prerequisite for the legitimization of any regime by the "Arab masses." Overbidding on the issue of Palestine, a constant feature of inter-Arab politics, was therefore destined to become a potent and effective instrument of propaganda warfare in the Nasser-Ba'th contest for popularity and regional leadership. As the events of May–June 1967 were to demonstrate, it could also have disastrous consequences.

In addition to practical political considerations, Ba'thist Syria's intransigence on this subject had ideological roots of its own that should not be underestimated. The role of ideology in determining the actual conduct of states is difficult to assess, but there is little doubt that the Syrian Ba'th has gone to considerable lengths in order to preserve some degree of ideological consistency in its actions, particularly whenever its civilian leadership has been in actual control of policy in Damascus. In its quest for "unity" and "socialism," and once in power in Syria, the party came to interpret the experience garnered in over two decades of political action throughout the Arab world, and particularly since the establishment of the United Arab Republic in 1958 and its eventual demise —the Ba'th having played an active part in both developments—as pointing to the central importance of the Palestine problem and to the insurmountable obstacle that the existence of Israel represents for any effective Arab unity. For the Ba'th, perhaps the fundamental lesson of the early 1960s in ideological terms was the need for a virtual rearrangement of priorities which would consecrate the primacy of the liberation of Palestine. This found expression in the

6. See Kerr, *Arab Cold War*, pp. 44–96.

report of the eighth national congress of the National Command of
the party, which met in early May 1965:

> The cause of Palestine is a fundamental starting point for de-
> fining the party's policy and plan of action both in and out of
> power. All other principles mentioned in the report are subject
> to and regulated by it. The cause of Palestine is more crucial than
> any other national issue and its consequences for the future and
> fate of the national cause are graver than those of the other prob-
> lems facing the Arabs and the party. Israel's continued existence
> means the impossibility of full achievement for any of the Arab
> nation's aims. Commitment to the Palestine issue means com-
> mitment to its liberation. . . . To give precedence to the libera-
> tion of Palestine means to condition our Arab and international
> policy in the light of the stand of foreign and Arab countries
> toward the issue of liberation.

The party also resolved to:

> Regard the Arab Palestinian people as the first and basic instru-
> ment for liberating Palestine through organizing them and lifting
> all restrictions which obstruct their course in fulfilling this role.[7]

Accordingly, when Ahmad ash-Shuqayri had set out in February–
March 1964 to organize the Palestine Liberation Organization, he
was well received in Damascus and was offered assistance and support. Palestinian officers in the Syrian army offered to train the
contingents of the future Palestine Liberation Army (PLA). It soon
became apparent to the Ba'thists, however, that the Palestinians
who would be called upon to meet in Jerusalem in May to establish
the PLO were being handpicked by Shuqayri from moderate "nonrevolutionary" circles, that the envisaged organization would be
"only an entity for propaganda and without any revolutionary
meaning," and that it would be financially and politically dependent on the summits, thus "link[ing] the fate of the Palestinian
Liberation movement to current Arab and international issues." [8]
By the time the PLO held its second congress in Cairo in June 1965,
the Syrians had long given up on the PLO, and Damascus Radio
was branding Shuqayri as "an agent for President Abdul Nasser"
who had turned the organization into "a machine obeying the
orders of certain very revolutionary regimes [meaning Egypt] to
cripple its revolutionary effectiveness and independence." [9]
Meanwhile, al-Asifah had started its operations from bases in

7. *Ath-Thawrah* (Damascus), May 5, 1965.
8. *Al-Ba'th,* editorial, April 15, 1964.
9. Damascus Domestic Service (in Arabic), June 15, 1965.

northern Jordan and Syria. Infiltration into Israel was usually across the Jordanian borders—and the Lebanese in very few instances—which were much longer, more accessible, and less well defended than the Syrian-Israeli lines. During the first few months of 1965, fedayeen raids were few and far between, and it was during this initial period that the often-mentioned disparity between the actual accomplishments of the guerrillas and the claims of their communiqués was most pronounced. By the end of the year, al-Asifah had issued thirty-nine statements, thirty-six of which were "military communiqués" containing news of over 110 operations within Israel. Israeli sources credit Fatah with a total of 35 "raids" in 1965.[10] Part of the difference in these figures, however, may be due to the fact that al-Asifah often mentioned as separate operations actions connected with the same raid, such as blowing up two different buildings in the same kibbutz (e.g., communiqués 20, 31)[11] or a commando group encountering two separate Israeli ambushes in the same location (e.g., communiqué 25).[12]

ARAB REACTIONS

The Syrian attitude throughout 1965 basically was one of wait-and-see. The commando warfare experiment was a novel one for them and, in the charged atmosphere of the Jordan waters diversion crisis, its consequences were difficult to foresee. The effectiveness of the commandos on one hand and the magnitude of the predictable Israeli response on the other had to be assessed. On the other hand, the Ba'th saw in al-Asifah's operations the opportunity to regain the initiative it had lost to Egypt in the Palestinian sphere and a new lever with which to affect the situation. On ideological grounds too, the idea of immediate action against the enemy and of a non-conventional revolutionary strategy based on direct mass participation advocated by Fatah struck a responsive chord among Ba'thists. The policy that evolved was one of tolerating and covertly assisting the fedayeen, while officially disclaiming any connections with them.

The Jordanian government, by contrast, was hostile to Fatah from the outset. Convinced that Jordan would be the target of Israeli reprisals, and wary of any activities that might provide a rallying point and encouragement for the restive Palestinian population on the West Bank, thereby threatening the shaky unity of the

10. Ehud Yaari, *Strike Terror: The Story of Fatah* (New York: Sabra Books, 1970), p. 76.

11. *Ath-Thawrah,* August 10, 1965; *Al-Ba'th,* October 10, 1965.

12. *Ath-Thawrah,* September 14, 1965.

country, King Hussein quietly but forcefully tried to prevent al-Asifah from operating on his territory. As Fatah was repeatedly to point out later on, the first one of its men to die in action was killed by Jordanian border patrols while his group was returning from a mission inside Israel. Similar incidents were to recur with increasing frequency. On July 22, 1966, Jordanian army units clashed with a group of commandos on their way to the Israeli border, killing four of them.[13] In this aspect, too, the situation that was to exist after 1967 was being foreshadowed in the prewar period. King Hussein first made the Jordanian attitude clear in a speech soon after his return from the third summit conference in October of 1965:

> We do not believe in or recognize the usefulness of any bodies or organizations undertaking impulsive and extemporaneous activities outside the framework of the United Arab Command and the joint Arab plan at a time when we are strengthening ourselves. This would hinder Arab planning, weaken Arab mobilization, open the opportunity for our enemies to commit aggressions against us, enable them to gain the initiative from the Arabs, and draw us into a battle before the proper time and before we have completed our preparation.[14]

Nor was Amman's attitude toward the Palestine Liberation Organization more forthcoming. Shuqayri demanded, among other things, that the PLO be allowed substantial freedom of political action among the Palestinians in Jordan, the recruitment and training of volunteers for the liberation army, and the arming and mobilization of frontier villages on the West Bank (for which purpose the PLO offered to supply small and medium weapons).[15] If granted, such measures would have soon resulted in the creation of a political authority within the country that rivalled that of the Hashimite monarch, had its own independent military resources, and appealed on the basis of differential nationalist sentiments to a sector of the citizenry that made up a majority of the population. Moreover, this new "Palestinian entity" derived its legal existence from sources external to Jordan and beyond its control—the decisions of the summit conferences—and already enjoyed the recognition of all Arab countries. In King Hussein's view, to permit the PLO to establish itself in the country would have put in question the legitimacy and future of the "Jordanian entity" brought into existence by his grandfather Abdullah in 1949 by merging the

13. Damascus Domestic Service, July 25, 1966.

14. *Al-Jihad* (Amman), October 5, 1965.

15. See the memorandum submitted by the PLO to the Jordanian government, text in *al-Muharrir*, February 23, 1966.

West Bank with the Kingdom of Transjordan. "The purpose of the PLO in its present form," he privately complained to President Nasser in July of 1966, "is the destruction of Jordan and of everything we have achieved throughout these long years for our nation and for Palestine. . . . We can no longer collaborate with this Organization." [16]

With the exception of Syria and Algeria, the view that Fatah's commando activity was reckless adventurism that could result in an untimely war was shared by the remaining Arab countries—not excluding "progressive" circles, most of which were of Nasserist inclinations and considered the PLO to be the only adequate framework for Palestinian action.[17] Official circles in the UAR were mostly silent on the issue, and Gaza, which was to become one of the principal springboards for Resistance operations after the June war, remained quiet throughout this early period. Only on the eve of the war were some raids undertaken by commandos of the PLO.[18] Arab representatives on the Mixed Armistice Commissions meeting in January 1966 demanded an end to activities by al-Asifah on grounds of their being ineffective, jeopardizing the peace prematurely, causing Israeli reprisals, and antagonizing world opinion.[19] Measures to curb such incursions were agreed on, and news of Fatah was played down. Early in September 1965 the Lebanese Army Command had already requested the country's press to stop publishing al-Asifah's communiqués and all news of its operations in Israel. In a memorandum submitted to the third summit conference at Casablanca later that same month, Fatah had called upon the Arab countries to "stop the persecution of the Liberation Movement forces in the different Arab states, whether they border or not on Israel, free those imprisoned without delay, remove the embargo placed on the publication of news of the Liberation Movement in many Arab countries, and refrain from attacking its men while they are carrying out their fedayeen operations or whenever

16. Text of letter from Hussein to Nasser dated July 14, 1966, was published in *al-Jihad* (Jerusalem), November 27, 1966.

17. Detractors of Fatah at this stage reportedly included the Palestinian branch of the Arab Nationalist movement, from which the PFLP and the Popular Democratic Front would emerge after the June war. See Khalil Hindi, Fuad Bawarshi, Shihadah Musa, and Nabil A. Sha'ath, *The Palestinian Resistance and the Jordanian Regime* (in Arabic) (Beirut: PLO Research Center, 1971), p. 23.

18. According to Israeli reports quoting captured fedayeen, the Egyptians clamped down on Fatah in the Gaza Strip following three raids carried out from there in February 1965. Yaari, *Strike Terror*, p. 67.

19. *Al-Hayat* (Beirut), January 14, 1966.

they . . . are compelled to seek refuge in neighboring countries." [20]

A strong boost to the position of Fatah in Syria came with the accession to power of the left wing of the Ba'th as a result of the February 23, 1966, coup against the Hafiz-Bitar-Aflaq old guard. The new leaders—Nur ad-Din al-Atasi, Yusif Zu'ayyin, Ibrahim Makhus, Lt. General Salah Jadid—shared a vaguely Marxist outlook unacceptable to the older nationalist leadership, were opposed to Syrian acquiescence in Nasser's summit policy of coexistence with the moderate regimes, and favored a more determined stand toward Israel. They consequently made it their business, on assuming control, to sabotage the summit spirit and bring about a conservative-revolutionary confrontation, on the one hand, and press ahead with the implementation of their share of the project for the diversion of the Jordan River's tributaries, on the other. Moreover, they officially adopted the strategy of "popular war of liberation" (*harb at-tahrir ash-sha'biyyah*) as the only adequate method for achieving not only the liberation of Palestine but also the eventual unification of the Arab world. The new leadership called an extraordinary meeting of the party's regional (i.e., Syrian) command from March 10 to March 17, 1966, which issued a report outlining the position of the regime on all aspects of domestic and foreign policy. On the issue of Palestine:

> The conference considers the Palestine question the main axis of our domestic, Arab, and international policies. It expresses its belief that the traditional line of policy regarding the liberation of Palestine has always been and remains a [device] fabricated to remove the boundaries existing between the progressive and reactionary forces and a constant justification for extinguishing the torch of struggle of the masses. The masses have become fully convinced that this traditional method of dealing with the issue means an evasion of the battle and a defeatism that has provided clear protection for many reactionary regimes. After all this time has been wasted, it has become clear that the liberation battle can only be waged by progressive Arab forces through a popular war of liberation, which history has proved is the only course for victory against all aggressive forces—regardless of the supremacy of their potential and methods. The popular war of liberation, which must be the result of scientific, cognizant, and accurate study of the various Arab potentials and the interconnected conditions of the popular battle—which depends on the people's vital struggling forces—will remain the certain road of the return, despite all pain and sacrifice. It will remain the final way for the

20. *Al-Ba'th*, September 10, 1965.

liberation of the entire Arab homeland and for its comprehensive socialist popular unification.[21]

It has been suggested that the neo-Ba'thist predilection for this strategy was due to the experiences of Atasi, Zu'ayyin, and Makhus in the Algerian revolution and the study by the new chief of staff, Ahmad Suwaydani, of Maoist doctrines of people's war during his stay in Peking as military attaché. In any case, the left wing of the Ba'th had preached since 1965 the advisability of starting the final showdown with Israel without further delay, since time was on the enemy's side. "It is quite possible that as a nation, and considering our present military capacities, we cannot liberate Palestine. But we can kindle the spark. . . . There is no sense in additional preparations, since Israel is also carrying on with its preparations and may obtain atomic weapons," said a restricted party circular dated November 3, 1965, and distributed to the regional command, which by this time had a majority of militant leftists on its executive committee.[22]

The role of the Palestinians in the conflict would be, in Suwaydani's words, that of "taking the initiative and opening the way"; it was readily acknowledged, however, that limited commando operations would be useless by themselves. The combined effort of all Arab masses would be needed, and a revolutionary leadership endowed with an adequate political and social ideology would be required to see the war of liberation through to victory. "Without this revolutionary content, and if the cause of Palestine is not considered a part of the total Arab revolution, the struggle of the Arab people of Palestine shall remain constrained within the scope of limited fedayeen military operations," said the new head of state, Atasi.[23] The struggle against Israel was in this manner directly linked to the revolution against the remaining conservative regimes in the Arab world, whose existence stood in the way of the full mobilization of Arab resources. The enemy was defined as consisting of the trilogy Zionism, imperialism, and Arab reaction. A new slogan became fashionable in Ba'th pronouncements, "the meeting of the progressive Arab forces," which emphasized the need for

21. *Ath-Thawrah*, April 4, 1966.
22. Quoted in Yaari, *Strike Terror*, p. 76. This, according to the author, appears to be one of the internal Ba'th party documents that fell into Israeli hands with the capture of the Golan Heights in 1967.
23. Speech commemorating the eighteenth anniversary of the loss of Palestine, *al-Ba'th*, May 15, 1965.

immediate confrontation with "reaction" by an alliance of the "progressive" regimes.

The left wing of the Ba'th thus went beyond Fatah in its orientation toward unconventional warfare and the potential it attributed to "popular war" for the task of defeating Israel, at least on the theoretical level. The Palestinians still believed that a total conventional effort could be successful, and thus conceived of themselves as the catalyst that would bring the reluctant Arab regimes to the battlefield through the medium of Israeli retaliation. Only after the 1967 defeat did the Resistance movement come around to the strategy of large-scale popular war, and only the extreme-left Popular Democratic Front of Nayif Hawatmah—and George Habash's PFLP (embodying the mainstream of the Arab Nationalist Movement) to some extent—went so far as to prescribe the elimination of the conservative regimes as a prerequisite for an effective war of liberation, while Fatah remained faithful to its principle of "noninterference in the internal affairs of Arab states."

COMMANDO RAIDS AND ISRAELI REPRISALS: THE TEMPO QUICKENS

On May 27, 1965, in reaction to Fatah's raids, the Israelis carried out their first act of across-the-border retaliation against Jordan since 1956. The attack was aimed at villages in the ash-Shunah, Jenin, and Qalqiliya areas. Its rationale was to impel the Jordanians to take even more stringent measures against Palestinian guerrillas operating from their territory. Though the Israelis clearly believed that the Syrians were to blame, as the statements of their spokesmen and press comments indicate, they apparently concluded that operations against the heavily fortified Golan sector would be too costly and their price out of proportion with the existing level of commando activities. They also believed that the Jordanians could put an effective damper on al-Asifah if sufficiently motivated to do so. In any case, the strategy of striking at Jordan in retaliation for commando activities regardless of their actual source was pursued throughout the pre-1967 war period almost without exception. The raid of May 27 was followed by another on Qalqiliya on September 5 and a third on April 26, 1966, against two villages in the Hebron district of the West Bank. The most destructive and important reprisal was that carried out on November 13, 1966, against the Jordanian village of as-Samu' and neighboring areas by two Israeli armored columns.[24] The net effect of this policy as far

24. For details see Fred J. Khouri, *The Arab-Israeli Dilemma* (Syracuse, N.Y.: Syracuse University Press, 1968), pp. 229–239.

as Damascus was concerned was to provide the Ba'th with further incentive for helping Fatah: fomenting trouble for the despised "reactionary" regime in Amman while avoiding Israeli reprisals.

Following the February 1966 coup in Syria, the number of commando operations increased substantially, after having subsided somewhat in the preceding months as a result of the measures taken by Jordan and Lebanon to seal their border areas. The internal leadership struggle in Damascus between the ruling National Command of the Ba'th and the left wing, which became critical in the last few months of 1965, may have also accounted for this slackening of fedayeen activity. Now the difficulties on the Lebanese and Jordanian borders led the new Syrian regime to allow al-Asifah to launch several operations from the Golan Heights. On July 14, 1966, Israeli warplanes strafed the Syrian diversionary works in retaliation following four Fatah mining operations close to the Syrian borders within a twenty-four hour period. From about this time on, Israeli accusations of Syrian responsibility for arming, training, and organizing Fatah became frequent, and Damascus gradually, but indirectly, came to acknowledge this responsibility, comparing itself to Hanoi [25] and praising the fedayeen for their exploits.[26]

After another two-month lull in commando operations during July and August—due to a conflict between Fatah and the new Syrian leadership, which according to some sources was caused by the latter's attempt to assume direct control of the commando organization [27]—the incidence and effectiveness of guerrilla raids shot up dramatically, a development which considerably alarmed the Israelis. On September 11 the army magazine, *Bamahane*, published an interview with General Itzhak Rabin in which Israel's chief of staff advocated a change of strategy for Israeli retaliation designed to strike at the "Syrian regime itself." On September 14, and again at a cabinet meeting on the eighteenth, Prime Minister Eshkol spoke of Syria's role in aiding the commandos. On October 11, Eshkol summoned the ambassadors of the four Great Powers to explain to them the grave border situation, and on the next day Israel lodged a complaint with the U.N. Security Council. After meeting and debating the situation during the balance of the

25. Damascus Domestic Service, August 14, 1966.

26. *Ath-Thawrah*, editorial, October 9, 1966.

27. At a meeting of Palestinians in Algeria in January 1972, Yasir Arafat disclosed that he had spent fifty-one days in the Mazza prison in Damascus in 1966, by way of illustration of the difficulties encountered by the Resistance in its relations with Syria. See *Africasia*, No. 58 (January 24, 1972). According to Yaari, *Strike Terror*, pp. 86–93, Arafat and eleven other top Fatah leaders were imprisoned for forty days by the Syrians.

month, the council attempted to pass a resolution considered favorable to Israel. This was vetoed by the Soviet Union. On October 29, Foreign Minister Eban accused the Security Council of moral weakness, and threatened that Israel would be forced to take action to insure its security. After twelve different incidents were announced by Israel between September 6 and November 12 (involving mine explosions, the derailing of a train, and the blasting of water pipelines), which were said to have killed seven and injured twenty-three Israelis, the Israeli army finally struck on November 13. Contrary to all expectations, however, the target was Jordan, not Syria. The village of as-Samu' underwent a three-hour attack by two armored columns protected by air cover. According to U.N. figures, the raid left 18 dead and 134 wounded and resulted in the destruction of 125 houses, a clinic, and a school. Significantly, six days earlier Syria and the UAR had signed a mutual defense treaty which committed either country to go to the defense of the other in case of armed aggression.

The main development in the regional political scene in 1966 was the renewal of the conflict between conservative and revolutionary regimes. This followed the failure of several attempts to end the war in Yemen, where Egypt and Saudi Arabia had been locked in a bloody and costly test of wills since 1962, and the reactivation by Saudi King Faysal of his plans for an Islamic alliance, a move which Nasser interpreted as a challenge to his leadership in the Arab world. When Jordan took the side of Faysal in the wake of the latter's visit to Amman in January, and Hussein's quarrel with Shuqayri over the scope of PLO activities in Jordan—which had been brewing since the previous year—grew increasingly bitter in mid-1966, it became clear that the Egyptian-Jordanian détente also was at an end. This coincided with the Syrian drive to align itself with Cairo and bring about the demise of the summit era of conciliation, an effort that, as we have seen, principally took the form of a more activist anti-Israel policy. With the renewal of the Arab "cold war" following Nasser's indefinite postponement of the summit meetings on July 22, 1966, a rapprochement between Syria and Egypt became an attractive proposition for both sides.

Notwithstanding these important incentives, it is very likely that the military agreement signed in November was brought about mainly by Cairo's desire to acquire a degree of control over Syria's hazardous tactics vis-à-vis Israel. Significantly, Fatah's activities subsided completely for more than a month following the as-Samu' raid. Cairo's restraining influence was not to last, however. The resistance of King Hussein to any type of Palestinian activism on the West Bank, even by the rather innocuous PLO, had again brought to the forefront of attention the crucial issue of confrontation with Israel. Compared with the situation in late 1963, when the problem had arisen as a result of Israel's completion of its national water-carrier project, the inter-Arab political scene now did not favor conciliatory face-saving attitudes; the Palestinians themselves had acquired, both through the PLO and the emerging fedayeen groups, the means to articulate their grievances and expose or even sabotage attempts by any one regime to evade its "responsibilities to the cause"; and—most important perhaps—Syria saw its best interests served by pressing the matter to the limit. In these circumstances, no compromise was possible. The outcome was a full-throttled campaign of political pressure, denunciation, and calls to subversion against the Jordanian regime, which became particularly bitter following the raid on as-Samu'. This anti-Jordanian campaign was joined by the Ba'th, the Arab Nationalists, the Egyptian press and radio, and eventually by President Nasser himself in late December 1966. In such an atmosphere, it was practically impossible for Cairo to withstand Syrian overbidding from the left and remain opposed to the activities of the Palestinian Resistance while upbraiding Hussein for having taken precisely such a stand. The new position of the UAR was described by Nasser on February 4, 1967: "With regard to the guerrillas, if the Palestinian people and the Palestine entity are organized, they have the right to fight for their country. Naturally there may be loss of life, but it is clear to the whole world that the Palestinian people are determined to insist on their rights and to shed their blood on behalf of these rights." [28]

Consequently, in mid-December commando operations were resumed, and now Fatah was joined by other small groups, also supported by Damascus, in forays across the border. One such group was known as the Heroes of the Return, whose first operation had been carried out on October 16. Responsible for it were leftist activists within the PLO of Arab Nationalist Movement inclination. Shuqayri himself seems to have had no part in setting up this organization, though by this time the difficulties he was facing in Jordan, and his loss of prestige because of the PLO's inactivity, had led him to express verbal support for guerrilla action.[29]

The rate of commando strikes in Israel escalated substantially in

28. *Al-Ahram*, February 2, 1967. At the same news conference, Iraqi President Arif, who was visiting the UAR, expressed his support for the fedayeen in similar terms.

29. See, for example, his message to King Hussein of November 22, 1966, *al-Muharrir* (Beirut), November 23, 1966. More information on divergences within the PLO can be found in Part II, pp. 68–69.

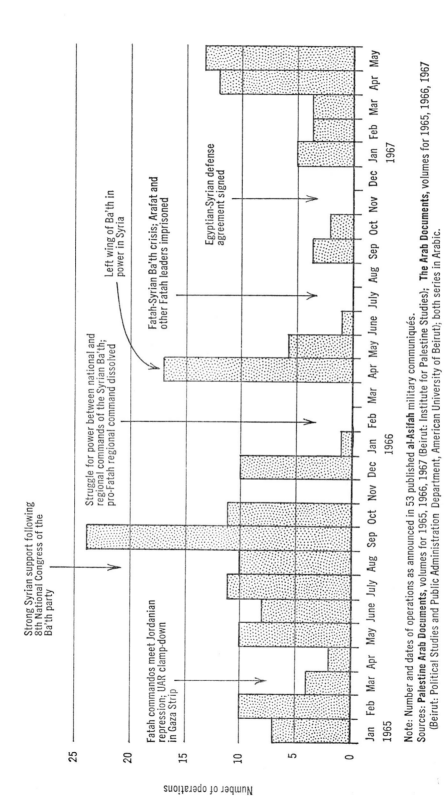

Note: Number and dates of operations as announced in 53 published **al-Asifah** military communiqués.

Sources: **Palestine Arab Documents,** volumes for 1965, 1966, 1967 (Beirut: Institute for Palestine Studies); **The Arab Documents,** volumes for 1965, 1966, 1967 (Beirut: Political Studies and Public Administration Department, American University of Beirut); both series in Arabic.

Fig. 4. Guerrilla Military Operations Carried Out by Fatah, 1965 to May 1967

the first six months of 1967, with an increase of 100 percent acknowl-edged by Israeli sources.[30] As a result, tensions between Israel and Syria continued to grow until, aggravated by armed clashes and veiled Israeli threats of invasion, they burst into the full-blown crisis of May 1967. This escalation was a natural development in view of the decrease in the severity of the constraints imposed upon feday-een activities by the political environment. The preceding survey has sought to describe some of these critical constraints and how they affected the degree of freedom of action that Fatah could muster at any given time. Figure 4 illustrates in graphic form the effect of these limitations on the level of al-Asifah's activities in the period January 1965 to May 1967. The situation obtaining at the begin-ning of 1967 remained substantially unaltered until the May crisis and the ensuing Six-Day War put an end to this first stage in the experience of the contemporary Palestinian Resistance movement.

THE DYNAMICS OF DEPENDENCE

What generalizations can be drawn at this point about the overall effects attributable to the inter-Arab political environment on the performance of the fedayeen during this period?

(1) The most important factor Fatah had to contend with in 1965–1966 was the lack of official and widespread popular support for its program of action. On the official level, this attitude was basically due to the unwillingness of the Arab governments to face the threat of a military confrontation with Israel, which commando activities were seen as bound to elicit and for which they considered themselves ill prepared. As for the masses, most Arabs continued to look to Cairo for political guidance and for leadership in any mili-tary undertaking. This factor was crucial because the geographic, political, and military conditions did not permit the development of an independent insurgent movement anywhere on the periphery of Israel that could dispense with external support. If Syria had complied with Unified Arab Command and Arab League recom-mendations to clamp down on al-Asifah, as the three other countries bordering on Israel had, the fedayeen movement would probably have ceased to exist—temporarily, at least—in the first half of 1965.

(2) This practically complete dependence of the commandos on one regime necessarily entailed a considerable surrender of their autonomy. Operationally, this resulted, first, in the forced ab-stention from raids across the Syrian-Israeli lines, which meant that

30. *The Arab War Against Israel: Statements and Documents,* Ministry of Foreign Affairs, Information Division, Jerusalem (June 1967), p. 45.

the fedayeen had to infiltrate across Jordan's west bank or the southeast of Lebanon to reach Israel's borders. More commandos were killed by the Jordanians and Lebanese while on their way to and from Israeli territory than by the Israelis during this period. This situation obviously placed severe limits on the number, magnitude, and efficacy of commando operations. Secondly, al-Asifah was able to function only on Syria's sufferance, and was forced into inaction whenever Damascus felt this was advisable. Witness the sudden cutoff following the as-Samu' raid, which came at a time of high momentum in commando activities and of critical importance for Fatah politically, as Palestinians across the ideological spectrum were then coming around to adopting its views and strategy. Nonetheless, Fatah was apparently successful in maintaining some degree of independence, particularly on the issue of noninterference in inter-Arab squabbles.

(3) The evident unwillingness of even "progressive" regimes to tolerate the existence of independent Palestinian militant organizations, and the facility with which they could isolate and neutralize any such groups when acting in unison, obviously impressed Fatah's leaders with the necessity of diversifying their sources of official support on the one hand, and of generating a protective cushion of mass popular backing on the other. Both of these objectives were to be actively, and successfully, pursued in the period of expansion following the June war. Fatah could not fail to observe that its continued existence throughout 1965–1967 had been a function of Arab dissension, and was therefore careful to cultivate relationships in both conservative and progressive camps. This rather delicate task was to be rendered feasible by Fatah's early insistence on the need for "total concentration on the Palestinian battleground . . . and forbearance of diversionary fires," [31] as well as its ideological moderation.

(4) In terms of achievements, Fatah's most notable accomplishment in perspective was that it laid the groundwork for the resurgence of the Resistance movement as a principal contestant in the aftermath of the June defeat. This it did by introducing and gradually asserting among the Palestinians the conception of guerrilla warfare as a viable alternative to action within the traditional framework of Arab political institutions, for the sterility of which the PLO stood as a prime example. Though the effectiveness of its operations against the Israelis was considerably limited, largely because of the obstacles placed in its path by most Arab regimes, it

31. See "Fatah Starts the Dialogue and Replies to the *Filastin* Article," in *Filastin,* No. 37 (March 24, 1966).

had succeeded by mid-1967 in what it considered a more crucial and fundamental task at this stage: attracting many Palestinians to the path of armed struggle and winning their confidence in its prescription for eventual victory. "We do not pretend at all that we have attained the stage of revolution in our operations. Our operations in the occupied territory can never attain the hoped-for revolutionary stage unless they rally around them all the sectors of the Palestinian people, who are the true stock for the battle of return. Our present operations are the candle that points to the correct path," [32] said a Fatah statement fourteen months after the launching of its activities. It is an index of this success that, when the Six-Day War began on June 5, at least four different organizations, representing a variety of political and ideological persuasions among the Palestinians, were engaged in commando operations on Israeli territory.

(5) Another factor illustrated by the preceding analysis, and probably the most significant because of the effects it had on the relationship between the Resistance movement and the Arab governments after the June war, is the central place occupied by the Palestine issue in the politics of the region. Unceasingly evoked and constantly played upon, the theme of the unavoidable confrontation with Israel and the eventual recovery of Palestine—whatever its political, strategic, or nationalist rationale, and regardless of the degree of purposefulness with which it has been practically pursued—was elevated through the dynamics of inter-Arab conflicts into one of the crucial tests of political legitimacy and acceptability for nearly every regime in the Arab world. The consequent semiautomatic commitment of the Arab capitals to the anti-Israel struggle was to provide the Palestinian Resistance movement with a valuable bargaining asset and a powerful lever for eliciting material and moral support following the war of June 1967.

32. *Ibid.;* see also the Fatah pamphlet entitled *How Will the Armed Popular Revolution Break Out,* in the series, "Revolutionary Lessons and Experiences," especially pp. 14–16.

2

THE ARAB WORLD
AFTER THE DEFEAT

THE SIX-DAY WAR AND THE RISE OF THE RESISTANCE

The swift events of June 5–10, 1967, with their far-reaching effects
on the military and political dimensions of the Arab-Israeli conflict,
fundamentally altered the terms of the relationship that had previously existed between the Palestinian guerrillas and the Arab
states. From an obscure, politically dependent and militarily insignificant coterie of commando bands, the Resistance movement
turned within months into a formidable political contestant and
pivotal element on the Arab scene, and a grass-roots movement with
few parallels in the contemporary history of the Middle East.

Prior to the June war, the fedayeen had lacked two basic requirements for the successful launching of a strong and self-assertive
Resistance movement: a convincing and inspiring strategy, and an
adequate manpower pool. Not only the Arab regimes directly involved in the confrontation with Israel but their peoples as well,
including the Palestinians, had looked upon their conventional
military forces as both their shield against Israeli aggression and the
eventual instrument for the recovery of Palestine. Throughout the
sixties, a large percentage of their GNP was expended by Egypt,
Jordan, and Syria on building up the armed forces. By the middle
of the decade, these forces were widely regarded in the area as
sufficiently strong to face a showdown with the Israelis. This esti-
mate was shared by the fedayeen themselves, who were bent on

provoking through their activities the desired military confrontation, in the belief that the outcome would be favorable to the Arab side. Their role in the envisaged strategy, however, was basically incidental. They would bring about the decisive battle and, once this was engaged, fight behind the enemy lines in traditional guerrilla fashion. But the task of liberation was ultimately to be accomplished by the conventional Arab armies in the field, presumably with the political aspects of the struggle fully under the control of the Arab capitals. In other words, even by their admission, the fedayeen—and the Arabs in general—still had to look toward Cairo, Damascus, and Amman for the fulfillment of their aspiration of recovering Palestine.

The absence of a stimulating alternative plan for liberation that could provide a focal rallying point and a basis for a powerful and politically significant Resistance movement was complemented by a second debilitating factor, namely, the limited recruitment base available. Even if Fatah had offered a viable and realistic alternative strategy based on a Vietnamese-style revolutionary war, it would have been hard put to raise sufficient manpower to develop into a significant threat to Israeli security. The natural manpower source would have been the Palestinian refugees still living in camps and urban slums in Jordan, Syria, and Lebanon (the Gaza Strip being under tight Egyptian control and therefore politically as well as geographically isolated). These were the Palestinians who had fled their land in 1947–1948 and who had failed to become economically integrated, either in the host countries neighboring on Israel or in other parts of the Arab world. They were extremely poor, mostly unemployed, and instilled with strong nationalist fervor. However, even in the unlikely event that Jordan and Lebanon would not have erected serious obstacles in the way of a large-scale mobilization of the refugees under their jurisdiction for irregular warfare against Israel, the recruitment pool provided by these disaffected elements was limited. The number of male Palestinian refugees in Jordan, Syria, and Lebanon between the ages of fifteen and forty-five who were presumably not self-supporting and who continued to receive full UNRWA rations as of May 1967 did not exceed 100,000 (out of a total refugee population of some 536,000 in this category above age fifteen),[1] and only a small portion of these would have

1. From the Report of the Commissioner-General of UNRWA for the period 1 July 1966 to 30 June 1967. The manpower readily available was probably even more limited than these figures suggest, as a substantial proportion of these male refugees were in fact gainfully employed and supporting their families. See Don Peretz, "The Palestine Arab Refugee

been sufficiently motivated to join the Resistance and physically fit for military action.

This situation was practically reversed following the June war. The quick defeat and almost complete destruction of Arab conventional forces, as well as the occupation of all of Palestine and substantial Egyptian and Syrian territories, left the Arab world in a stunned, traumatic state in which all defenses were down, and all options—except submission to the accomplished fact—seemed to be foreclosed. The costly conventional war machine in which so much confidence had been placed lay in ruins, and all hopes for the restoration of Palestine in the foreseeable future, nurtured for two long decades, were suddenly dashed. The ensuing vacuum was not just military; it was primarily political. The sudden defeat shattered the prestige and moral leadership of conservative and revolutionary regimes alike. The evident lack of coordination between the centers of political decision during the fighting, and the deception practiced in the first days of the war only to be immediately replaced by the shocking admission of the magnitude of the debacle, greatly undermined the authority and credibility of the established governments, already badly tarnished by the defeat itself. Even further discredit came as a result of the vacillation and political maneuvers that prevented for almost three months the holding of the summit meeting that the UAR and Jordan had called for as early as June 6 to coordinate Arab action in face of the Israeli onslaught. In the disconcerting aftermath, while Israel consolidated its newly acquired gains, the Arab leadership appeared busily engaged in the traditional motions of the intraregional political game.

In this atmosphere of utter official disarray and almost total popular political disorientation and fluid allegiances, the renewed call of the Palestinian fedayeen to armed resistance at the beginning of October 1967,[2] coupled with the actual resumption of commando operations in the preceding month, was embraced with enthusiasm by most Arabs and particularly by the largely augmented bulk of displaced Palestinians. The practicality of commando warfare in conditions of complete Israeli military superiority was not even questioned—with one or two notable exceptions.[3] Moreover, it was

---

Problem," in Hammond and Alexander, eds., *Political Dynamics in the Middle East.*

2. See the political statement issued by Fatah in *al-Hurriyah* (Beirut), October 2, 1967.

3. See, for instance, Muhammad Hasanayn Haykal's article in *al-Ahram,* August 16, 1968, in which a comparison is drawn between demographic and topographic conditions in Algeria, Vietnam, and Palestine.

argued that, with more than a million Palestinians now under Israeli control, a classical movement of national resistance based on the local population could be launched. On the popular level, the fedayeen strategy of guerrilla war was finally consecrated in March 1968 with the battle of Karameh, in which an Israeli armed column trying to destroy guerrilla bases on the eastern bank of the Jordan met with resistance by the fedayeen, aided by Jordanian forces, and sustained comparatively heavy losses in men and equipment. Hailed as the first Arab victory over the Israeli army since 1948, Karameh enhanced even further the prestige of the Palestinian commando groups, particularly Fatah, and brought them increased backing on the government level. The number of supporters seeking to join the ranks of the Resistance multiplied rapidly for the remainder of the year, and so did financial contributions, which poured in from Palestinian circles.

By February of 1969, when the leadership of the Palestine Liberation Organization was taken over by Fatah—and the guerrilla movement thereby became the official representative of the Palestinian people—the fedayeen had become a leading political force in the Middle East, with a distinctive ideology, a clearly defined program of action, a set strategy, and political as well as military means for their execution.[4]

The established regimes had to come to terms with this force in one way or another, but could no longer afford to ignore it. The commando groups that operated from Gaza in 1955–1956 and Syria/Jordan in 1965–June 1967 had acted under the aegis and strict control of Cairo and Damascus respectively. Their dependence on the regimes, resulting from their inherent physical weakness plus the lack of popular support, turned them into instruments of the host governments, even when they were not the latter's creation (as they had been in the case of the Gaza commandos). The main Resistance organizations that came to the fore in the aftermath of the June war were largely autonomous, newly organized groups that rose in critical circumstances to fill a political vacuum and answer emotional popular needs. This rapidly led to their acquiring a substantial degree of legitimacy and mass support. These two assets soon enabled the fedayeen movement to assert itself as a coequal of the established regimes and claim the exclusive right to determine the future of the Palestinian people.

This emphasis on the popularity of the commandos should not be allowed to obscure the plain fact that the Resistance remained highly dependent on official Arab backing, particularly—but not

4. See Part II, pp. 52–74.

exclusively—by Syria and Egypt. This backing fulfilled an essential role and was expressed basically in two forms: political guardianship —protecting the movement from antagonistic governments; and material assistance—providing the guerrillas with the funds and weapons that enabled them to develop into a strong force in a short period of time. But this dependence was not without its price, which the Resistance paid largely in terms of governmental interference in its internal affairs, both directly and through government-sponsored fedayeen groups. The proliferation of commando organizations witnessed during 1968 and 1969 is traceable partly to ideological splits and partly to the desire of various Arab regimes to extend their influence within the growing Resistance by creating groups that would represent their interests and be counted on to follow their directives. The Vanguards of the Popular War of Liberation (better known as Sa'iqa) and the Arab Liberation Front, which rank in terms of military strength among the larger commando groups, were set up and trained, armed and financed by Syria and Iraq respectively. While perhaps independently established, other smaller organizations were so dependent on one source of financial support that they were practically under the political control of their sponsors. Such was the case of the Action Organization for the Liberation of Palestine and the Organization of Arab Palestine, both of which were funded by the UAR.[5] In general, this had the effect of increasing internal squabbling in the movement and sharpening conflict over vital issues of organizational integration and ideology.

CONTINUITY AND CHANGE IN THE ARAB POLITICAL SCENE

The basic pattern of inter-Arab politics was not substantially affected by the 1967 war. Only two important shifts became evident in the second half of that year. Both, however, were to have considerable impact on the relationship between the fedayeen and Arab governments.

First, the Israel issue naturally became the overriding concern of several Arab countries, particularly those bordering on Israel, as a result of the territorial losses incurred and of the strategic implications of the new status quo for security. The new balance of forces underscored the fact that containment of Israel could no longer be relegated to second place; it also lowered the threshold of risk and

5. Predictably, these two organizations were the only fedayeen groups to express support for Cairo's acceptance of the Rogers peace initiative in the summer of 1970.

was bound to make the regimes wary of destabilizing elements—such as the Palestinian commando organizations—that might cause them to lose control of the situation.

Second, there was a strong rapprochement between Cairo and Amman, virtually a political alliance born of the shared interest of the two regimes in recovering the territories lost in the Six-Day War, and the realization that if either reached a separate settlement with the Israelis, this could be disastrous for the other, while a joint negotiating stance would be advantageous to both. The precarious viability of Jordan's economy following the loss of the West Bank and the sudden influx of some 215,000 new refugees into the East Bank lent credence to reports circulating in the aftermath of the war to the effect that King Hussein would not be averse to seeking some form of unilateral peaceful solution with Israel. Moreover, it was clear that a united front and close consultations would have to be maintained if a political settlement was to be sought by the two governments over the opposition of other conservative and revolutionary Arab regimes that could afford a more militant and uncompromising stance. The value of King Hussein as a channel of communication and bridge with the West was duly appreciated by President Nasser,[6] and in several instances the Jordanian monarch sounded out ideas and initiatives in the West that originated in Cairo. Though this Cairo-Amman axis was subject to occasional stress, and eventually broke down in the aftermath of Jordan's suppression of the Resistance in September 1970, it proved to be unusually resilient while it lasted, and did considerably affect the relationship between the fedayeen and the Jordanian government, mainly in the direction of allowing the regime more leeway in its attempts to control the guerrillas than it would have otherwise enjoyed.

Aside from these developments, there was a basic continuity of both the major issues and the behavioral patterns that have characterized inter-Arab politics for nearly two decades. The ideological rift between moderate and conservative regimes friendly to the West and socialist, radical governments was not resolved but merely papered over in the postwar drive for a unified stand to "eliminate the consequences of the setback." The bitter exchange of slogans

6. On June 7, 1967, the third day of the war, Nasser instructed the Joint Arab Command chief of staff, General Abd al-Mun'im Riyadh, who was in charge of the eastern front, that "there is no need for Jordan to sever relations with America and Britain." Text of cable is in Sa'd Jum'ah, *The Conspiracy and the Battle of Destiny* (in Arabic) (Beirut: Dar al-Kitab al-Arabi, 1968), p. 248.

and invective that periodically erupted in the past between the two camps was not immediately renewed, primarily because the main source of friction between Saudi Arabia and the UAR throughout the sixties, the Yemen civil war, was eliminated following the disengagement agreed to in August 1967 at the Khartoum summit conference. A cornerstone of this détente were the subsidies paid by Saudi Arabia, Kuwait, and Libya to the UAR and Jordan to the tune of £135 million sterling per year in compensation for losses stemming from the closure of the Suez Canal and the Israeli occupation of the West Bank.[7] The oil-rich countries thereby secured the abandonment of the partial oil embargo clamped down after the June war and the rejection of an Iraqi plan submitted to the Khartoum conference which called for further "utilization of the Arab oil as a weapon against the countries that supported the aggression." [8] Though on the surface the fever of the ideological conflict seemed to have temporarily abated, the failure of diplomatic endeavors to bring about Israeli withdrawal, the strengthening of the "progressive" block by the accession of Libya and the Sudan in 1969, and the rise of leftist Palestinian organizations professing Marxist-Leninist ideas and openly promoting social revolution throughout the Arab world as well as the overthrow of existing regimes, are all factors that have accentuated the ideological motif in regional politics and resulted in an increased radicalization of thought and expectations among the politically aware.

More recently, the picture has become somewhat more complex. In the wake of Nasser's death in September 1970, Egypt has perceptibly moved toward a moderate-centrist position under the more "Egyptian" rule of President Anwar as-Sadat. The latter, far from attempting to step into the role of standard-bearer of militant Arab nationalism, has strenuously sought to achieve a peacefully negotiated and comprehensive settlement of the Arab-Israeli problem through the medium of the West, principally the United States, even at the price of drastically reducing the militarily and politically valuable, perhaps irreplaceable, connection with the Soviet Union. On the inter-Arab political scene, Sadat has projected a relatively low profile, and domestically he has attempted to liberalize the regime. This new Egyptian posture and the disappearance of Nasser's restraining influence have permitted other Arab regimes to lower their guards, and a gradual realignment of forces has occurred

7. Libya ended payments to Jordan after September 1970, and Kuwait, after some vacillation, did likewise in the spring of 1971.

8. Details of the Iraqi plan were published in *al-Ahram*, August 4, 1967.

and still continues. Some salient manifestations of this trend are the substantial rapprochement between Egypt and Saudi Arabia, and the opening to the West of the Sudan and the Republic of Yemen—symbolized by their resumption of diplomatic relations with Washington in the summer of 1972.

Anti-Israel verbal bellicosity continued to provide fertile ground for political maneuver, particularly by leftist regimes. Despite its poor performance in the June fighting, Ba'thist Syria persisted in assuming the role of zealous guardian over the rights of the Palestinians and champion of the Resistance, spawning a fedayeen organization of its own whose political leadership was entrusted to former Syrian Prime Minister Yusif Zu'ayyin. Unconditional support for the commando movement was voiced also by another aspirant to leadership in the progressive camp—Algeria. Both countries refused to accept the principle of a political settlement, or the notion that the state of war be ended and recognition of Israel be granted by the Arabs in exchange for Israeli withdrawal.[9] Syria was the only Arab country to boycott the Khartoum summit, which the semiofficial daily, *ath-Thawrah*, described as "the latest podium for the advocates of the liquidation of the Palestine cause."[10] Algeria sent its foreign minister, who took no active part in the proceedings. Shortly afterwards, the mouthpiece of the Algerian ruling FLN called, in an editorial, for the adoption of a strategy of people's war against Israel, while stating that "the struggle against Zionism has not only patriotic content; it has ideological content as well: the progressive regimes against those regimes that are not."[11] Syria sounded similar summons to immediate resumption of military hostilities through a pooling of the resources of the progressive states (identified as the UAR, Iraq, Algeria, and Syria) and joining "the ranks of popular resistance throughout the great Arab nation, transform[ing] it into armed resistance, and bring[ing] about total confrontation with any support that colonialism may have in the Arab world, whether political, economic or social."[12] Thus, the conflict with Israel and the strategy of guerrilla warfare were seen as an integral part of a larger struggle pitting the revolutionary Arab socialist bloc against Western-oriented, traditionalist

9. See the statement by the foreign minister of Syria, I. Makhus, in *an-Nahar*, August 17, 1967; the speech of the Algerian president, Boumedienne of August 30, 1967, in *al-Mujahid* (Algiers), September 3, 1967.

10. *Ath-Thawrah* (Damascus), August 30, 1967.

11. *Révolution Africaine* (Algiers), September 10, 1967.

12. "Statement of the National Command of the Syrian Ba'th Party on the Proceedings of the Ninth Extraordinary National Conference," *al-Ba'th*, September 18, 1967.

regimes. Both instances further illustrate the close connection between the Palestinian policy of any particular Arab government and its intraregional political and ideological interests—with the latter taking clear precedence—that was pointed up by the Syria-Fatah relationship before the June war.

The conservative regimes have been hardly less extreme in their pronouncements. Saudi Arabia refused to recognize the cease-fire of June 8, 1967, which ended the war on the Jordanian and Egyptian fronts, and took a similar stand on the United Nations Security Council Resolution of November 22, 1967, vowing unceasing war against Israel until the Palestinians recover their full rights and the Muslim holy places in Jerusalem are retrieved. This attitude was shared by Kuwait, whose prime minister stated shortly after the war that his country "will never agree to cessation of hostilities" and that "there is no question of negotiations, direct or indirect." [13] An obvious role is played by such declaratory policies, by the subsidies paid to the front-line countries, and by the substantial financial aid provided to moderate Palestinian organizations in quieting down objections of Arab radicals to these countries' friendly relations with the West and in minimizing disruptions to the flow of oil.

In general, the net practical effect of the rigid, formalistic stands taken by these governments, be they radical or conservative, toward the Palestine problem has been to render even more difficult any agreement on joint action among Arabs, and to accentuate further their chronic disunity. Intended primarily for domestic consumption, these postures have lacked credibility, either because they have not been backed by corresponding capabilities, or because they are out of tune with the broader policies and commitments of the states concerned. Nevertheless, they have succeeded in setting limits to the flexibility and room for political maneuver of those countries—primarily Egypt and Jordan—that felt a pressing need to recover the territories lost in 1967 and have therefore been ready to compromise where necessary.

Had it not been for President Nasser's enormous personal prestige and considerable political acumen, it is doubtful whether such compromise proposals as the November 22 U.N. resolution or the Rogers plan of June 1970 would have had much currency in the Arab world. The Khartoum conference adopted the principles of "no peace with Israel, no recognition of Israel, no negotiations with Israel, and that the Arab nations shall take action to safeguard the right of the people of Palestine to their homeland." [14] Even this

13. *Ar-Rai al-Aam* (Kuwait), June 29, 1967.
14. Texts of Conference Statement and Resolutions in *al-Ahram,* September 2, 1967.

restrictive formula was reached over the vigorous objections of the Palestinian representative, PLO chairman Shuqayri. (Shuqayri eventually withdrew from the meeting after an acrimonious debate with King Hussein and the Sudanese premier, Muhammad Mahjub, and as a result of the conference's failure to adopt a set of principles submitted by the PLO, which included, among other injunctions, a refusal to negotiate even indirectly with Israel, recognize even the pre-June 5 status quo, or reach "any settlement that may affect the Palestine cause." [15]) When the November 22 resolution was passed less than three months later, embodying far-reaching concessions to Israel, Egypt found it acceptable, however, and gradually made it the basis of its negotiating position. For those regimes that urged unyielding militancy, Nasser had caustic words similar to those the Egyptians were to address to Iraq in the summer of 1970 when the Baghdad Ba'thists tried to capitalize on Cairo's acceptance of the Rogers plan: "We are not prepared to listen to those who advocate immediate war. These people have never been in a war in their lives, and they have no intention of being in one." [16] In the same speech, he repeatedly affirmed his determination to seek a political solution.

In short, by the end of 1967 it was clear that the forces that had shaped the inter-Arab political scene before the June war—the constant tensions between conservative and revolutionary, the challenges to Egypt's regional leadership from both the right and the left, the manipulation of the Palestine issue—continued unabated in the aftermath of that conflict.[17] They have constituted to a large extent the political environment in which the emergent Palestinian Resistance movement has had to operate, and have defined the constraints that the different fedayeen organizations have had to grapple with in their quest for unhindered action combined with overall Arab support and assistance.

15. *Al-Muharrir*, September 18, 1967.

16. In a speech at the opening of a new session of the National Assembly, *al-Ahram*, November 24, 1967.

17. For a more detailed treatment, see Malcolm H. Kerr, "Regional Arab Politics and the Conflict with Israel," in Hammond and Alexander, eds., *Political Dynamics in the Middle East.*

3
THE ARAB REGIMES
AND THE PALESTINIAN
REVOLUTION

POST-JUNE 1967 ALIGNMENTS

Three more or less well-defined groupings gradually evolved among the Arab countries as they faced the consequences of the Six-Day War and redefined their future policies and their attitudes toward the Palestine problem. The first grouping consisted of the UAR, Jordan, and regimes close to Cairo, such as the Sudan and Iraq (then under the rule of Abd ar-Rahman Arif). It had as its overriding objective the recovery of the Israel-occupied territories, and was willing to envisage political solutions to this effect and compromise on issues that had been fundamental to the Arab position since the establishment of the Jewish state in 1948, including the recognition of Israel and the conclusion of a definitive peace. These governments were naturally reluctant to destabilize the situation or reinforce Israeli feelings of insecurity and motivations for territorial annexation by adopting intransigent postures. Consequently, they did not look with favor upon a strong, militant Palestinian movement with irredentist aspirations, though they could not directly disavow it because of its popular support. Other Arab countries that adhered to this position were Lebanon, Tunisia, and Morocco. As the commandos gained strength and popularity and the prospects of a political solution faded during 1968, the UAR came to see in the Palestinians a welcome partner in the military confrontation

186

that was developing and granted the commandos material aid, training facilities, and use of its radio stations. The UAR also came down on the side of the Resistance in the several crises that later developed with Jordan and Lebanon, a position dictated not only by Cairo's interest in maintaining the viability of the guerrillas but also by its obligations as leader of the progressive camp toward an ideologically kindred movement. The fedayeen realized early on, however, that this alliance was doomed to be temporary, that Egypt was interested in retrieving the lands lost in 1967, not in liberating the whole of Palestine, and that Cairo considered them to be merely an "instrument for tactical pressure" on Israel.[1]

A second group was composed of Saudi Arabia, Kuwait, and Libya (the latter until September 1969 when the new Qadhafi republican regime aligned itself with Egypt). These countries were mainly interested in protecting their vital oil exports and maintaining a modicum of friendly relations with the West, on both of which the stability of their regimes is largely dependent.[2] At the same time, complete isolation from the Arab world had to be avoided to keep pressure from the Arab left and internal opponents within tolerable limits. A compromise formula was evolved and tacitly ratified at the Khartoum summit, whereby the three oil countries would provide £135 million sterling to Egypt and Jordan in exchange for continuance of unimpeded oil supplies to Western countries. As noted earlier, on the Palestine front, these regimes have sought to neutralize radical criticism by voicing opposition to political solutions and applauding the activities of the Resistance. In spite of the ideological gap that separates them from the mainstream of Palestinian Resistance thought, both Saudi Arabia and Kuwait have provided substantial financial aid to the fedayeen. The aid has been channeled almost exclusively to Fatah, whose moderate nationalist ideology made it the least threatening of the

1. See, for instance, the interview with PLO spokesman Kamal Nasir in *Jeune Afrique*, July 14–21, 1969, p. 37. "As for President Nasser, who uses the Palestine cause to suit his own policies . . . we have never trusted him during the past two years and have not taken seriously his promises to free Palestine," said an article in the Fatah publication *al-Asifah*, August 1969.

2. Saudi Arabia, for example, obtains 80 percent of its total income from the oil industry, and is largely dependent on foreign experts and technicians, mostly West European and American, for local management and essential services, such as water and electrical supplies, development projects, etc. See Tom Dammann, "Saudi Arabia's Dilemma: An Interview with King Faisal," in *Interplay* (New York), September 1970, pp. 16–19.

important commando organizations.[3] In the final analysis, notwith-standing their rhetorical militancy, both of these countries can be expected to support a political settlement once it is reached, and would not regret the demise of the guerrillas, particularly in view of the apparent increasing radicalization of the Resistance groups, including Fatah, since early 1970.

Syria, Algeria, and Iraq—the latter following the Ba'thist coup of July 17, 1968, which overthrew the pro-Egyptian Arif regime—make up the third grouping, which has been characterized by an outspoken rejection of all nonmilitary solutions to the Arab-Israeli conflict, and an insistence on the viability and adequacy of a total war of popular liberation of the Vietnamese type as the only "win-ning" strategy against Israel. These governments consistently ex-pressed strong, unreserved support for the Palestinian Resistance. Yet, on the level of action, this backing has not been unconditional, as both Syria and Iraq have had to weigh the effects of their posture and of a large fedayeen presence in their countries on the shaky stability of their regimes. Since the takeover of power by General Asad in Syria in late 1970 and the union of this country with Egypt and Libya in the Federation of Arab Republics in September 1971, the position of the Damascus government regarding a political settlement has softened considerably. As for Algeria, its geographi-cal remoteness and its increasing concentration on economic devel-opment since 1969—which has led Boumedienne's government to adopt a more pragmatic stance in foreign affairs—have limited the extent of the Algerian connection with the Resistance, although moral support and some material aid have been regularly main-tained.[4]

THE NEED FOR A SECURE BASE

The active backing of some first-line Arab governments and at least the tacit acquiescence of others have proven indispensable for the survival and growth of the Palestinian commando movement.

3. During a visit to Saudi Arabia in June 1969, Yasir Arafat is reported to have criticized the blowing up by the PFLP of the petroleum pipeline transporting Saudi oil to the Sidon terminal in Lebanon as "contrary to the general interests of true fedayeen action." *Al-Hayat* (Beirut), June 13, 1969.

4. Some friction developed between Algeria and the PFLP in Septem-ber 1968 following the Front's hijacking of an El Al airliner to Algiers. In general, Algeria has tended to favor Fatah and in 1969 undertook a promotional campaign in Western Europe on its behalf. *Le Monde*, February 27, 1969.

The struggle waged thus far by the fedayeen against Israeli occupation has not conformed to the model of traditional guerrilla warfare or popular war of liberation, as the Palestinian commandos themselves acknowledge. A slim chance of launching a popular war in the West Bank existed in the second half of 1967, while the Israeli hold on this area was still weak and mobility across the Jordan River was relatively unimpeded. Though Fatah tried to develop a climate of widespread civil disobedience, smuggled arms into the West Bank, and created an incipient underground network, the attempt to bring about a general insurrectionary situation eventually misfired. Whatever the reasons for this failure—principal among which probably was the fear on the part of the local inhabitants that large-scale revolt would provide the Israelis with a handy excuse for their wholesale ejection—the fedayeen had no recourse but to fall back on their pre-June war strategy of commando-type, hit-and-run raids across the cease-fire lines as their main mode of operation.

The smallness of the enemy theater and the tight Israeli military control over both Israel proper and the West Bank and Gaza Strip made it impossible for the guerrilla units to stay in enemy-held territory longer than was necessary to complete their assignments. The existence of nearby sanctuary areas thus became essential if a steady level of operations was to be maintained once the option of locally based armed revolution was foreclosed. These sanctuaries or "secure bases" were obviously needed for training, regrouping, and logistic resupply as well. Needless to say, the bases had to be located in the periphery countries—Jordan, Syria, Lebanon—and this automatically raised the crucial dilemma of the inevitable dependence of the Resistance in matters vital to its survival on factors and centers of decision external to itself and liable to be sharply antagonistic.

The large potential for confrontation between the guerrilla organizations and the host regimes arose both from the natural operational requisites of any large-scale paramilitary organization— which by themselves would be sufficient to cause substantial friction —and the policy of across-the-border retaliation that Israel had developed since the 1950s to counter fedayeen activities. This policy was bound to exert great pressure on the host regimes, given the Israeli military preponderance after the Six-Day War, which rendered the Arab countries on the eastern front practically defenseless.

At the end of 1967, once it became clear to the commando leadership that the revolutionary situation in the West Bank had failed to materialize, Fatah decided to establish its "secure bases" in regions beyond Israeli control. Some of the key specifications for these sanctuaries were that they should be (1) under the total control of the Resistance; (2) near enemy territory so as to enable the commandos to carry out their operations; (3) in areas populated by large numbers of Palestinians, who would naturally be the main sources of support and manpower, the "feeding ground" denied them on the West Bank; and (4) in locations that would "enable the revolutionaries to resist the siege and annihilation operations of the enemy," that is, at a safe distance from the cease-fire lines.[5] The obvious choice was the East Bank of Jordan, in view both of the long borders with occupied territory and of the large numbers of Palestinians there, which had swelled with the postwar influx to fully two-thirds of the kingdom's population. Great efforts were devoted throughout 1968 to building up this "secure base," with training camps established by the different commando groups the length of the Jordanian territory, from Tiberias in the north to the areas south of the Dead Sea. This task was greatly facilitated by the battle of Karameh, which gave an enormous boost to the prestige of the Resistance and obliged King Hussein to become more tolerant of fedayeen activities within Jordan.

The fedayeen presence in Lebanon developed in 1969 and was triggered mainly by the diverse measures taken by the Israelis along the Jordan River to impede commando infiltration, including ambushes, patrols, minefields, and electronically monitored fences. The south of Lebanon also offered topographic features favorable to guerrilla warfare and was not separated from the relatively industrialized and heavily populated northern part of Israel by any natural barriers. In attempting to establish permanent bases there, the fedayeen broke one of their own rules, however, by disregarding the fact that there were practically no Palestinians residing in the border areas of southern Lebanon. Though the local Lebanese were initially sympathetic and cooperative, the onset of systematic Israeli retaliation in the second half of 1969, in the form of artillery barrages, extended raids on border villages, and air strikes, soon strained relations between the commandos and the local inhabitants, in some instances to the breaking point.[6] The exodus of large numbers of southerners to the Lebanese interior, particularly the Beirut area, which by early July 1970 had reached 22,853 persons,[7] created

5. *Fateh* (Beirut), April 17, 1970.

6. On January 15, 1970, an office belonging to the Sa'iqa organization was burned down by the inhabitants in the southern town of Nabatiyyah, and demonstrations took place in this and other towns protesting the commando presence. *An-Nahar* (Beirut), January 16, 1970.

7. Official figures announced by the governor of southern Lebanon on July 4, 1970. *An-Nahar*, July 5, 1970.

an atmosphere that worked to the disadvantage of the commandos and henceforth enabled the army and the government to progressively tighten restrictions on their freedom of movement and even attempt to dislodge them forcefully from their positions in the south and the southeast of the country.

Despite strong Syrian backing for the Resistance, the cease-fire lines in the Golan area remained mostly quiet in the period after the June war. There appeared to be a continuity of the arrangement prevailing before the war between Fatah and the ruling Ba'thists. The post-June situation differed from the prior one, however, in the sense that the fedayeen movement was no longer under the tutelage of Damascus, or at its mercy. Its main forces, bases, and command structure were now in Jordan, and the new Syrian-Israeli lines were substantially longer and more easily penetrable than the heavily fortified borders along the Golan Heights. This suggests that the fedayeen's abstention from using Syria's territory to launch operations against the Israelis was not simply due to Syrian injunction or Palestinian impotence but was a mutually agreeable and tacitly established policy designed to insure the Syrian regime's support for the Resistance.

Although the Resistance movement sought sanctuary and territorial control on the Jordanian East Bank—which it largely obtained during 1968–1969—its actual *secure* base has always been in Syria, where such stronghold has taken a political rather than a territorial form. The commando leadership knew from past experience that a powerful and independent fedayeen presence would not be tolerated in the long run by the Jordanian and Lebanese regimes for varied reasons, particularly if it became effective enough to trigger large-scale Israeli retaliation, and that there would be attempts at its expulsion or liquidation. Strategically located and ideologically compatible, Syria could provide adequate sanctuary from Arab threats and could serve as an essential logistics supplier and rear base. This was fully borne out by the events of September 1970 in Jordan, when the assistance rendered by Syria to the commandos, both in terms of matériel supplies and participation in the fighting, enabled the latter to stand their ground against the Jordanian army for several days and retain control temporarily of some areas and towns (such as Jarash and Ajlun) in the northwestern section of the country. Significantly, a number of subsequent clashes between Jordanian military and the fedayeen were caused by the Jordanians' repeated attempts to cut off the road that linked the guerrilla strongholds with Syrian territory.[8] The importance of Syria's support was finally underscored by the fact that, as Resis-

8. *New York Times,* October 19, December 7 and 9, 1970.

tance spokesmen duly admitted, she was the only Arab country to come to the aid of the Palestinians in that critical showdown.[9]

THE FEDAYEEN AS A DOMESTIC FACTOR

As a result of the growing strength of the Palestinian Resistance after 1968, as well as the implications of its activities for the security of the states bordering on Israel, the nature and extent of the fedayeen presence in each of these countries was bound to become a contentious domestic issue. The commando presence itself proved to be a strongly destabilizing element in polities that have seldom known other than the most precarious political stability. This was particularly evident in Jordan, where this presence posed a long-term challenge to the very existence of the Hashemite regime and the integrity of the state, even under the optimal conditions of a return to the territorial status quo of June 4, 1967. The impact on Lebanon was slightly less upsetting.

Lebanon

The commando buildup in Lebanon that began in October 1968 soon became highly visible and had serious consequences. As in Jordan, fedayeen political and organizational activities were quickly extended to the refugee camps sprawling on the outskirts of the main cities—Beirut, Sidon, Tripoli. Border raids on Israeli settlements and mortar barrages from Lebanese territory became a frequent occurrence. By April 1969, the Palestinian Resistance was on the verge of turning Lebanon for the first time since 1948 into an active and direct participant in the Arab military confrontation with Israel. This soon jeopardized the continuity of the political system by undermining the uneasy domestic consensus on Lebanon's political relationship to the Arab world as first embodied in the National Pact of 1943,[10] and plunged the country into the longest and most critical government crisis in its history (aside from the 1958 civil war), bringing on once again the threat of prolonged internal strife. At the same time, fedayeen actions undercut the here-

9. See the statement by PLO spokesman Kamal Nasir in *Le Monde,* September 27–28, 1970.

10. This "gentlemen's agreement" between the Christian and Muslim leadership specified that, though Lebanon would consider itself part of the Arab world, it would maintain a neutral stance in inter-Arab affairs and friendly relations with both East and West. For an analysis of the crisis between the Resistance and the Lebanese government, see Michael Hudson, "Fedayeen are Forcing Lebanon's Hand," *Mid East* (Washington, D.C.), Vol. 10, No. 1 (February 1970), pp. 7–14.

tofore "successful" Lebanese defense policy of minimal military preparedness that had permitted Lebanon to avoid armed encounters with Israel in the past. From late April through November, the country remained without a regular government as Prime Minister Rashid Karami repeatedly failed to form a cabinet willing and able to take a stand on the issue of Palestinian activities from Lebanese territory. This tense period was punctuated by several clashes between the army on the one hand and the Resistance forces and Palestinian refugees on the other. Nonetheless, by November 1969, the fedayeen had succeeded in extracting from the Lebanese government, in what became known as the Cairo agreement, a formal recognition of their autonomous presence in the country and of their right to engage in operations from Lebanese territory subject to the principle of "coordination" with the government.

The successful penetration of Lebanon by the Resistance movement provides a persuasive example of its main asset at work: popular support. Though the number of Palestinians in the country does not exceed 14 percent of the total inhabitants, the fedayeen were able to capitalize on the strong backing of the Muslim half of the population, which identifies itself closely with pan-Arab national (qawmi) issues, and on the strong general feeling of dissatisfaction with the government's reaction—or, rather, lack of it—to the devastating Israeli raid on the Beirut airport on December 28, 1968. Moreover, the growing number of disaffected intellectuals of all creeds who have become estranged from the political system because of its administrative inefficiency, the immobilism fostered at all decision-making levels by the confessional balance on which the system rests, and the closed nature of the political arena, which continues to be dominated by the traditional zu'ama (notables) of the landed and moneyed classes, found in the issue of freedom of action for the fedayeen from Lebanon a rallying cause with which to challenge the "establishment." [11] Together with parties and organizations of the left, these elements made up the "Lebanese na-

11. A public opinion poll conducted by an-Nahar in November 1969 shortly after the Cairo agreement was concluded showed that a surprising 85 percent of the Lebanese public favored commando operations in general, but only 62 percent were in favor of fedayeen operations from Lebanese territory. Cited in ibid., p. 14. A later survey of opinions of the fedayeen is reported in Halim Barakat, "Social Factors Influencing Attitudes of University Students in Lebanon Towards the Palestinian Resistance Movement," Journal of Palestine Studies, Vol. 1, No. 1 (Autumn 1971). Barakat found that, among Lebanese students, "sectarianism is the most highly significant determining factor of attitudes" toward the Resistance.

tional forces" which, as the PFLP's periodical *al-Hadaf* repeatedly pointed out, were the Resistance's main protection against the regime.

Syria

In Syria where, from mid-1968 on, a contest for control of the regime developed between the ruling civilian wing of the Ba'th party under Salah Jadid and the military wing led by Defense Minister Hafiz al-Asad, the Palestinian commandos became one more lever in the hands of the different factions locked in the struggle for power. Support for the Resistance was turned into an issue of internal party politics, and Sa'iqa quickly developed into a major organization of several thousand combatants in the course of 1969 and was used by the civilian leadership as a counterbalance to the military's support of the Asad group. Domestic political considerations were not the only ones in determining the Syrian decision to set up Sa'iqa. Aware of the potential effects of a strong Palestinian commando presence on the internal balance of power, the Syrian Ba'thists—and the Iraqis as well, in the case of the ALF—sought to contain and limit the local influence of the Resistance movement by creating their own guerrilla organization, while simultaneously curtailing the activities of other fedayeen groups. Throughout the 1967–1970 period, Fatah did not have a strong presence in Syria, and it faced Syrian demands for the removal of its training camps to Jordan after the creation of Sa'iqa. In the latter part of 1968, the organ of the left wing of the Popular Front for the Liberation of Palestine (PFLP), *al-Hurriyah,* reported that Damascus had even imposed border controls aimed at hindering the free movement of fedayeen across the borders with Jordan,[12] while George Habash, the leader of the main branch of the PFLP, spent over seven months in Syrian jails in 1968, accused of plotting to overthrow the regime. Yet, mindful of the substantial dependence of their movement on the continued support of Damascus, and facing major opposition in Jordan and Lebanon, the main Resistance organizations did not seek an open confrontation with the regime, which continued to lend them strong political support and material aid in their activities outside Syria. Furthermore, Fatah later found in Sa'iqa a useful ally against the PFLP in the protracted struggle that developed be-

---

12. *Al-Hurriyah* (Beirut), September 16, 1968. In Iraq, when the Arab Liberation Front was set up by Baghdad in March of 1969, the government proceeded to close down local Fatah offices and even prohibited rallies commemorating the battle of Karameh.

tween these two organizations for the leadership of the guerrilla
movement.

Jordan

The Jordanian regime's attitude toward the Palestinian armed
struggle was strongly antagonistic in the wake of the June war,
just as it had been before it. On September 4, 1967, soon after Fatah
had resumed its operations, King Hussein expressed his opposition
to the fedayeen on the grounds that their activities would increase
Israeli repression, which would drive the inhabitants of the occupied areas to flee their homes and seek refuge in neighboring Arab
countries: "I regard it as a crime that any quarter should send so-
called commandos to engage in activities which . . . can only assist
the enemy in his attempts to break the spirit of resistance to the
temporary occupation. . . . Inasmuch as I am opposed to such
methods, it is my duty—and the duty of every citizen and every
Arab—to resist them with all my power." [13] Hussein was as good as
his word. A Fatah statement released a few weeks later accused the
Jordanians of "opposing, hunting down, and arresting the commandos." [14] Similar charges were regularly made in the following
months as Jordan undertook a stiff but unsuccessful campaign to
eradicate the guerrillas from the East Bank. As pressure increased,
on February 19, 1968, barely a month before Karameh, Fatah issued
a statement in reply to another attack by King Hussein,[15] pledging
that the Resistance would not permit "anyone or any regime" to
prevent its operations.[16] Despite Jordanian opposition, the commandos were by this time firmly established in the Jordan valley,
and were progressively stepping up their raids into Israeli-occupied
territory. These drew increasing threats of retaliation from Israel,
and finally the large raid on Karameh on March 21.

The popular support that accrued to the fedayeen after the
battle of Karameh, and the increased official backing of the UAR
and other Arab governments, forced Jordan to reverse its position
and grant the commando organizations greater freedom to establish
training camps, carry out open recruitment and organizational activities, and launch operations into the occupied territories. As

13. Interview with the Jordanian News Agency, *ad-Dustur* (Amman),
September 5, 1967.
14. *Al-Hurriyah*, October 2, 1967.
15. In a special message to the Jordanian public denouncing guerrilla
activities as detrimental to the overall Arab cause, text in *ad-Dustur*,
February 17, 1968.
16. *An-Nahar*, February 21, 1968.

hopes of an early political settlement weakened during 1968 and armed clashes became more frequent on the cease-fire lines, a degree of military collaboration developed between the guerrillas and the Jordanian troops stationed along the Jordan River, with army fire covering in many instances the crossings of commando squads to and from the West Bank.

This honeymoon period was to prove short-lived. The growth of the Resistance and the challenges this brought in its wake to the security of the state as a result of Israeli retaliation, and to the authority of the regime as the guerrilla organizations attempted to extend their de facto control over the areas they occupied, set the commando movement and the Jordanian government on a collision course which eventually led to the major clashes of November 1968, February and June 1970, and the civil war of September 1970. Innumerable minor skirmishes punctuated this whole period, as tension gradually built up between guerrillas determined to secure unrestricted freedom of action and military forces that remained by and large unquestioningly loyal to the monarchy.

On the Palestine side, the situation was progressively rendered more inflammable by the actions and pronouncements of organizations of the militant left, particularly the PFLP of George Habash and the Popular Democratic Front of Nayif Hawatmah. Ideologically committed to *social* revolution in the Arab world as a prerequisite for waging a successful popular war of liberation against Israel, these groups of Marxist-Leninist orientation openly advocated the overthrow of all moderate and conservative Arab regimes, including the Jordanian, which they considered to be allied with "Western imperialism" by their common interests, and therefore indirectly with Israel and Zionism as well. Only the restraining influence of the largest organization, Fatah, which conceived of the current struggle as a *national* revolution whose primary goal was the liberation of the Palestinian homeland, made possible the series of agreements regulating the uncertain *modus vivendi* between the Resistance and the Jordanian government achieved in November 1968.

Regardless of the ideological coloration of the Resistance, Hussein's determination to control the commando movement or, alternatively, to eliminate its hold over the Palestinian population in the cities and curtail its freedom of movement and viability by restricting it to sparsely inhabited areas, was dictated by several considerations. In the first place, the establishment on the East Bank of a "secure base" for the armed struggle, which the fedayeen defined as "a place where the revolutionaries have complete control and authority" [17] with the ultimate goal of mobilizing the population politically and militarily for a popular war of national liberation [18] entailed a corresponding curtailment of the government's "authority and control" that was bound to elicit a strong reaction from the regime, particularly since Palestinians make up such a large proportion of the population. In addition to undermining the king's authority in this fashion, the commandos provoked massive Israeli reprisals against Jordanian towns, villages, and vital installations (such as the East Ghor irrigation canal in the north, which assured the livelihood of several tens of thousands of people in the Jordan valley) that further eroded the influence of the regime by repeatedly exposing its inability to protect the lives and property of its citizens from the enemy.

Furthermore, the Resistance movement's claim to being the only genuine representative of the Palestinian people and protector of its rights posed a direct challenge to the legitimacy of King Hussein's own jealously protected claim to guardianship over the Palestinians in a much more forceful manner than the similar challenge presented by Shuqayri's PLO in 1965–1966. This claim has been a cornerstone of the Hashemite state since the annexation of the rump of Palestine—the West Bank—following the establishment of Israel. In reasserting the separate identity of the Palestinian people and couching the revolution in nationalistic terms and aspirations, the Resistance movement offered an alternative set of allegiances to the Palestinian Jordanians and presented a fundamental threat to the integrity of the Jordanian state that transcended the present conflict over the future of the territories occupied in 1967 and struck at the roots of Hussein's rule.[19] The king's offer, first set forth clearly in 1969 and reaffirmed in the United Arab Kingdom project announced by Hussein in March 1972, to grant the Palestinians local autonomy on the West Bank after the latter's return to Jordanian control was clearly an attempt to contain and accommodate within the framework of Hashemite sovereignty the Palestinian national aspirations reawakened by the fedayeen.

Last, but not least, a strong guerrilla movement placed enormous obstacles in the way of a peaceful solution to the Arab-Israel prob-

17. *Fateh*, April 17, 1970.

18. A Fatah leader has described this objective as "to politicize the military struggle and militarize the political struggle. The goal is not to have just a group of guerrillas but to have a fighting people." *Klassekampen* (Oslo), May 1970.

19. "Hussein has no right to speak on behalf of the Palestinians and no authority to negotiate a settlement affecting Palestine." *Al-Asifah*, August 1969.

lem, which has ranked as the highest priority of the Jordanian government since June 1967. All the major commando groups have always been adamant in their determination to sabotage any peace
plans that fail to meet the national demands of the Palestinians and
satisfy their grievances. As advanced by the Resistance, these demands are totally incompatible with Israeli interests. Hence, any
multilateral political solution acceptable to Israel and its neighbors
was bound to provoke a showdown between the host Arab governments and the Resistance. It has long been tacitly understood by
the Arab capitals, and explicitly pointed out by the Israelis, that any
final settlement must include the cessation of hostile acts, including
Palestinian commando operations, by all states concerned. In other
words, it would be the responsibility of the Arab countries bordering on Israel to put an end to the activities of the Resistance ema-
nating from their territories. Thus, there was a basic underlying
inconsistency in the position of those governments that purported
to support the Palestinian armed struggle and simultaneously
pressed forward with attempts to effect a compromise settlement.
These two policies remained compatible only so long as no such
compromise settlement appeared imminent.

4

THE RESISTANCE
IN CRISIS

The presentation by the United States of a new set of proposals for a peaceful solution of the Middle East conflict in June 1970, and the acceptance of this so-called Rogers plan by the Egyptian and Jordanian governments, plunged the Palestinian Resistance movement into the most dangerous crisis in its short history. Unfortunately for the movement, this challenge came at a time when, though at the peak of its military strength, it was rent by deep-seated divisions among its main component groups and was suffering from a steady decline in its effectiveness and even in its popularity. The chronic problems of disunity and ideological diversity were taking their toll:

> Each commando group continued to carry out its own operations and to put out its own military communiqués. Decline was reflected too in a steady loss of credibility: when the fighting broke out in September, people had almost ceased to believe what the resistance spokesmen had to say, military bulletins had become all but unreadable, and confidence even in the fighting ability of the commandos had been shaken. While a year earlier the *fedayeen* had enjoyed the wholehearted support of almost all social strata, now only the refugee population and the poorer elements in the towns remained loyal to the resistance movement.[1]

1. Hisham Sharabi, "Palestine Resistance: Crisis and Reassessment," *Middle East Newsletter* (Beirut), January 1971.

President Nasser's unconditional acceptance of the American plan and the immediate implementation of its cease-fire clauses were seen by the fedayeen as justifying their worst fears and suspicions regarding the intentions of the Arab states to conclude a definitive peace settlement with Israel that would signal the final surrender of Palestinian national rights. Faced with this prospect, and confident of their strength and position in Jordan, the fedayeen made no secret in August and early September of their determination to impede at all costs the seemingly impending settlement. An emergency session of the Palestine National Congress met in Amman on August 27–28, but could not decide on a unified strategy to achieve this goal. For the extreme-left organizations, this could best be achieved by seizing power in Jordan, and the PFLP as well as the PDFLP openly called for the overthrow of the monarchy.[2]

Whether the circumstances were actually propitious for a final showdown with Hussein's regime was a different matter. On the wider Arab level, many capitals, including those most in favor of the Resistance, were critical of the commandos in the wake of the June events in Jordan. Responsibility for this latest major clash had been attributed to the commandos, particularly the PFLP, and not the Jordanian government. The Arab states feared that it had strengthened the extremists in both camps, Palestinian and Jordanian, further deepened the rift between the main Resistance organizations, and threatened the stability of the whole area by almost toppling the Jordanian monarchy. Furthermore, Egypt was embarking on a diplomatic offensive following its acceptance of the United States proposal and would be certain to oppose any attempts at altering the situation in Jordan.

"Nasser felt that King Hussein and the Palestinian Resistance had by necessity to co-exist," later wrote the editor of *al-Ahram*, Muhammad Hasanayn Haykal. "The liquidation of the Resistance would have rendered it impossible for King Hussein to rule, while the fall of the throne would have inevitably provoked an American intervention." [3]

Locally, the prospects were even less favorable. Following the imposition of the cease-fire with Israel in August, several units of the Jordanian army had been redeployed around Amman and King Hussein had reinstated General Zayd Bin Shakir—who had been dismissed in June at Palestinian request—as deputy chief of staff.[4]

2. *New York Times,* September 1, 1970.
3. *Al-Ahram,* December 26, 1970.
4. *Washington Post,* August 17, 1970.

The available evidence suggests that Fatah and the majority of the organizations affiliated with the PLO favored a wait-and-see attitude, despite their bitter denunciation of Cairo's move. Hence their disapproval of the PFLP's mass hijacking operation in the first week of September, which led to the suspension of the Popular Front's membership in the central committee of the Resistance. Nonetheless, the spirit animating the guerrillas in general was one of defiance, and the lack of unity and discipline within the movement, which had become increasingly acute during 1970, made it practically impossible for PLO chairman Arafat to restrain the more extreme elements indefinitely.[5]

On the Jordanian side as well, the hard-liners among Hussein's advisers gradually gained the upper hand. They recommended swift action not only to restore the badly eroded authority of the king but also to arrest the growing disaffection among the military. During the first two weeks of September, the commando presence in the southern part of Jordan was quickly and quietly eliminated.[6] On September 15, spurred by the hijacking incidents, Hussein appointed a military government under Brigadier General Muhammad Dawud—a Palestinian—and ordered it to take all necessary measures to "restore security, order, and stability" to the country.

THE CIVIL WAR AND THE ARAB ROLE

The formation of the military government virtually signalled the start of the civil war, which raged in Amman and the north of Jordan until September 25, when a cease-fire worked out with the assistance of several Arab leaders, particularly President Ga'far an-Numayri of the Sudan, was accepted by the warring parties.[7] The Jordanian government agreed to the cease-fire only after great pressure was applied in the later stages of the fighting by President Nasser and the leaders of Libya, Kuwait, Syria, the Sudan, Yemen, Southern Yemen, Tunisia, and Lebanon, who had hastily assembled in an informal summit meeting in Cairo. On September 27 a fourteen-point agreement on a *modus vivendi* was hammered

5. "By the summer of 1970 there was a serious breakdown in discipline. There were ugly incidents in which civilians and members of the Jordanian armed forces were subjected to rough or insulting treatment at the hands of fedayeen. . . . On the eve of what was to be the Jordan civil war, the Palestine resistance was divided as never before." Sharabi, "Palestine Resistance."

6. *An-Nahar Arab Report,* September 21, 1970.

7. For details of the fighting, see Part II, pp. 126–128; also *Mid-East Review,* December 1970, pp. 21–24; *Times* (London), September 25, 1970.

out in Cairo between King Hussein and Yasir Arafat.[8] An inter-Arab follow-up committee chaired by Premier Bahi Ladgham of Tunisia was formed to supervise the implementation of the Cairo agreement, and a large military mission consisting of Egyptian, Kuwaiti, Saudi, Sudanese, and Syrian elements was assembled under General Ahmad A. Hilmi of Egypt to monitor the cease-fire. The Cairo agreement was supplemented on October 13 by a further protocol signed in Amman by Jordan and the Resistance.

Despite large-scale Syrian intervention in aid of the commandos in the north of Jordan, the outcome of the ten-day fighting was highly unfavorable to the Resistance, which eventually lost a large portion of its manpower and weapons, effective control over the large towns, including the capital, and a good deal of its prestige and popularity. The attitudes of the different Arab governments toward the Resistance both during and after the September events showed few substantial differences from the past. If any major discrepancy was evident during the crisis, it was between the expectations of concrete aid from several "progressive" regimes and the unfolding reality of little practical support. As often in the past, the Palestinians again fell victims to traditional inter-Arab outbidding, this time principally on the part of Iraq, which failed, despite repeated Palestinian appeals, to make good its promise of putting at the disposal of the Resistance the Iraqi contingent of twelve thousand men stationed in northern Jordan. Even in the case of Syria, which did come to their aid, the intervention was camouflaged in such a manner as not to commit the Syrian government militarily on the side of the guerrillas. Moreover, it was basically a move in the internal struggle for power between the civilian and the military wings of the ruling Ba'th party, and this also was detrimental to the effectiveness of the Syrian action.

On the other hand, there is little doubt that the Jordanian victory would have been even more conclusive, and its cost to the Resistance movement in lives and equipment substantially higher, had it not been for the strong, in some cases violent, disapproval evinced by several Arab leaders toward Jordan and the determined general stand in favor of the Palestinians taken by practically all Arab governments. Both Libya and Kuwait stopped their much-needed financial aid to Jordan that had been agreed upon at Khartoum in 1967, and the Libyan government broke off relations with Amman, Qadhafi threatening at one point to send troops to succor the fedayeen.[9] Collective retaliatory action had been threatened on

8. Text in *An-Nahar Arab Report,* October 5, 1970.
9. *Fateh,* September 21, 1970.

September 26 by the heads of state who had assembled in Cairo after the onset of the fighting. Earlier, and perhaps more significantly, President Nasser had invoked the possibility of military intervention to stop the war in a private message to Hussein on September 20, which was not made public at the time. "I want you to know honestly that we will not allow liquidation of the Palestine Resistance," warned the Egyptian leader. "No one can liquidate it, and instead of fighting the enemy, we will find ourselves involved in an Arab civil war." [10] To underscore his concern, Nasser had also airlifted the Palestine Liberation Army brigade stationed on the Suez front to Syria to join the remaining PLA forces assembled there. At a Cairo news conference on September 26, following two trips to Jordan at the head of a mediation team, President Ga'far an-Numayri of the Sudan had accused Hussein of "genocide" and blamed him for the continuation of the fighting and the breaches of the several cease-fire arrangements concluded by his team. Finally, a military intervention of sorts had actually materialized when a large contingent of tanks bearing the insignia of the PLA—but consisting mainly of Syrian units—crossed the border into northern Jordan on September 19–20 and remained in control of the Irbid-Ramtha region until dislodged by Jordanian armor and air force units two days later and forced to withdraw back into Syria on the twenty-third. The weight of this generalized Arab disapproval was clearly reflected in the Cairo and Amman agreements, particularly the latter, which, coming a fortnight after the cease-fire and concluded under the aegis of the inter-Arab commission already deployed in Jordan, was substantially more favorable to the Resistance than was warranted by the outcome of the fighting and the ensuing balance of forces.

Yet verbal disapproval carried little weight on the battlefield, and apart from high rhetoric, noisy threats, and the limited Syrian intervention, the various Arab leaders had been unwilling—or unable—to assist the Palestinians with much else. Here, the Egyptian posture had been crucial. Committed to the preservation of the status quo in Jordan, Nasser had devoted all his efforts—in the last political act of his life—to the arduous task of marshalling sufficient pressure on Amman to obtain a cease-fire that safeguarded the integrity of the fedayeen as a political and military factor. At the same time, he sought to maintain open channels to Hussein and a suffi-

10. Text of letter published in *al-Ahram*, December 25, 1970; reproduced in English in *New Middle East*, No. 29 (February 1971), pp. 49–50. According to *al-Ahram* editor Haykal, the message was kept secret at Hussein's request.

ciently conciliatory attitude to preserve the post-1967 political "alliance" between the two countries. Also, the reactions of the United States and Israel to Syria's incursion had alerted him to the possibly grave repercussions of active external intervention. The resulting restraint in Cairo's position had dictated the tenor of the summit's reaction and virtually precluded more forceful aid to the Resistance. If the prospect of a peaceful solution to the Middle East conflict to be reached at their expense had prompted the Palestinians to seek a showdown, as the hostilities progressed they were to discover to their discomfiture that, from Egypt's viewpoint, the logic of the peaceful solution dictated the preservation of Hussein's ascendancy in Jordan. "The supreme irony" of Nasser's career, a perceptive observer has noted, "was that he died in the act of shielding his old enemy Husayn, at the expense of his old clients, the Palestinians." [11] Despite its seeming incongruity, the dilemma that had faced the Egyptian leader in September 1970 was symbolic of the ambiguous and equivocal attitude displayed by all Arab regimes toward militant Palestinian nationalism throughout its existence.

The Decline of the Fedayeen in Jordan

In the months that followed the civil war, the position of the fedayeen in Jordan continued to deteriorate as the Jordanian army, taking advantage of the weakness and disorganization of the guerrillas, progressively extended its control over most of the country. An agreement concluded between the Resistance and the government on January 15, 1971, after several days of clashes in Amman and northern areas still occupied by guerrillas, stipulated that weapons held by the Palestinian militias in the towns were to be surrendered and stockpiled in arsenals, which would, however, remain under commando supervision. Since the militias represented the major remaining armed Palestinian presence in the cities, this measure further undermined the Resistance. By mid-February 1971, Jordanian officials estimated that the number of commandos throughout the country had dwindled to five thousand men, or 25 percent of the pre–civil war figure.[12] In the meantime, the government formed shortly after the crisis under the premiership of hard-liner Wasfi at-Tal—a man widely considered to have masterminded the Jordanian victory in September—proceeded to weed out elements sympathetic to the Resistance from the bureaucracy and the armed forces, and gradually but effectively consolidated government control over the

11. Malcolm H. Kerr, *The Arab Cold War*, p. 153.
12. *Washington Post*, February 15, 1971.

urban centers. In December, the guerrillas lost the towns of Zarqa and Jarash, in March the army took over Irbid—the second largest city in the country—and finally in April the fedayeen had to evacuate Amman itself. In mid-July, constant pressure by the army against the remaining Resistance strongholds in the hilly and forested Jarash-Ajlun region, halfway between Amman and the Syrian border, culminated in a final, determined drive that resulted in the dislodgement of most of the remaining commando forces from Jordan.[13]

This deliberate and well-planned rollback and eventual elimination of the fedayeen presence in the kingdom—which only months before had appeared so well entrenched as to call into serious question the continuity of Hashemite rule—was conducted literally in the face of the Ladgham-Hilmi mission, which had been sent to Jordan on behalf of almost the entire community of Arab states presumably to prevent a further erosion of the Palestinian position. The mission faced a generally unyielding and uncooperative attitude on the part of the Jordanian civil authorities, as well as harassment and obstruction by the Jordanian army in the field. In the weeks and months that followed the civil war, it became increasingly apparent that, while breaches of the cease-fire, ambushes, raids, searches, and other incidents were being perpetrated by both sides, the initiative had largely passed to the government and the army, who fully exploited every incident to extract further concessions from the dwindling guerrilla forces. By January, Bahi Ladgham was threatening to resign if "acts of provocation" and military operations by the Jordanians against the fedayeen were not stopped;[14] by early April, he was openly accusing the Amman government of wanting "to liquidate the Palestinian Resistance in stages"[15] in the wake of the fall of Irbid to the army after substantial fighting with the PLO militias. Later that month, following Ladgham's resignation and the pullout by Cairo of its military observer group in protest at the developing situation, the inter-Arab mission in Jordan folded.

Despite the strongly critical attitude of the Ladgham-Hilmi team toward the Jordanian regime, which was reflected in public pronouncements and in its reports to the governments that had guaranteed the Cairo agreement, most Arab capitals maintained a restrained, wait-and-see stance throughout this period that belied the

13. See pp. 137–141 above for a more detailed description of these events.

14. See *Times* (London), January 12, 1971; *Le Monde*, January 13, 1971.

15. *Le Monde*, April 5, 1971.

forceful commitment to the survival of the Resistance expressed the previous September. Harsh words of condemnation were certainly not lacking, but at no time did Wasfi at-Tal find it necessary to back-track or grant the Resistance any concessions under pressure from Arab capitals. The Cairo agreement, worked out at a summit meet-ing and endorsed by eight governments, had literally stipulated that in case of violations by either the Jordanians or the Palestinians, "all the Arab countries signatory to it will take unified and collec-tive measures against the violating side." This undertaking, and the creation of the machinery for its implementation in the form of the inter-Arab mission, effectively amounted to the extension of a joint Arab custodianship over the Resistance movement. Yet it was under the umbrella of this custodianship that the Jordanian regime was able to deliver its sharpest and most crippling blows. Certainly, the September defeat had rendered the remaining military and political structure of the Resistance extremely vulnerable, and the reasser-tion of the government's control was perhaps unavoidable. But the supervisory mission's presence in Jordan blunted the edge of Arab disapproval of the Jordanian measures—which were carried out un-der the cover of cooperation with the mission—and, by allowing the regimes the appearance of dutifully protecting the Resistance, it precluded the need for further intervention on their part. More-over, it served to muffle Palestinian protestations and worked to de-prive the guerrilla leaders of the option of appealing to a wider Arab audience by providing an intermediate on-the-spot means of dealing with their grievances. As long as its actions fell short of a direct, open assault on the Resistance—and the "salami tactics" of the Tal government prior to the final onslaught of July 1971 were in the main carefully limited in their scope—the Jordanian regime correctly estimated that no significant opposition from other Arab governments was likely to materialize.

The reasons for this lack of serious concern for the fate of the commandos must again be sought in the wider political environ-ment. The very real divergence in the interests of the Resistance and the frontline governments had been submerged in the wake of the 1967 war by the latter's initial reluctance to seek openly a po-litical accommodation with Israel, and by Cairo's tactical need in 1969–1970 for an active eastern front while it conducted its unsuc-cessful war of attrition over Suez. But in the latter part of 1970 and throughout most of 1971, diplomacy, bargaining, and peaceful set-tlement became the predominant themes as Nasser's successor, An-war as-Sadat, mounted a determined diplomatic campaign, effected a partial but significant rapprochement with the United States, and granted unprecedented concessions in order to obtain Israel's withdrawal from the occupied territories, including a public commitment to sign a peace agreement with Israel guaranteeing "the inviolability and political independence of every state in the area, including Israel." [16] In this he had the support of practically every Arab government, including Syria. Only the sulky Iraqi regime—isolated from the mainstream of Arab politics since its bitter attacks on Nasser's acceptance of the Rogers plan—and, to a lesser degree, Algeria continued to speak out against the peaceful solution. The major opponent to this course of action was the Palestinian Resistance, however, and it had demonstrated in the summer of 1970 the extremes to which it would go to disrupt any prospective settlement.

The September civil war had by no means completely eliminated the power of the commando movement, but it had reduced it to a level that had compelled the fedayeen to reevaluate their position on fundamental issues and adjust their expectations to the new reality. This reevaluation was most evident in regard to the basic question of peaceful settlement with Israel. As of January 1971, the main body of the Resistance, as represented in the central committee of the PLO, no longer opposed the efforts of Egypt and other Arab regimes to recover through peaceful means the territories occupied in 1967 "so long as these attempts do not compromise the rights of the Palestinian people" and do not interfere with its armed struggle. This shift in policy by Fatah was necessary to normalize relations with Egypt, on which the movement remained heavily dependent for weapons, ammunition, medical services, and political backing against rival organizations and external enemies. Despite this apparent concession—to which the leftist guerrilla groups in any case remained adamantly opposed—it was clear that Palestinian interests would be involved in practically any arrangement to be negotiated with the Israelis, and that even a moderately strong Resistance movement could constitute a serious obstacle.

A long-standing source of support for the commandos was jeopardized by developments in Syria during the fall of 1970. On November 20, several prominent leaders of the ruling Ba'th party in Syria were ousted from power in a shake-up that was probably one of the more important side effects of the Jordanian civil war. The change

16. Interview with Arnaud de Borchgrave, *Newsweek,* February 22, 1971, p. 41. In a similar interview ten months later Sadat affirmed his willingness "to agree to direct negotiations for the drafting of a peace treaty" on condition that "Israel agrees to withdraw to international borders." *Newsweek,* December 13, 1971, p. 47.

of regime came when the military strongman of the party, Defense Minister Hafiz al-Asad, removed the neo-Marxist group of civilians headed by retired Lieutenant-General Salah Jadid, together with whom he had taken over the government in February 1966. The internal power struggle between Asad and Jadid had been a prolonged one, but it was the Syrian intervention in Jordan instigated by Jadid, presumably over Asad's opposition, that appears to have brought matters to a head.[17] The new government soon set out to establish closer relations with Cairo, and in the spring of 1971 became a founding member of the Federation of Arab Republics along with Egypt and Libya. More willing to entertain the possibility of a negotiated settlement with Israel than its predecessor, and more skeptical about the effectiveness of "popular wars of national liberation," the new regime's backing of the fedayeen was bound to be more qualified. Syrian relations with Jordan improved under Asad, to the extent that Damascus sought to mediate between Jordanians and Palestinians in the April and July 1971 clashes. In March 1972 the Syrian president publicly acknowledged his willingness to accept a political solution on the basis of U.N. Security Council Resolution 242, provided "the rights of the Palestinians were recognized." [18] What these "rights" consisted of in Asad's view was left undefined. Nonetheless, pressure from the rival Ba'thist regime in Iraq, the domestic left, and the Resistance organizations prompted the Syrians to break relations with Amman and close the borders after the Jarash-Ajlun incidents and subsequent Jordanian military actions on Syria's borders.

The final blow dealt to the Palestinian commandos in Jordan in July 1971 caused the second major crisis in Hussein's Arab relations within less than a year. The demise of the follow-up committee had removed a largely ineffectual yet "bothersome" constraint on the regime's actions, but it had again made it necessary for the Arab governments to deal with the Jordanian situation at the highest level. Now, however, opposition to Hussein came almost exclusively from the "progressive" camp. The popularity and visibility of the Palestinian organizations had markedly decreased in the wake of the civil war, and domestic public pressure on the governments to react against Jordan was considerably less than it had been in September. Even among the "progressives," support of the Resistance was mixed. Most notably, Egypt—as well as Libya and Algeria—was strongly in favor of the unification of the commando organizations under

17. This is confirmed by an unidentified Syrian official in *War/Peace Report* (New York), February 1971, p. 6.

18. *Christian Science Monitor,* March 10, 1972.

Fatah's leadership, since in Cairo's view it had been the fractionalization of the movement and the rashness and extremism of the leftist groups that had brought about the September debacle. To this effect, Sadat had even been willing to close his eyes to whatever repressive measures Hussein might take against the PFLP and the Popular Democratic Front. He had actually agreed with the Jordanian monarch, he disclosed in a speech on July 23, 1971, "to cooperate together so as to give a chance to the clean fedayeen elements, such as Fatah, to take their [proper] place and to cleanse fedayeen action and incriminate the agent elements and the suspect elements." [19] Syria and Iraq, on the other hand, generally supported the Marxist organizations and were also unwilling to see Fatah take over their own home-grown Palestinian groups, Sa'iqa and the ALF.

It was very unlikely in these circumstances that joint Arab action could have been undertaken to stave off the final collapse of the guerrilla position in Jordan. In April, shortly after the events surrounding the occupation of Irbid by the Jordanian army had demonstrated the inability of the follow-up committee to protect the Resistance, President Sadat convened the representatives of governments that had signed the Cairo agreement; yet, after several delays and a one-day session, the meeting dissolved without even issuing a statement critical of Hussein. The Jordanian situation was also discussed on several occasions by the leaders of the Federation of Arab Republics, who were at times joined by President Numayri of the Sudan, a prospective member of the federation, and PLO chairman Arafat.

The July crackdown on the last guerrilla redoubts in the Jarash-Ajlun hills finally prompted President Qadhafi of Libya to call a second summit conference, which met on July 30 in Tripoli and was attended by five countries only: Egypt, Libya, Syria, and the two Yemeni republics, as well as the PLO. Saudi Arabia had opposed holding the conference,[20] to which King Faysal, as well as King Hussein and King Hassan of Morocco had not even been invited by Qadhafi. The bloody coup attempted against the Moroccan monarch on July 10 had earlier clouded relations between "conservatives" and "revolutionaries," and the short-lived communist putsch of July 19–22 in the Sudan certainly did not help to clear the atmosphere. Lebanon, Tunisia, and Kuwait refused the invitation, and for different reasons so did Algeria, which, faithful to its long-held position, pointedly observed through Radio Algiers that there was a "contradiction between the desire to defend the Palestinian cause and acceptance of the Rogers plan," and that it was

19. *Al-Ahram,* July 24, 1971.   20. *Le Monde,* July 31, 1971.

consequently futile to hold the conference.[21] The summit did condemn Hussein for his disregard of the Cairo and Amman agreements but rejected Qadhafi's proposal for military action against Jordan, which was supported only by Arafat.[22]

Although the "progressive" governments found themselves unable to dissuade the Jordanians from chasing out the Resistance organizations, they vented their pique and compensated for their impotence, at least in the eyes of their domestic publics, by making life difficult for the "reactionary" Hashemite regime. By the time the Tripoli conference met, Algeria, Libya, and Syria had broken or suspended their diplomatic relations with Amman, Iraq had recalled its ambassador, and both Iraq and Syria had closed their borders and airspace to all traffic to and from Jordan.[23] This blockade, which was to last for many months, did cause some temporary harm to the already badly shaken Jordanian economy, and doubtless increased Hussein's receptiveness to the Egyptian-Saudi mediation efforts begun in mid-July to restore some form of Palestinian commando presence in Jordan. But to the fedayeen these face-saving measures were little consolation. In its issue of July 16, the guerrilla newspaper *Fatah* reproached the Arab governments for "not having done anything to stop the massacre of the Palestinian people in Jordan," while the PDFLP's organ, *al-Hurriyah,* accused them of collusion with Amman: "They waited until the Resistance had been liquidated in a bloodbath to react, although they were aware of all the plots being hatched against the Palestinian people." [24]

THE EGYPTIAN-SAUDI MEDIATION

The failure of the Ladgham follow-up committee to normalize relations between the PLO and the Jordanian government did not mark the end of Arab mediation efforts. Both during the April and the July clashes, Syria had sent top-level delegations to Amman to renegotiate the implementation of the Cairo and Amman agreements. These eventually unsuccessful efforts had been applauded and sup-

21. *Ibid.*   22. *Le Monde,* August 1–2, 1971.

23. Egypt also severed its diplomatic relations with Jordan in April 1972, shortly after the announcement of the Hussein Plan. Cairo refused to join the aerial blockade, however, which substantially undermined its effectiveness.

24. Cited in *Le Monde,* July 29, 1971. Similar charges would be voiced by the PLO chairman Yasir Arafat himself later on. "Yes, we suffered a serious defeat in Jordan," he admitted to a meeting of Palestinians in Algiers in January 1972, "but the operation was not purely Jordanian. It was an Arab plot." *Africasia* (Paris), No. 58 (January 24, 1972), p. 27.

ported in the other Arab capitals, which were eager to see an end to the embarrassing situation in Jordan. Egypt in particular was desirous of a settlement that would stabilize relations between Jordan and her neighbors sufficiently to permit the reorganization of the shattered eastern front, and would allow the fedayeen to resume their operations against Israel.[25] Shortly after the failure of the second Syrian mediation attempt in July, Egypt and Saudi Arabia launched an intensive effort to bring representatives of the PLO and the Amman government face-to-face to work out a permanent agreement that would restore to the commandos some bases in Jordan on condition that they would operate exclusively against Israel and would fully respect the authority of the Jordanian regime. Both mediators appeared determined to ensure the success of their efforts, and great pressure was applied on the two sides, particularly as the chances for a peaceful Arab-Israeli settlement receded in the latter part of 1971.[26] Two series of meetings, September 14–22 and November 8–26, were eventually held in Jeddah, but to no avail. The two critical issues that proved most intractable were the question of who is to represent the Palestinian people—the Resistance or the Jordanian monarch—and the degree of freedom of political and military action that the fedayeen would be allowed in Jordan. The vengeful assassination by the newly created "Black September" group of the Jordanian premier, Wasfi at-Tal, in Cairo on November 28 destroyed whatever slim chances of success the Egyptian-Saudi initiative had offered.[27] On December 17, Amman officially accused Fatah of having engineered both Tal's murder and the attempt on the life of Jordan's ambassador to London, Zayd ar-Rifa'i, two days later,[28] thus declaring war on the only major Palestinian group it had continued to consider a *bona fide* Resistance organization.

THE UNCERTAIN FUTURE

Throughout 1972, the likelihood of an early return of the Resistance to Jordan on other than King Hussein's own terms seemed

25. *Christian Science Monitor*, August 23, 1971.

26. At one point, the Saudi foreign minister, Omar as-Saqqaf, threatened to close his country's borders with Jordan and suspend its annual financial subsidy of $35 million if the Jordanians did not prove cooperative. He also said Saudi Arabia would stop its aid to Fatah if the latter did not join the mediation effort. *Al-Anwar* (Beirut), September 13, 1971.

27. For a summary account of the Jeddah negotiations, see *Journal of Palestine Studies* (Beirut), Vol. 1, No. 1 (Autumn 1971), pp. 167–170; No. 2 (Winter 1972), pp. 142–144.

28. Amman Domestic Service Broadcast, December 17, 1971.

practically nonexistent. Their forces weakened, their mystique tarnished, and their ranks divided, the fedayeen were back in Syria, whence they had set forth in 1965, with their "secure base" again limited mainly to one country, and therefore once more heavily dependent on the good will of the rulers in Damascus. But this time around, they encountered in Damascus a less sympathetic mentor. The ideologically inspired, militantly uncompromising party-liners of the neo-Ba'th had now been replaced by a more traditional, military-controlled regime, jealous of its authority and unwilling to tolerate any forces that might challenge it.

Unlike the pre-June war situation, however, they now maintained a limited yet significant presence in Lebanon as well, from where they launched raids and mortar attacks against northern Israel during 1971 and the first half of 1972. But the general weakness of the fedayeen jeopardized their positions everywhere. Their border activities produced repeated Israeli retaliatory incursions into Lebanese territory. Major reprisals included a full-blown four-day invasion of southeastern Lebanon in February of 1972 and, in June, air as well as artillery strikes against several villages, including the towns of Hasbayya and Marja'yun, both actions taking a heavy toll in Lebanese civilian lives and property. These Israeli attacks produced the desired effect of precipitating one more confrontation between the Resistance and the Lebanese government over the issue of the guerrilla presence in the south. At the same time, amid signs of increasing tension and hostility between the fedayeen and the local population in the border areas, voices were raised from the Christian right—which included those of the deputy premier, Albert Mukhaiber, and of Raymond Edde, leader of the National Bloc party—calling for abolition of the 1969 Cairo agreement. To this the Resistance, with the support of the Lebanese left, was adamantly opposed, as was to be expected, and the fedayeen threatened an armed showdown over this question. Lebanon was now the only front-line country in which they retained some freedom of action and a presence legitimized by inter-Arab agreements, and the preservation of these gains was crucial to their credibility as a surviving political-military force, both on the Palestinian and on the larger international levels. The leadership of the PLO, however, understood the precariousness of the local guerrilla position in the south, and was ready to salvage the situation by compromising on the terms of implementation of the Cairo accord while preserving its formal status intact.

The government, for its part, was unwilling to risk a confrontation that could potentially degenerate into a renewed national crisis, was reluctant to appear to be giving in to blatant Israeli pressure, and did not relish the prospect of facing the same kind of political isolation Jordan had been undergoing since the 1970 civil war. Following the large-scale Israeli raid on the Arqub area in February, Prime Minister Salam had already broached the possibility of amending the Cairo agreement while allowing it to stand. "We shall honor any agreement that carries Lebanon's signature," he had said, adding elliptically, "but this does not mean that the Cairo agreement is an inviolable constitution which prevents us from constantly appraising the situation in a positive manner." [29] On the ground, this process was already under way: the Lebanese army had moved into the Arqub region—under guerrilla control since 1969—on the heels of the withdrawing Israelis. The new relationship was formalized in a quick series of meetings at the end of June between Arafat and Salam, as a result of which the chairman of the PLO agreed, within the framework of the Cairo agreement, to suspend all military operations against Israel from Lebanon and to withdraw the guerrillas from certain specified areas; he also assumed the responsibility for preventing any guerrilla organization from breaking this arrangement.

The stability of this new setup was likely to be severely tested in the future, not only by dissident guerrilla groups loath to abide by arrangements imposed by the Fatah-dominated PLO under Arafat and needing to show some achievements in the armed struggle to maintain themselves in being,[30] but also by the Israelis, who would continue to apply military pressure on Lebanon at any provocation to placate domestic opinion and to goad the Lebanese into effectively sealing their borders. Moreover, as the events surrounding the Black September operation against the Israeli Olympic team at the 1972 Games in Munich and its sequel of further Israeli retaliatory attacks against Lebanon were to demonstrate, the trend toward increasing Palestinian acts of terror abroad consequent upon the military ineffectiveness of the fedayeen in the Palestine area itself could easily take matters beyond the control of both the mainstream leadership of the Resistance movement and the Arab host governments.

Thus, despite the setbacks and retreats suffered by the Palestinian guerrillas since 1970, they still retained an undeniable capability to

29. *Al-Anwar*, March 9, 1972.

30. Immediately after the Arafat-Salam agreement of 27 June, the PFLP (General Command) and the Sa'iqa organizations announced that they did not consider themselves bound by the agreement. The first of these groups had earlier claimed responsibility for the operation that had brought about the latest Israeli reprisal. *Arab Report and Record* (London), June 16–30, 1972.

affect seriously, in one way or another, the course of events in the Middle East. Unfortunately, as in Munich, this capability progressively tended to manifest itself in negative, perhaps eventually self-destructive ways. The Resistance movement could, however, point to other solid achievements. It had revived in the scattered Palestinian diaspora a clear sense of national belonging and imbued its members with a forceful pride in their identity. It was widely accepted in the Arab world as the genuine spokesman for the Palestinian people, and had established a political presence, including representatives, information, and broadcasting media, in several Arab and foreign countries. It had forcefully staked a claim to a Palestinian say in any final settlement of the Middle East conflict.

Yet these are not necessarily permanent gains. The record suggests that only a strong Resistance movement, with a solid base of mass political support, reasonably smooth relations with host governments, and an effective military arm capable of independent action against its enemies, can continue to uphold them. But these prerequisites, though all essential, are in the final account mutually exclusive—and therein lies the Palestinians' basic dilemma. A guerrilla movement with a substantial popular base, an activist social-political program, and a viable military force would present an intolerable challenge and threat to the existing political systems in Jordan, Lebanon, and Syria, and is therefore bound to clash with the central authorities. The stronger the movement grows, the more destabilizing a factor it becomes, both as a radical, militant challenger on the internal political scene, and as a potential trigger of large-scale Israeli reprisals against the host country's territory. In light of this fact, the crises of April–November 1969 in Lebanon and June–September 1970 in Jordan were predictable developments. That Syria has thus far been spared a similar confrontation despite the large guerrilla presence there is due to the tight rein successive Damascus regimes have kept on the Palestinians, their vocal political support for the Resistance, and their willingness to apply considerable pressure on their Lebanese and Jordanian neighbors—even to the point of outright military intervention—if necessary to protect the position of the fedayeen in those countries. These actions have had the welcome result of providing non-Syrian jumpoff points for guerrilla actions against the Israelis.[31] Moreover, the fedayeen are conscious of the vital need to maintain good relations with at least one of the countries on Israel's eastern periphery.

31. Not only did the Syrians go to the support of the Palestinians with an armored thrust into Jordan during the September 1970 civil war, but they also sent large contingents of Sa'iqa forces into Lebanon in the spring

The solution to this dilemma appears practically limited to either of two general directions. One option would be for the Palestinian organizations to deemphasize their role as an agent for social-political change within the Arab countries and concentrate on rebuilding the Resistance as a fighting force, with the objective of regaining the initiative through the resumption of widespread guerrilla activities against Israel, primarily from within the occupied territories. It was the military performance and promise of the fedayeen at Karameh and in the subsequent period up to the beginning of 1970, and their appearance as a key to war or peace in the region, that had earned them the allegiance of the Arab public and the grudging support of most Arab governments. However, the resurgence of the Palestinians as a major combatant appears remote in the aftermath of their collapse in Jordan, despite their sporadic harassment of Israeli border areas from Lebanon. Even in Syria, their staunchest ally, the change of regime in November 1970 brought in a leadership that has taken a tougher line toward the Resistance. Evidence of the reluctance of Asad's government to tolerate a strengthening of the guerrillas' firepower was given in the summer of 1971 by the Syrian confiscation of a large shipment of arms sent by Algeria to the commandos through the port of Lataqiyah.[32] Only a renewal of protracted large-scale fighting in the area, for instance between Israel and Egypt, might afford the fedayeen the opportunity to rebuild their military potential on a significant scale.

The alternative—and perhaps more feasible—path would seem to point in the direction of a stronger reliance on political means in order to solidify the gains thus far achieved by the movement and secure a role in the representation of Palestinian interests in any prospective negotiations. This would not imply a renunciation of the armed struggle, source of the movement's ethos and mainstay of its popular support. It would entail the development of a clear political program—and making the necessary institutional adjustments—that would fit the circumstances of the current phase in the Resistance effort, and would provide adequate guidelines for whatever supportive military action is required. The reassertion by King Hussein of his authority over the Palestinians in Jordan, his plan, announced in March 1972, for reintegration of the Palestin-

---

and summer of 1969, which bolstered the guerrillas' control of the southeastern part of the country and fought repeated clashes with the Lebanese army.

32. For the Algerian reaction, see the article by the Algerian ambassador to Lebanon, Muhammad Yazid, in *an-Nahar*, August 17, 1971 (English translation in *New Middle East*, November 1971, p. 30).

ians into his kingdom on a new basis of local autonomy within an overall Hashemite suzerainty,[33] and the recent movements among the inhabitants of the West Bank toward a more active participation in decisions affecting their future, have placed in great jeopardy the credibility of the Resistance movement's claims and ability to represent the Palestinian people. To regain the momentum lost in their confrontation with Jordan sufficiently to rebuild their movement as an autonomous political force was the main challenge facing the Resistance leadership in 1973 and beyond.

In dealing with this challenge, the Palestinian Resistance must endeavor to overcome or at least minimize the basic problem of dependence that has accompanied the movement since its inception. Perhaps the fundamental conclusion to be drawn, not merely from the Jordanian civil war and its aftermath, but from the entire history of the Resistance and its relations with the Arab regimes, is that the factor of dependence has been the main impediment to the growth of the movement into a military as well as political force able to pursue its goals with the possibility of success. Some causes of this dependence—the smallness of the conflict area, the military power of the enemy, the lack of any real "sanctuaries," the hostility of most Arab governments—admittedly are beyond the control of the fedayeen organizations. Others, mainly of an internal nature, are not. Primary among these have been the plurality of organizations and ideological differences. While the valuable asset of popular support has permitted the Resistance to counteract in many instances the weakening effects of dependence, the Palestinian national movement is likely to remain at the mercy of the dynamics of inter-Arab politics—as it has been since its inception—so long as it lacks a substantial degree of structural unity and ideological cohesion.

33. For details of the Hussein Plan and the Palestinian response, see texts of King Hussein's speech of March 15 and the statement by PLO spokesman Kamal Nasir in *Journal of Palestine Studies*, Vol. 1, No. 4 (Summer 1972), pp. 166–170.

BIBLIOGRAPHY

HISTORICAL BACKGROUND ON PALESTINE

Books and Articles

Abcarius, M. F. *Palestine through the Fog of Propaganda*. London: Hutchison, 1946.

Abu-Lughod, Ibrahim, ed. *The Transformation of Palestine*. Evanston: Northwestern University Press, 1971.

Alush, Naji. *Arab Resistance in Palestine, 1914–1948* (in Arabic). Beirut: Palestine Research Center, 1967.

Antonius, George. *The Arab Awakening*. Philadelphia: Lippincott, 1939.

Barbour, Nevill. *Nisi Dominus: A Survey of the Palestine Controversy*. London: George G. Harrap, 1946.

Bell, J. Bowyer. *The Long War: Israel and the Arabs Since 1946*. Englewood Cliffs, N.J.: Prentice-Hall, 1969.

Darwazah, Muhammad I. *The Palestine Case at its Different Stages* (in Arabic). Sidon, Lebanon: Manshurat al-Maktaba al-Asriyyah, 1951. 2 vols.

Friedman, Isaiah. "The McMahon-Hussein Correspondence and the Question of Palestine." *Journal of Contemporary History*, Vol. 5, No. 2, 1970.

Furlonge, Sir Geoffrey. *Palestine is My Country: The Story of Musa Alami*. London: John Murray, 1969.

The Future of Palestine. Beirut: Hermon Books, 1970.

Hattis, Susan Lee. *The Bi-National Idea in Palestine during Mandatory Times*. Haifa, Israel: Shikmona, 1970.

Haykal, Yusif. *The Palestine Case* (in Arabic). Jaffa, Palestine: n.d. (1937).

Himadeh, Said B., ed. *Economic Organization of Palestine*. Beirut: American Press, 1938.

Hurewitz, J. C. *The Struggle for Palestine*. New York: Norton, 1950.

Jeffries, J. M. N. *Palestine: The Reality*. London: Longmans, Green, 1939.

217

John, Robert, and Sami Hadawi. *The Palestine Diary*. Vol. I and II. Beirut: Palestine Research Center, 1970.

al-Kayyali, Abd al-Wahhab (ed.). *Documents on Palestine Arab Resistance against the British Occupation and Zionism, 1918–1939* (in Arabic). Beirut: Institute for Palestine Studies, 1968.

al-Kayyali, Abd al-Wahhab (ed.). *A Modern History of Palestine* (in Arabic). Beirut: Arab Institute for Studies and Publication, 1970.

Kedourie, Elie. "Sir Herbert Samuel and the Government of Palestine." *Middle Eastern Studies*, Vol. 5, No. 1, January 1969.

Khalidi, Walid, ed. *From Haven to Conquest: Readings in Zionism and the Palestine Problem until 1948*. Beirut: Institute for Palestine Studies, 1971.

Kirkbride, Alec S. *A Crackle of Thorns*. London: John Murray, 1956.

Klieman, Aaron S. *Foundations of British Policy in the Arab World: The Cairo Conference of 1921*. Baltimore: Johns Hopkins Press, 1970.

Mansur, George. *The Arab Worker under the Palestine Mandate*. Jerusalem: Commercial Press, 1937.

Mogannam, Matiel. *The Arab Woman and the Palestine Problem*. London: Herbert Joseph, 1937.

Monroe, Elizabeth. *Britain's Moment in the Middle East*. Baltimore: Johns Hopkins Press, 1963.

Polk, William R., David H. Stamler, and Edmund Asfour. *Backdrop to Tragedy: The Struggle for Palestine*. Boston: Beacon Press, 1957.

Rose, Norman Anthony. "The Arab Rulers and Palestine, 1936: The British Reaction." *Journal of Modern History*, Vol. 44, No. 2 (June 1972), pp. 213–231.

Sharabi, Hisham. *Arab Intellectuals and the West: The Formative Years, 1875–1914*. Baltimore: Johns Hopkins Press, 1970.

Shimoni, Jacob. *The Arabs in Israel*. Translated by the Human Relations Area Files, Yale University, New Haven, 1956.

Simson, H. J. *British Rule, and Rebellion*. London: William Blackwood and Sons, 1938.

Storrs, Sir Ronald. *Orientations*. London: William Blackwood and Sons, 1938.

Sykes, Christopher. *Cross Roads to Israel*. London: Collins, 1965.

Tibawi, Abdul Latif. *Arab Education in Mandatory Palestine*. London: Luzac, 1956.

Toynbee, Arnold. "The McMahon-Hussein Correspondence: Comments and a Reply." *Journal of Contemporary History*, Vol. 5, No. 4, 1970.

Yasin, Subhi. *The Great Arab Revolt in Palestine 1936–1939* (in Arabic). Cairo: Dar al-Kitab al-Arabi, 1959.

Archives:

British Museum, London: Newspaper Collection, *Palestine Bulletin* and *Palestine Post*, Jerusalem (English), 1926–1928, 1932–1939.

Central Zionist Archives, Jerusalem: Files of the Political Department of the Jewish Agency (S25) and the Central Office of the Zionist Organization, London (Z4).

Israel State Archives, Jerusalem: Chief Secretary's Office papers; Arabic documents.

Public Record Office, London: correspondence files of the War Office

(1917–21), Foreign Office (1917–21, 1939), and the Colonial Office (1921–40); Cabinet Papers; Parliamentary Command Papers.

St. Antony's College, Oxford: Collection of Private Papers, Middle East Centre.

CONTEMPORARY PALESTINIAN NATIONALISM

Books and Articles

Alush, Naji. *The Palestinian Revolution: Its Dimensions and Issues* (in Arabic). Beirut: Dar at-Taliah, 1970.

Black September. Beirut: P.L.O. Research Center, Palestine National Liberation Movement, Fatah, 1969.

Chaliand, Gérard. "Le Double Combat du F.P.L.P." *Le Monde Diplomatique,* July 1970.

Chaliand, Gérard. *La Résistance Palestinienne.* Paris: Editions du Seuil, 1970.

Denoyan, Gilbert. *El Fath Parle: Les Palestiniens contre Israel.* Paris: Editions Albin Michel, 1970.

A Dialogue with Fateh. Interview with Salah Khalaf, Palestine National Liberation Movement, Fateh, 1969.

Dodd, Peter, and Halim Barakat. *River without Bridges: A Study of the Exodus of the 1967 Palestinian Refugees.* Beirut: Institute for Palestine Studies, 1968.

"The Fall of the Fifth Summit: Reasons, Details and Results" (in Arabic). *Al-Hadaf,* January 3, 1970.

Francos, Ania. *Les Palestiniens.* Paris: Julliard, 1968.

Hammond, Paul Y., and Sidney S. Alexander, eds. *Political Dynamics in the Middle East.* New York: American Elsevier, 1972.

Harkabi, Yehoshafat. *Arab Attitudes to Israel.* New York: Hart, 1972.

Harkabi, Yehoshafat. *Fedayeen Action and Arab Strategy.* Adelphi Papers, No. 53. London: Institute for Strategic Studies, December 1968.

Harkabi, Yehoshafat. "Three Articles on the Arab Slogan of a Democratic State" (mimeo), 1970.

Hindi, Khalil, et al. *The Palestinian Resistance and the Jordanian Regime* (in Arabic). Beirut: PLO Research Center, 1971.

Hudson, Michael. "Fedayeen Are Forcing Lebanon's Hand." *Mid East,* February 1970.

Hudson, Michael. "The Palestinian Arab Resistance Movement: Its Significance in the Middle East Crisis." *Middle East Journal,* Vol. 23, No. 3, Summer 1969.

Hudson, Michael. "The Palestinian Resistance: Developments and Setbacks, 1967–71." *Journal of Palestine Studies,* Vol. 1, No. 3, Spring 1972.

International Documents on Palestine, 1967 and 1968. Beirut: Institute for Palestine Studies, 1970 and 1971.

Jum'ah Sa'd. *The Conspiracy and the Battle of Destiny* (in Arabic). Beirut: Dar al-Kitab al-Arabi, 1968.

Kerr, Malcolm H. *The Arab Cold War: Gamal 'Abd al-Nasir and His Rivals, 1958–1970.* 3rd ed. New York: Oxford University Press, 1971.

Khouri, Fred J. *The Arab-Israeli Dilemma.* Syracuse, N.Y.: Syracuse University Press, 1968.

"Lessons and Tasks of One Year in the Battle" (on the fedayeen in Lebanon) (in Arabic). *Al-Hadaf,* April 25, 1970.

Maqsud, Clovis. "New Palestine: Grievance Redressed, Justice for Arab and Jew." *Mid East,* June 1970.

"Multiplicity in the Palestinian Struggle" (in Arabic). *Al-Hadaf,* January 10, 1970.

On the Crisis of the Palestinian Resistance Movement (in Arabic). Documents submitted by the PDFLP to the Sixth National Congress, September 1969. Beirut: Dar at-Taliah, 1970.

Palestine Arab Documents (in Arabic). Vols. 1–4, (1965, 1966, 1967, and 1968). Beirut: Institute for Palestine Studies, 1966, 1967, 1969, 1970.

The Palestine Yearbook (in Arabic). Vols. 2–4 (1965, 1966, 1967, and 1968). Beirut: Institute for Palestine Studies, 1967, 1968, 1969, 1971.

The Palestinian Resistance Movement in Its Present Reality (in Arabic). Introduction by Nayif Hawatmah. Beirut: Dar at-Taliah, 1969.

"The Palestine Revolution and the Jews" (mimeo). New York: Palestine Liberation Organization, 1969.

Peretz, Don. "The Palestine Arab Refugee Problem." In Paul Y. Hammond and Sidney S. Alexander, eds., *Political Dynamics in the Middle East.* New York: American Elsevier, 1972.

Peretz, Don, Evan M. Wilson, and Richard J. Ward. *A Palestine Entity?* Washington, D.C.: Middle East Institute, 1970.

"Periodicals and Pamphlets Published by the Palestinian Commando Organizations." *Journal of Palestine Studies,* Vol. 1, No. 1 (Autumn 1971).

Political and Armed Struggle. Palestine National Liberation Movement, Fateh, n.d. (1969).

Revolution Until Liberation: The Political Manifesto of the Arab Liberation Front. 1969.

Revolution Until Victory. Palestine Liberation Movement, Fateh, n.d. (1969).

"Secrets of the Armed Struggle in a Frank Discussion with the Leaders of Fatah." *Al-Ahram,* January 3, 1970.

Sharabi, Hisham. *Palestine and Israel: The Lethal Dilemma.* New York: Pegasus, 1969.

Sharabi, Hisham. *Palestine Guerrillas: Their Credibility and Effectiveness.* Washington, D.C.: Center for Strategic and International Studies, Georgetown University, Supplementary Papers, 1970.

Sharabi, Hisham. "Palestine Resistance: Crisis and Reassessment." *Middle East Newsletter* (Beirut), January 1971.

Yaari, Ehud. "Al-Fath's Political Thinking." *New Outlook* (Tel Aviv), Vol. 2, No. 9 (November–December 1968), pp. 20–32.

Yaari, Ehud. *Strike Terror: The Story of Fatah.* New York: Sabra Books, 1970.

Journals and Newspapers

Action (New York), Action Committee on American-Arab Relations.
Africasia (Paris).
Al-Ahram (Cairo).
Arab News and Views (New York), Arab Information Center.
Arab Report and Record (London).

Christian Science Monitor, especially articles by John Cooley.
Fatah (Amman, weekly, in Arabic); *Fatah* (Amman, daily, in Arabic).
Fateh (Beirut, in English).
Al-Hadaf (Beirut), PFLP.
Al-Hurriyah (Beirut), PDFLP.
Jeune Afrique (Paris), especially articles by Abdallah Schleifer.
Journal of Palestine Studies (Beirut).
Al-Jumhuriyah (Cairo).
Al-Katib (Cairo), Arab Socialist Union.
Le Monde (Paris).
Mid East (Washington, D.C.).
Al-Muharrir (Beirut).
Al-Mujahid (Algiers, in Arabic).
An-Nahar (Beirut)
An-Nahar Arab Report (Beirut, in English).
New Middle East (London).
New York Times.
Observer (London).
Palestine Affairs (Beirut, in Arabic).
Ar-Rai al-Aam (Kuwait).
Révolution Africaine (Algiers).
At-Taliah (Kuwait).
Ath-Thawrah (Baghdad).
The Times (London).
Washington Post, especially articles by William Touhy.

News Agency Releases and Radio Broadcasts

Iraqi News Agency (INA).
Middle East News Agency (MENA).
Syrian Arab News Agency (SANA).
Voice of Fatah (Cairo and clandestine broadcasts).
Voice of the PLO Central Committee (Damascus and Baghdad).

SELECTED RAND BOOKS

Averch, et al. *The Matrix of Policy in the Philippines.* Princeton, N.J.: Princeton University Press, 1971.

Bagdikian, Ben. *The Information Machines: Their Impact on Men and the Media.* New York: Harper & Row, 1971.

Becker, Abraham S. *Soviet National Income 1958–1964.* Berkeley and Los Angeles: University of California Press, 1969.

Canby, Steven L. *Military Manpower Procurement: A Policy Analysis.* Lexington, Mass.: D. C. Heath, 1972.

Clawson et al. *The Agricultural Potential of the Middle East.* New York: American Elsevier, 1971.

Cooper, Charles A., and Sidney S. Alexander. *Economic Development and Population Growth in the Middle East.* New York: American Elsevier, 1972.

Dalkey, Norman (ed.). *Studies in the Quality of Life: Delphi and Decision-making.* Lexington, Mass.: D. C. Heath, 1972.

Goldhamer, Herbert. *The Foreign Powers in Latin America.* Princeton, N.J.: Princeton University Press, 1972.

Gurtov, Melvin. *Southeast Asia Tomorrow: Problems and Prospects for U.S. Policy.* Baltimore: Johns Hopkins Press, 1970.

Hammond, Paul Y., and Sidney S. Alexander. *Political Dynamics in the Middle East.* New York: American Elsevier, 1972.

Langer, Paul, and Joseph J. Zasloff. *North Vietnam and the Pathet Lao: Partners in the Struggle for Laos.* Cambridge, Mass.: Harvard University Press, 1970

Leites, Nathan, and Charles Wolf, Jr. *Rebellion and Authority: An Analytic Essay On Insurgent Conflicts.* Chicago: Markham Publishing Company, 1970.

Moorsteen, Richard, and Morton I. Abramowitz. *Remaking China Policy: U.S.–China Relations and Governmental Decision-making.* Cambridge, Mass.: Harvard University Press, 1971.

Nelson, Richard R., T. Paul Schultz, and Robert L. Slighton. *Structural Change in a Developing Economy: Colombia's Problems and Prospects.* Princeton, N.J.: Princeton University Press, 1971.

Pascal, Anthony H. (ed.) *Racial Discrimination in Economic Life.* Lexington, Mass.: D. C. Heath, 1972.

Pascal, Anthony H. *Thinking About Cities: New Perspectives on Urban Problems.* Belmont, California: Dickenson Publishing Company, 1970.

Robinson, Thomas W. (ed.). *The Cultural Revolution in China.* Berkeley and Los Angeles: University of California Press, 1971.

Schurr, Sam H., et al. *Middle Eastern Oil and the Western World: Prospects and Problems.* New York: American Elsevier, 1971.

Stepan, Alfred. *The Military in Politics: Changing Patterns in Brazil.* Princeton, N. J.: Princeton University Press, 1971.

Wolfe, Thomas W. *Soviet Power and Europe 1945–1970.* Baltimore: Johns Hopkins Press, 1970.

INDEX

Abdallah, Amir, 36, 42, 49
Abd al-Hadi, Awni, 23–24, 31, 32
Abu Ammar. *See* Arafat, Yasir
Abu Ayad. *See* Khalaf, Salah
Abu Ali Ayad, 141
Abu Garbiyya, Bahjat:
  as head of Palestinian Popular
    Struggle Front, 67, 89
  as leader of PLO, 87, 92, 130, 140
Abu Jihad. *See* al-Wazir, Khalil
Abu Lutuf. *See* al-Qaddumi, Faruq
Abu Said. *See* al-Hassan, Khalid
Abu Shilbayah, Muhammad, 145,
  146n
Abu Sittah, Hamid, 87, 91, 92, 130, 137,
  140
Action Organization for the Libera-
  tion of Palestine (AOLP), 66, 67,
  72, 129, 180
Adwan, Kamal, 84, 130, 132, 134
Agricultural Parties, Zionist-subsidized,
  14, 18
al-Alami, Musa, 35, 40–41, 42n
al-Alami, Zuhayr, 83, 92, 137
Algeria:
  and Fatah, 188n
  as supporter of commando move-
    ment, 183–184, 188
  independence of, and Palestinian re-
    sistance, 158
Amir, Ali Ali, 160
Amman protocol (1970), between Jordan and fedayeen, 202
Amr, Yasir, 91, 92, 137
Anglo-American Committee of Inquiry
  (1946), 41

al-Ansar:
  representation of, at Palestine Na-
    tional Congress (1971), 137
  sponsorship of, by Arab Communist
    Parties, 66, 67
al-Aqsa Fedayeen Front, 63
Arab congresses:
  1919 (Damascus), 4
  1920 (Damascus), 26
  1920–1921 (Haifa), 14–15
  1936 (Bludan, Syria), 23–24
  1938 (Cairo), 24
  1944 (Alexandria), 40
Arab Executive (1920–1934):
  dissolution of, 34
  early activities of, 20–28 *passim*
  Grand National Meeting, 32
  increasing radicalization of, 29–33
Arab Higher Committee (1936), 20–21,
  34–40 *passim*, 41
Arab-Israeli conflict:
  after British withdrawal, 41–42, 47–
    48
  casualties, since June 1967, 120–123
  Palestinian objections to settlement
    of, 3, 73, 124, 133–135, 198, 206–
    207
  See also Palestinian national resis-
    tance movement; Six-Day War
    (June 1967)
Arab League:
  formation of, 40–41
  and Palestinian national movement,
    24, 50
Arab Liberation Army, as League-
  sponsored guerrilla arm, 41